THE
TACTICS
OF
HOPE

HOW SOCIAL ENTREPRENEURS
ARE CHANGING OUR WORLD

THE
TACTICS
OF
HOPE

HOW SOCIAL ENTREPRENEURS
ARE CHANGING OUR WORLD

WILFORD WELCH

WITH DAVID HOPKINS, CONTRIBUTING EDITOR

EARTH AWARE
San Rafael, CA

To my wonderful wife, Carole, who also thrills me, and to my extraordinary daughters Ashley and Shandy. Each is devoted to making the world a better place: Carole through her Cross Cultural Journeys Foundation work with women in Africa and Asia, Ashley in the field of corporate social responsibility and Shandy through her work to create better health care delivery systems.

TABLE of CONTENTS

FOREWORD
by Desmond Tutu

The most important thing you can do is live a meaningful life, and being of service to others is one of the greatest ways to make life meaningful. The potential and power of individuals throughout the world to bring about positive change is enormous, and never before have we lived in an era so ripe with opportunities to make a difference.

Some are fortunate to be born into circumstances of relative comfort. Others are less fortunate, having been born into circumstances most dire. This second group grows up without the things many of us take for granted, such as access to clean water, shelter, health services, protection from the cruelty of others, and even the most rudimentary education. Nine hundred million people live like this every day, in extreme poverty, yet they have as much potential as the rest of us to live productive, meaningful lives. As the stories in this book demonstrate, they can and will do so if they have access to some of the basics they need to build their lives.

As I travel through my home country of South Africa and around the world, I am awed and humbled by the work that millions of individuals have undertaken to enable those less fortunate to build lives of dignity, security, and hope. It is a beautiful thing to see. It is one of the greatest gifts one can give to another human being—and to oneself.

It is quite clear that our collective home is being depleted by our past and current practices. The world our children and grandchildren inherit will be much less hospitable than we might have hoped. This calls for all of us—rich and poor, black and white, Christian, Jew, Muslim, Hindu, Buddhist and those of all other faiths—to become better stewards of our home, the Earth. The good news is that there are many individuals who are already answering this call, providing leadership and creating initiatives that the rest of us can learn from and emulate. The stories of some of these noble individuals and their initiatives are told in these pages.

This book is inspiration and guide for those who want to be informed, those who want to begin to take their first steps, and those who truly want to realize the potential we all have to make a difference.

—Desmond Tutu
Cape Town, South Africa
January 2008

—ACKNOWLEDGMENTS—

Explorers of world affairs as well as mountaineers can benefit from guides, and I have had many extraordinary guides over the years. My initial interest in the world was fostered by my father and mother, who took their five children on wonderful trips abroad. Then came Jack Crocker, who introduced me to the notion of service to others during my formative years at Groton School. "Uncle Sid" Lovett, the former Chaplain of Yale University, who was the head of the Yale-China program during the years I taught in a Chinese refugee college in Hong Kong, helped me put that notion of serving others into practice. Bill Bundy and Marshall Green, both the top diplomats for East Asia in the U.S. Department of State, provided me with many insights and connections in the world of diplomacy. James Gavin and Bill Krebs proved to be wise mentors during my ten years as the head of Asia for Arthur D. Little International. Crocker Snow became a close colleague and friend during my many years at *The WorldPaper*, where we constantly traveled the world to uncover stories that would give clues to emerging global trends and challenges. Michael Hoffman, who also lives and breathes world affairs, has been a constant companion along the way and brought me on the board of Columbia University's School of International and Public Affairs (SIPA) where I met many extraordinary students and faculty from around the world, most notably Dean Lisa Anderson. And most recently, I have been honored with the friendship and guidance of one of the world's wisest and most courageous human beings, Nobel Peace Prize Laureate Desmond Tutu of South Africa, who has been at my side during each of the Quest for Global Healing gatherings.

I have also been blessed when it came to writing this book: David Hopkins, the Contributing Editor, being the most important blessing. David interned with me during his last two summer vacations from Middlebury College, and after he graduated in 2007, worked with me on this book day and night for nearly a year. I deeply appreciate all his support, hard work and commitment to the field of social entrepreneurship. I am particularly proud of the fact that David, who is one-third my age, has been such a close partner on this journey. This speaks to the potential and power of intergenerational collaboration. This book might never have become a reality if Raoul Goff, the publisher of Earth Aware Editions, had not had the instinct that I had this book in me, and editor Alan Rinzler had not taken on the task of bringing greater coherence to my writing. I also thank my sister Carolyn Chadwick, who for seventeen years has produced the extraordinary *Radio Expeditions* programs for National Public Radio and The National Geographic Society, for introducing me to Raoul. And, I also want to thank her daughter Hadley for the research she undertook.

Writing this book has been a profoundly humbling experience for which I am most grateful. Exploring in some depth the plight of the extremely poor who barely survive each day with little hope for a better future has been deeply disturbing. They do not need our pity, but our respect, as well as clean water, access to a basic education, healthcare, and personal safety, and they will have a foundation from which to build better lives. Witnessing the work of each of the creative, passionate and selfless individuals profiled in this book, who are truly making a difference, also fills me with awe and hope for the future.

I also want to thank Rory Riggs for his financial support of the companion website to this book, and Davis Hammon for his extraordinary ability to turn our ideas about an open source website into a powerful tool for individuals to use to address their social and environmental concerns.

No one walks on this earth alone. I have been honored with great guides, my wife Carole Angermeir-Welch, being my greatest source of strength, love and wisdom.

Fatima Gailani (center), president of the Afghan Red Crescent Society, with the author (right) and Carole Angermeir-Welch (left).

INTRODUCTION

Social entrepreneurs combine street pragmatism with professional skill, visionary insights with pragmatism, and ethical fiber with tactical thrust. They see opportunities where others only see empty buildings, unemployable people and unvalued resources. Radical thinking is what makes social entrepreneurs different from simply 'good people.' They make markets work for people, not the other way around, and gain strength from a wide network of alliances. They can 'boundary-ride' between the various political rhetorics and social paradigms to enthuse all sectors of society.

—John Catford

A hundred years from now, people may look back at this time—the cusp of the new millennium—and note that it marked the beginning of a dramatic shift in human consciousness regarding our social and environmental actions on earth. They may conclude that around this time occurred a collective realization that our current practices were not sustainable. And, they may give credit to the actions taken by millions of concerned individuals around the world, particularly people called "social entrepreneurs," who used new technologies, business methods and a lot of determination to overcome age-old social and environmental challenges.

This book seeks to encourage individuals to claim their power and take action to address the environmental and social challenges that concern them. It argues that social entrepreneurs are essential to the restoration of a sustainable planet and the improvement of the lives of the 900 million people living in extreme poverty. It argues that these two issues—a recovering environment and social justice—are critical challenges of our era that most people are ignoring at their peril. It suggests that if you are not concerned about these issues you may want to reconsider your point of view. It contends that governments and multilateral institutions like the United Nations and the World Bank are critical to the solution of these issues, but if left to their own devices will not have enough political will or creativity to achieve the level of results necessary. It also contends, however, that there is hope—hope in the form of individuals from all corners of the world who are taking it upon themselves to step forward in whatever ways they can to address these challenges.

What can I do? you may ask. A lot, as it turns out. Most of the barriers that previously prevented your making a difference no longer exist. The only major barrier that remains is the voice that says, "I am but one and the problems are so many." The reality is that your ability to leverage your impact on the world has never been so great.

Millions of people are already taking action. Some are taking small yet important actions such as reducing their consumption of gasoline, or helping out at the local homeless shelter. Others, such as the individuals behind the twenty-seven organizations highlighted in Chapters 3–9, have established major initiatives that are leading to systemic changes to overcome age-old challenges.

Ann Cotton

Ann Cotton, for example, founded the Campaign for Female Education, which now supports the education of over 400,000 poor girls in sub-Saharan Africa, while Priya Haji, the founder of World of Good, is helping poor artisans in thirty-four developing countries gain fair trade access to the U.S. market. And there are so many others, some of whose stories are told in this book.

Iqbal Quadir is another good example of a social entrepreneur. In 1971, he was a young boy living in rural Bangladesh. One day he journeyed ten kilometers by foot to fetch medicine for his brother who was sick. After a full day's passage, he returned home defeated and empty handed. The pharmacist, whom Iqbal had traveled all day to see, was not there.

Twenty-two years later in New York, one of the busiest and most wired cities in the world, the computer network crashed at an investment bank on Wall Street. Among the bankers was Iqbal, who had received a scholarship to study business and engineering in the United States before entering the financial world as a venture capitalist. A light went on within Iqbal. He was reminded of his rural home growing up, a place with no phones or electricity. In that moment he saw an opportunity to help the poor of his native Bangladesh while creating a profitable enterprise.

Connectivity is productivity, he realized, whether in a modern office in New York or a poor village in Bangladesh. In the years that followed, Iqbal put his skills to work, turning his realization into action. He raised seed money in New York and moved to Bangladesh to enlist the help of Grameen Bank, established by Muhammad Yunus, who in 2006 would receive the Nobel Peace Prize for his own groundbreaking initiative. The Bank provided microcredit to the poor so that they could purchase cows or other assets that would generate income and enable them to pay back their loans. In essence, Iqbal reasoned that poor villagers who wanted to borrow money to buy a cow could borrow money to rent or buy a mobile phone and could sell minutes of phone use to other villagers. After spending years searching for a telephone company that would invest in his idea, in 1995 he convinced the Norwegian phone company Telenor to do so. Seeing Telenor's interest, Grameen Bank also decided to invest and lent its name to the new phone company. GrameenPhone enabled rural microcredit borrowers, primarily women—"phone ladies" as they are now called—to provide retail telephone services in their communities. These women were able to repay their loans over time, and support themselves and their families while increasing the connectivity and productivity of those living in isolated villages.

Iqbal Quadir

During the next seven years, GrameenPhone sold or rented mobile phones to over 300,000 phone ladies through its Village Phone Program, enabling over 60,000 rural villages to become connected to one another and to the rest of Bangladesh, in effect helping 100 million people. In addition, GrameenPhone built a telephone subscriber network of over 15 million individuals, making it the largest phone company in Bangladesh. In 2004, the American investors sold their small stake in GrameenPhone to Telenor for $33 million.

Iqbal is a successful social entrepreneur who took it upon himself to help alleviate poverty by empowering the poor villagers of Bangladesh. This innovative approach was particularly effective because poor governments often struggle to invest in communications or other infrastructure projects, especially in rural areas. In looking for a profitable business opportunity, he improved the lives of millions of people and also did well for himself. Many other social entrepreneurs highlighted in this book are introducing new and highly effective tactics to address our most pressing social and environmental problems.

A lot of young men and women feel passionate about something, but struggle to turn their passion into powerful initiatives, and better still, financially rewarding ones. But Mark Hanis did just that. In 2005, when he was still an undergraduate student at Swarthmore College, Mark became enraged by what he felt were generations of American politicians failing to honor their commitment to stand up against genocide around the world. The grandson of European immigrants who had faced the threat of genocide during the Holocaust of the Second World War, Mark was particularly sensitive to the lackluster response of the United States government to the ongoing genocide in the Darfur region of the Sudan. Instead of just writing a paper or arguing about it in the classroom, Mark leveraged email and the social networking power of the Internet to ask fellow students across the United States to give what they could to help protect the women and children of Darfur who were the victims of mass murder. He also asked for their help to lobby the U.S. Congress on this issue.

In less than a year, Mark raised over $250,000, which he used to establish the Genocide Intervention Network. Within months of its establishment, the Genocide Intervention Network increased U.S. awareness of the genocide in Darfur and put sufficient pressure on both congressional and executive branch decision makers to bring about a significant change in U.S. foreign policy.

Mark Hanis would never have been able to affect U.S. national policy so quickly and effectively fifty years ago. He was able to take advantage of a tool, the Internet, which had only recently become available. This shift in global communications has forever improved the potential individuals have to come up with new approaches to age-old challenges.

Around the same time that Mark was changing the American government's commitment to Darfur, Curt DeBerg, a university accounting professor in northern California, began using the Internet to link high school students from all over the world into a single organization called SAGE, Students for the Advancement of Global Entrepreneurship. SAGE has already trained 4,000 students from two hundred high schools in more than ten different countries to start and maintain entrepreneurial businesses that generate both financial and social value to their communities. As part of this effort, SAGE has held global competitions in countries as diverse as China, Ukraine, the United States and Nigeria. With funding from such corporations as Allstate, Walgreens, Bank of the West, Chevron and Wells Fargo, Curt continues to leverage the power of corporate social responsibility to fund his vision. SAGE is now an effective agent of change in school programs globally.

Social entrepreneurs look for opportunities in what many consider to be the most difficult and widely discussed challenges of our era. They are establishing initiatives that provide access to health care and education for the poor, protection of their human rights and access to credit and fair trade for the goods they produce for world markets. They are creating programs that help individuals reduce their emissions of CO_2 that contribute to global warming.

We hear about these issues all the time in the media, but often do not know how to take meaningful actions within the constraints of our time and resources. The stories of individuals like Ann, Priya, Iqbal, Mark and Curt may suggest ways in which you too can play a role in the solution, and not contribute to the problem. Harking back to the epigraph of this introduction, if social entrepreneurs see opportunities where "others only see empty buildings," then the ways in which they work to address those opportunities are, to be sure, the tactics of hope.

In 1980, Bill Drayton, a management consultant working for McKinsey & Company, coined the term "social entrepreneur." Drayton quit his job and has dedicated his life to lead and grow Ashoka, the first foundation to identify and support thousands of social entrepreneurs throughout the world. Drayton, a global champion for social entrepreneurship, recognized that a major shift was occurring in how we typically categorize and work with nonprofits, for-profits and governments. He noticed that social entrepreneurs do not see such distinctions. In fact, they ignore these differences, bringing players from all three sectors together to create change, using methods that are often financially self-sustaining and even profitable.

Bill Drayton

Social entrepreneurs think "out of the box." They don't care if their initiatives are nonprofit or for-profit, nongovernmental or corporate; they build partnerships with members from any sector that will help them turn their visions into reality. Like the business entrepreneur, they are not afraid to fail, adjust their approach and try again. They demand social change, and put the importance of solving social problems before making money for themselves. Increasingly, however, they are doing both at the same time—making money while changing the world. In the history of capitalism there has rarely been such a widespread and effective paradigm shift, moving from pure competition to collaborative competition as the driving force among companies and individuals looking to invent new models and products that benefit the social whole.

Former President Bill Clinton uses the phrase "private people doing public good." Sergey Brin and Larry Page, the founders of Google, have said that Google.org, which seeks to address social issues with new technologies and business methods, will have an even greater impact in the world than Google.com, which made them their billions. Oprah Winfrey recently celebrated the work of social entrepreneurs on her television show. President Bush used the term *social entrepreneur* in his January 2007 State of the Union address. Klaus Schwab, the founder of the World Economic Forum, the largest summit of its kind in the world, has created a fellowship, foundation and line of study in its name, working to help companies bridge the delicate balance between returning profits to shareholders and generating a greater social return.

We are all much more closely interconnected and interdependent than ever before, with people and events on the other side of the globe increasingly affecting our lives. There is no place to hide, at least for long. In the twenty-first century, nations large and small are realizing that while the current worldview of "we" against "them" is still a prevalent doctrine, it may not lead to our long-term survival. "We" is the planet we share, and "we" may be the only species ever to have existed on earth in such a misguided way as to accelerate our own extinction through self-inflicted environmental destruction, genocide, disease and poverty. Our children will inherit even greater problems if we do not change our ways.

The Tactics of Hope highlights the extraordinary initiatives of teenagers and retired executives, poor villagers and wealthy philanthropists, Hollywood movie stars and advertising executives, medical doctors and Internet engineers. They are based in tech-savvy offices in California, undeveloped villages of sub-Saharan Africa, the rocky peaks of the Himalayas, the destitute slums of a Brazilian city and the coral reefs of Indonesia, among other places.

This book suggests tools you might use to help redefine your career, choose a new one, support someone else's or find your passion among the many social and environmental challenges that are out there. This is true whether your passion be the socioeconomic improvement of your own neighborhood, the resolution of religious and military conflicts in the Middle East, the removal of land mines in Asia, the prevention of HIV/AIDS in sub-Saharan Africa or the preservation of rainforests in the Amazon. The book is organized so that you can read any chapter at any time, depending upon your interests.

In reading *The Tactics of Hope* and visiting the companion website— www.TacticsofHope.org, and those of the many other social entrepreneurs noted in Part III—you will find options and strategies regarding how best to take action in ways that address your concerns and are within your capacities. You can indeed make a difference, no matter where in the world you live, whether you are male or female, young or old, rich or poor.

PART I

THE POWER OF INDIVIDUALS TO TRANSFORM OUR WORLD

CHAPTER 1

Hope and Possibility

We are seeing a 'revolution in the organization of human society.' Characterized by the emergence, in country after country, of 'the same sort of open, competitive-yet-collaborative relationships that marked the birth of the modern competitive business sector three centuries ago,' this social entrepreneurial revolution has gone little noticed by politicians or the press. 'Nevertheless, when the history of these times is written, no other change will compete with it in terms of importance . . .'

—Sally Osberg
Skoll Foundation President and CEO,
quoting Bill Drayton, Founder of Ashoka

Every era has its unique challenges. During the last century, over 100 million people were killed or injured during the First and Second World Wars. Other military conflicts took countless more lives of armed combatants and civilians. The century also witnessed an epic struggle for world domination between the forces of communism and democratic capitalism, each side's ideological arsenal backed by the threat of nuclear holocaust that could have annihilated millions of people and destroyed entire nations.

Now, in the twenty-first century, one major challenge of our era is the "war on terror," with its epicenter in the Middle East. It dominates the headlines, with the result that many other important issues of our time receive less attention.

The restoration of a sustainable planet and the eradication of extreme poverty are two such major challenges that also can and must be overcome. So far, despite the fact that more and more organizations have come into being to tackle these issues since the Second World War, the challenges are far from being solved. The winners or losers in these battles carry no military weapons nor are they fighting for any one nation's government; collectively, these challenges are for all of us to solve.

Before 1945, only national and colonial governments had authority over the health and safety of the people, as well as the stewardship of the natural world within their borders. People at the bottom rungs of most societies, particularly those in poorer countries, were given little help, and were often abused by the governments that were allegedly there to protect them. Environmental protection was not a priority to national governments at that time, despite the fact that it often was a priority to the native populations of each country. The natural world was perceived to be filled with an unending supply of resources to be exploited at will.

The good news is that progress has been made over the past fifty years to recognize and address these challenges. The bad news is that the progress made has not been nearly enough. Since 1945, increased attention has been paid to these challenges by the following entities: multilateral organizations; nongovernmental organizations; TV, print media and the Internet; documentary films; academic institutions; foundations; and multinational corporations. The role each has played is summarized below.

Multilateral Organizations—
Soft power and trickle-down economic development rather than empowerment from below

The United Nations and the World Bank Group were established in 1945 with mandates to address many of these challenges. In reality, they had little real enforcement powers to protect the human rights of the impoverished or the environment, only "soft" moral authority. In the 1950s and 1960s, during the middle of the cold war between the United States and the Soviet Union, foreign aid to the poorest countries flowed directly to governments. What was intended to help the poor was based on a "trickle-down" approach to economic development, but most of the money did not trickle down very far. The motivation behind the allocation of foreign aid by the major cold war powers was often political—to woo governments into one ideological camp and keep them out of the others. And since many of the recipient governments were corrupt, the money was often siphoned off before it trickled down to those most in need of it.

Nongovernmental Organizations (NGOs)—
Making a difference

Although a few nonprofits, such as the International Committee of the Red Cross, were already in existence, it was not until the 1970s that nongovernmental organizations, or NGOs, began emerging to address the root causes or outcomes of extreme poverty and environmental degradation. Médecins Sans Frontières (Doctors without Borders), for example, was founded in 1971, and Human Rights

Watch in 1978. When President Clinton went to Russia in January of 1994 for his first official visit with President Yeltsin, there were a handful of NGOs operating there. Ten years later there were 63,000. Now there are over 500,000.

TV, Print Media and the Internet—
Gradually raising our awareness

Over the past fifty years, fundamental shifts have occurred with regard to who controls the news, where the news and commentary come from and the technologies and channels utilized to distribute the news. Before the 1980s, most of the international media focused on events in the Western world for a Western audience. Conversely, events in the developing countries that were not perceived to have a direct impact on the Western world were given limited coverage. Virtually all of the international media, such as the *International Herald Tribune* and *The Economist*, were owned by Westerners, and written for a Western audience, and most of the broadcast and print journalists reporting on these issues were also Westerners.

This began to change around 1980. *The WorldPaper*, established in 1979, was a world affairs supplement carried by local publications in twenty-seven countries in six language editions featuring "the voices of the world speaking for themselves on issues of global concern." Most of the writers were native to the regions they wrote about.

CNN, created in 1980 by Ted Turner, also had strong international coverage. Its reporters were initially Westerners reporting from a Western point of view. CNN is now ubiquitous on television around the world, with extensive coverage of world affairs from a number of perspectives. During the 1990s, other players joined the field and now provide an even greater array of perspectives. They include Al Jazeera, providing Middle Eastern perspectives, and the Internet, enabling near-instant access to information through the World Wide Web and its blogs and vlogs created by locals all over the world.

In Thomas Friedman's book *The World Is Flat*, he notes the profound transition taking place across multiple forms of media due to computers, email, fiber-optic networks, teleconferencing and dynamic software. He argues that this can be seen as a "shift from a primarily vertical—*command and control*—system for creating value to a more horizontal—*connect and collaborate*—value-creation model," a process that will blow away the "frictions, barriers, and boundaries [that] are mere sources of waste and inefficiency."

Documentary Films—
Shining greater light on the dark side of the human condition

The growth of documentary films about human rights and social justice abuses and environmental challenges has also increased over the years. There have been many important films recently of this nature, among them *Born into Brothels*, which chronicles the lives of children living in Indian brothels; *Darwin's Nightmare*, about the destruction of the local African ecosystem in Lake Victoria due to the exploitation of the fish and arms trade in Europe and Russia; *Water*, documenting the plight of women in India trapped by the caste system into which they are born; and *An Inconvenient Truth*, focused on global warming.

Academic Institutions—
From training diplomats to training global citizens

Graduate schools have existed for years to train government officials for international service, but few of them prepared students for other international careers. In recent years, this has shifted substantially. There has been significant growth in international affairs and international public policy programs offered to students interested in working for multilateral organizations, NGOs, the international media and multinational corporations. The School of International and Public Affairs at Columbia University, SIPA, is an impressive example, from which more than 650 students from one hundred countries graduate every year. The London School of Economics, the Institut des Hautes Études Sciences Politiques in Paris and the Lee Kuan Yew School of Public Policy at the National University of Singapore, now all have such programs, as do Johns Hopkins, Yale, Harvard, Tufts, Princeton and Stanford, to name a few. Columbia University recently established the world's first five-year PhD program in sustainable development, evidence of academia's increasing commitment to this issue.

In the early 1970s hardly any business school in the world offered courses in international business, or on the international aspects of finance, accounting or the other subjects they offered. Today, business schools give considerable emphasis to the international aspects of each subject. Many colleges and even high schools now provide courses on international issues, including language training and study abroad programs. Courses in social entrepreneurship are also being introduced.

Foundations—
Gradually going global

Foundations have also emerged as important players in dealing with global poverty and sustainability challenges. The Ford and Rockefeller foundations have been operating internationally for decades. The Bill & Melinda Gates Foundation and Google.org are major new players, and foundations as a whole will undoubtedly make greater and greater contributions to solving global challenges. The 71,000 U.S.–based grant-making foundations annually allocate over $40 billion to charitable causes, of which approximately $4 billion, or 10%, goes internationally. Foundations are clearly giving more attention to international issues and seeking to figure out ways to do so more strategically, entrepreneurially and collaboratively. The Global Philanthropy Forum is playing a very significant role in helping bring about these changes.

Multinational Corporations—
A major part of the problem can be a major part of the solution

Multinational as well as local businesses in each country are often justifiably criticized as being part of the problem. It is clear, however, that the major challenges of our era cannot, and will not, be addressed effectively without the business sector recognizing that it is in their enlightened self-interest to become part of the solution. The most recent entities on the international scene to focus on the plight of the poor and the importance of a sustainable planet are a few farsighted multinational corporations with strategies to achieve a "triple bottom line," referring to "people, profits and planet." The evolving role of multinational corporations is explored in Chapter 10.

While the increased awareness, capabilities and actions taken by each of the seven groups mentioned above are impressive, one out of seven people in our world still lives in extreme poverty, and the environmental stress caused by population and consumption pressures on our planet has reached a critical point. While governments and multilateral institutions remain pivotal to solving these challenges, they have reached the limits of their capacity to do what is required given their current practices. Their track record does not inspire confidence. There has been more talk than action. Now, the stakes are too high to assume that they will develop the political will, allocate the resources and implement the programs necessary to achieve success.

The following statistics highlight the current realities of the human condition today:

- More than 900 million people live in extreme poverty, defined as earning less than $1 per day. Each is seeking to survive without access to any of the basic services that many take for granted, such as clean water, health clinics, education and housing.

- An estimated 50,000 people, the majority of whom are women and children, die every day due to poverty-related causes.

- The world as a whole has been on a nonstop consumption binge over the past half-century, consuming more natural resources since the end of the Second World War than in all human history up to that point.

- The richest 10% of adults in the world own more than 85% of the world's assets, while the bottom half of the world's adult population owns just 1%.

- The gap between the rich and the extreme poor continues to grow, largely because the rich have the ability to use their knowledge and their money to make more money; meanwhile the extreme poor are trapped in circumstances that make it nearly impossible for them to dig their way out of poverty without access to services such as an education or financial loans.

Some argue that the world's material resource sustainability problems are largely due to rapid population increases in the poorer countries of the world, and this has certainly contributed to the problem. But, those 900 million extreme poor consume less than 2% of the world's resources and are clearly not the cause of the world's sustainability challenges.

Some argue that technological advances will allow us to create more with less, and thus enable us all to grow and consume at current rates. But, despite the creativity of human beings and the wonders of technology, the current levels of consumption by the "haves" of the world are not sustainable even if the more impoverished countries stopped their population growth and remained at their current minimal rates of consumption.

Some argue that the funds are not available to end extreme poverty. That is a contrived argument by vested interests focused on other priorities, such as defense spending. Professor Jeffrey Sachs of Columbia University's Earth Institute and author of *The End of Poverty*, who played a major role in the development and promotion of the United Nations Millennium Goals, estimates that a mere

0.7% of the GNP (gross national product) of rich countries is all that is required financially to eliminate extreme poverty. The United States currently spends roughly seven times that amount on its military each year, and the Iraq War alone costs far more than 0.7% of U.S. annual GNP. The reality is that extreme poverty has not as yet generated sufficient concern and the political will necessary to bring about a shift in priorities.

The UN Millennium Goals, signed by 189 heads of state in 2000, was a significant step forward in the world's acknowledgement of the problem. It called for a 50% reduction in the number of people living in extreme poverty by 2015. In addition, nearly all the world's heads of state agreed to achieve universal primary education, to promote gender equality and the empowerment of women, to reduce child mortality, to improve maternal health, to combat HIV/AIDS and to ensure environmental sustainability. Chapters 3–9 of this book highlight twenty-seven extraordinary initiatives developed to address these issues by social entrepreneurs around the world.

THE COMING ANARCHY—
Driven by the World's Poor with Little to Lose

> *October 6, 2007*
> *I have just returned from Eastern Chad, where I visited the camps for Darfuri refugees and the internally displaced persons (IDPs) of Chad. The region is burdened not only by poverty, but by outbreaks of malaria, yellow fever, dengue fever—and both criminal and political violence. More than 240,000 refugees from Darfur have resettled in Chad this year. An additional 180,000 have been internally displaced by the spreading chaos. The crises in Sudan and Chad are interlinked, and could spread to the Central African Republic. Warring ethnic groups span the borders, and rebel militias supported by each country's president wreak havoc in the other's fragile and lawless state.*

> —Jane Wales,
> President of the North American World Affairs Council,
> to the board of trustees

Not only should we be concerned about the extreme poor for obvious humanitarian reasons, we should also be concerned for geopolitical reasons. While there are many poor people in the advanced countries, the extreme poor living in developing countries are often the victims of, and sometimes even partially the cause of, failed states like Somalia, Sudan, North Korea, Zimbabwe, Palestine and Chad. States that collapse are not only the cause of violence and enormous dysfunction within their borders, but they also destabilize neighboring countries, thereby affecting the whole world's geopolitical structure, as was the case in Afghanistan. If the chaos and bloodshed becomes too great for the world to ignore any longer, some states and international organizations will have to step in and spend a great deal of money in the process of getting things under control.

Fifty years ago, the desperately poor were more isolated and less aware of what they lacked. Increasingly they have become aware of the gap between what they have and what others have. That awareness is a growing source of instability in a world that touts economic growth and the "more is better" message behind it. Many of the extreme poor have moved to cities where consumption and consumerism are much more pervasive. Many of those living in isolated areas now have some access to TV and radio, which are largely driven by consumer-oriented advertising or programming that depicts the rich and famous. The extreme poor thus have reason to feel disenfranchised, and at times may feel that they have nothing to lose if they try to acquire, or destroy, what others have.

Economic disparity is a destabilizer, the genocide in Cambodia during the late 1970s being just one of many examples. Organized by Pol Pot, the leader of the Khmer Rouge, disenfranchised Cambodian peasants were stirred up and directed to find and kill those who appeared to show signs of affluence, such as anyone who wore glasses or had gold fillings. Before the genocide ended, 1.8 million Cambodians had died, many massacred in "killing fields" by their fellow Cambodians. I once asked Arn Chorn Pond—a Cambodian friend who at the age of nine was forced to play the flute during the killings—how many people he had witnessed being killed or who he had been forced to kill himself. He thought for a while and then murmured "maybe 5,000." As unimaginable as that sounds, it happened. To put this in perspective, between the age of nine and twelve, Arn had witnessed the killing of more of his fellow Cambodians than the total number of U.S. military killed in both Gulf wars.

In his book *The Coming Anarchy*, Robert Kaplan presents a possible future in which gangs of disenfranchised urban poor ravage large areas. Although presented as a worst-case scenario, it is not one to be taken lightly. For example, on May 15, 2006, the BBC reported just such a situation from Sao Paolo, Brazil: "Masked men attacked bars, banks and police stations with machine guns. Gangs set buses on fire, and inmates at dozens of prisons took guards hostage in an unprecedented four-day wave of violence around South America's largest city that left more than eight dead."

Unfortunately, the advances of technology that have helped the process of globalization and economic growth have also made it easier for the disenchanted

The first picture of the Earth from space, taken by the Apollo 17 crew on December 7, 1972.

to lash out by using weapons unimaginable fifty years ago. While those who flew planes into the World Trade Center and the Pentagon on 9/11 were quite well educated—as are Osama Bin Laden and the leaders of Hamas and Hezbollah—those they convince or coerce to blow themselves up for the greater good are often very poor and have little education and little to lose.

WE ARE ALL IN THIS TOGETHER

A fundamental shift is taking place in people's awareness of these challenges and in their desire to take personal responsibility and action to address them. William James Durant, the twentieth-century American philosopher and author of *The Story of Civilization*, wrote that we would only realize that "we were all in this together" if we were threatened by aliens. Similarly, Edgar Mitchell, the sixth man to stand on the moon, said that a fundamental shift occurred in the way he saw humankind and our small, vulnerable planet, when he was returning from the moon in the Apollo 14 spacecraft in 1971. That epiphany led him to establish the Institute of Noetic Sciences (IONS) that scientifically explores consciousness. Another global shift in awareness and consciousness occurred on December 7, 1972 when the crew of the Apollo 17 spacecraft took a photo of Earth from outer space (previous page). It showed us all how relatively small, fragile, and interconnected our home is. It is one of the most widely distributed photographs in history.

Genetically, 99.9% of the makeup of all human beings is identical, but we spend most of our time focusing on our differences. It may now be time for us to focus on what binds us together, such as our shared concerns. Since it is not practical for all 6.6 billion of us to go to the moon to experience such a shift in worldview, we will have to reach the "tipping point" in our collective consciousness by other means, if indeed we do. Human brains are designed to respond to sudden threats, not gradual changes. Global warming, for example, would cause many more people to take action if millions of people in the United States or Western Europe suddenly were at risk of losing their land and livelihoods due to the ocean rising, as occurred during Hurricane Katrina in New Orleans. A nuclear device set off by terrorists who felt they had nothing to lose might also act as a drastic call to action. This book is suggesting that we not wait for such atrocities, and that to prevent such outcomes for our children, we must act now, not by responding to a disaster, but by acting voluntarily when we have the opportunity to do so.

Is More Better—or Sustainable?

The conventional measure of a nation's "progress" is the growth of its gross national product, or GNP. Included in GNP, however, are many revenue-generating activities that pollute the earth and destroy the lives of others. People often measure their own success by their personal financial growth rate and total assets just as nations do. But a shift in perspective is occurring. In today's world, more and more people are questioning the notion that "more is better"—or sustainable. They are also questioning how we measure "progress." For example:

- Since 1994 the California-based organization Redefining Progress has been challenging traditional ways in which economic, social and ecological impacts are conceptualized and measured. Its measure is called the Genuine Progress Indicator (GPI). It starts with the same accounting framework as the gross national product, but then makes some significant distinctions. For example, it includes the economic contributions of household and volunteer work, but subtracts factors such as crime, pollution and family breakdown that result in activities that decrease a nation's gross national product.

- The United Nations Development Programme (UNDP) has created the Human Development Index (HDI) that emphasizes the social development aspects of each country's development agendas.

- *The WorldPaper* created the Wealth of Nations Index in the early 1990s using sixty-three variables to measure each country's progress along three dimensions: economic, social and information exchange. The underlying premise is that those countries with great strength and balance in all three dimensions are those that will make the greatest and most sustainable progress.

- Futurist Hazel Henderson has produced a similar index, as has the government of Bhutan. The Bhutanese call theirs the "Gross Happiness Index" which is their attempt to measure quality of life in more holistic and spiritual terms than gross national product.

- The World Social Forum was established in 2001 in reaction to the big business–oriented World Economic Forum held in Davos, Switzerland each year. The World Social Forum's seventh annual gathering, which took place in Nairobi, Kenya in January of 2007, had 66,000 registered attendees, and 1,400 participating organizations from 110 countries.

- The Earth Charter, created in the 1990s, is a declaration of fundamental principles for building a just, sustainable and peaceful global society in the twenty-first century. It seeks to inspire a sense of global interdependence and shared responsibility for the well-being of the human family and the living world. Thousands of people and organizations from virtually all of the countries of the world collaborated in the development of these principles.

These and other initiatives are clearly having an impact on how we view our world and how we view our own responsibilities to deal with global challenges such as the restoration of a sustainable planet. Some have been tracking this shift for many years. In 1986, Paul Ray, a PhD sociologist, started doing research in the United States, tracking the attitudes and actions of people he labeled "cultural creatives." The attributes of cultural creatives include caring deeply about ecology and saving the planet, human relationships, peace, social justice, self-actualization, spirituality and self-expression. They are inner-directed and socially concerned. They are activists, volunteers and contributors to good causes.

Ray's research found that there were only 2 million cultural creatives in the United States in 1964. By 2000 the research indicated that that number had grown to 50 million in the United States and 80–90 million in the European Union. While cultural creatives have not emerged as a political group, much less a party, this data also suggests that a fundamental shift has been taking place below the political surface with an increasing number of people challenging prevailing worldviews and becoming more socially active.

Unintended Consequences

Some argue that those who live in cities, as half the world does, and those who are consumed by a desire to have more and more are becoming increasingly out of balance with the natural world and with each other. *The Last Child in the Woods,* by Richard Louv, explores the problems developed by children who have little exposure to the natural world. Louv calls it "nature deficit disorder." Further, an article published in the *American Sociological Review* in June 2006 reported that the number of people in the United States who have no one to confide in has more than doubled to 25% since 1985, suggesting that our individualistic, transaction-oriented society is resulting in many people feeling alienated and alone.

The Balinese appear to be more conscious of the need for balance in their lives. Indeed, the Balinese concept *Tri Hita Karana* means to be in balance with the natural world, with each other in community and with spirit. While the Balinese may have little to teach the rest of the world about economic growth, they have much to share about living lives of balance and harmony. And, it seems that more and more people are listening.

Agung Rai, the founder of the Agung Rai Museum of the Arts (ARMA) in Bali, invites foreign visitors to explore ways of leading lives based on such balance. He notes that the Balinese phrase *angkaramurka* refers to the damage people inflict upon themselves when they are never satisfied with what they have and always want more. He mentions the Balinese word *moksa,* which means to seek balance between the material and the spiritual. *Angkaramurka* may be hardwired into the world's operating system without most people being aware of the consequences.

In 1949, Tarzie Vittachi, a young Indian reporter, had an opportunity to interview Mahatma Gandhi and asked him, "How are you going to build an Indian nation that will satisfy the wants of the Indian people?"

"I am going to teach them to reduce their wants and satisfy their needs," Gandhi responded. That seems an appropriate approach to be considered by the entire world in the coming years of global resource challenges and serious concerns about global sustainability.

The Emergence of Individual Responsibility

It is now possible for more people than ever to collaborate and compete in real time with more people on more different kinds of work from more different corners of the planet and on a more equal footing than at any previous time in the history of the world.

—Thomas Friedman, *The World Is Flat*

Given the challenges we face, you may feel overwhelmed and not believe that individuals like you can make a difference. Again, there is good news. Friedman's *The World Is Flat* documents how the Internet has fundamentally changed what individuals as well as organizations can do globally to find information, collaborate in ways never previously possible, and thereby take greater responsibility.

The Internet makes it possible for any individual anywhere in the world with access to a computer and the web to explore virtually any topic of interest, and then to find and collaborate with other individuals they have never met before.

Let's assume you want to research organizations working in Uganda to assist women who are infected with HIV. That is no longer the complicated research task it would have been five years ago. On the contrary, you can go to WiserEarth.org or one of several other websites mentioned in Part III of this book, and with just a few clicks of your mouse have the names, websites and contact information of organizations seeking to address that challenge.

Or maybe you have experience in retailing, your ancestors came from Azerbaijan and you would therefore like to lend $100 to someone there who wants to open a small retail operation. That too is now only a few clicks of a mouse away. Just go to Kiva.org (profiled in Chapter 5) and look at the photos of those in Azerbaijan looking for loans and a description of their projects. Take out a credit card and designate on your screen to whom you want your $100 loan to go to in Azerbaijan, thereby establishing a relationship with someone across the world. To date, Kiva has had a 98% repayment rate.

Or you may have become intrigued while reading in this book's introduction about Mark Hanis's initiative to address genocide in the Sudan and want to know more. Your first step could be to log on to GoogleEarth.com where you can view satellite images of the Sudanese villages that have been destroyed and where villagers were slaughtered.

Mark Hanis, founder of the Genocide Intervention Network.

Because travel from one continent to another is now so fast, it is possible for someone in Asia to contract a disease such as SARS or bird flu on Monday and travel halfway around the world by Wednesday, weeks before the disease is detected and tracked to its source. The exciting development here is that "bottom up" information systems using the Internet are already enabling citizens to report diseases to international health organizations and NGOs long before local governments have collected the data, made it public, and taken remedial action.

Soon, someone is likely to create a system for using GPS coordinates instead of postal codes to instantly locate rural villages around the globe. Think how valuable this could be to emergency rescuers rushing to drive overland to a remote area hit by a disaster in Africa, Asia or anywhere around the world. Just as exciting might be the notion of your creating a for-profit company that offers this service. You might make a difference in the world while making an excellent livelihood.

THE INTERNET AS THE GREAT DEMOCRATIZER

In fact, the Internet has become the great democratizer. In a world in which big government and big business seem to dominate our lives, the Internet now makes it possible for any individual to have his or her voice heard around the world and to take action and make a difference. If you want to contact someone in Uganda, Afghanistan or the Sudan and have been reluctant to do so because of the high cost of international phone service, set up Skype or a similar Internet-based phone service on your computer and speak to them for a fraction of what you would have paid for the same call a few years ago, or today using traditional phone services. Near instantaneous transmission of information in almost any form can also connect us simultaneously as never before, as when Live 8 and Live Earth concerts take place around the world on the same day.

An aspiring film producer with a video camera and access to the Internet can post clips on YouTube.com for the world to see. The number of clicks on the film clip equals, in effect, a popular vote for its content. Live in the woods and publish your book online and see if anyone will pay for it. Start a small business that collects and sells used books and make a deal with Amazon to sell your books through their huge channel of distribution.[1]

So, for those who want to "get on with it" and move from concern to action in addressing such issues as extreme poverty and a sustainable planet, there are no excuses. The very good news is that people all over the world are indeed doing just that. They are joining the "civil society movement," which some argue is the fastest growing movement in human history.

---

[1] Read *The Long Tail* by Chris Anderson and get an additional glimpse at how the Internet is making it possible for individuals with powerful ideas but without their own distribution systems to piggyback on the established distribution systems of others to achieve their goals.

And of all those getting on with it, young adults and retired older people are likely to surprise us with their energy, commitment, collaborative skills, creativity and effectiveness. Impatient but well-informed young adults want to take action, not just talk about the problems. Many retired professionals and other adults who are living longer lives than previous generations want to stay engaged and use their professional expertise to make a difference.

YOUTH RISING

Nicholas D. Kristof, a *New York Times* columnist, writes extensively about those living in extreme poverty and of those social entrepreneurs, young and old, who are energetically and creatively addressing age-old challenges in ways that bring about systematic solutions. He argues that these young social entrepreneurs are the twenty-first-century version of the student protestors of the 1960s.

Mark Hanis and his Genocide Intervention Network, mentioned in this book's introduction, are good examples. The following are a few more, all suggesting that this is not an isolated phenomenon but indeed the rising power and effectiveness of youth around the world.

- The eighty-four youths from twenty-six countries who found their way to the second Quest for Global Healing gathering in Bali in May of 2006. They spent three days by themselves before the formal gathering began, and when they arrived for the first day of the major gathering of 650 individuals from forty countries, they wanted to come up with solutions, not just talk about the problems. The tenacious Rim Nour, a twenty-eight-year-old woman from Tunisia was among them. She found out about the gathering through the Internet, arranged for a scholarship, worked out the complicated visa and travel arrangements and made the journey alone from Tunis, through Rome, Frankfurt, Bangkok and Singapore, before arriving in Bali. She was not looking for excuses, but rather to collaborate with others in finding solutions to many of the world's challenges.

- The 1,000 graduate students from over one hundred countries studying international public policy or international affairs at SIPA, the School of International and Public Affairs at Columbia University in New York. They go on to work for the UN, international NGOs, international investment banks, their own foreign ministries or they become international social entrepreneurs. They are bright and totally committed to taking action, rather than just talking about the challenges.

- The 550 instructors at the National Outdoor Leadership School. Based in Wyoming and operating in fourteen countries around the world, NOLS is the world's leading school teaching wilderness skills and is the organization that developed the "Leave No Trace" practices for venturing into the natural world. On the west coast of the United States, the instructors at the Yosemite National Institutes share that same commitment to and respect for the natural world.

Phoebe Coburn in Nepal at the Magic Yeti Library.

- Jeffrey Buenrostro, an MBA student at the Stanford Graduate School of Business, is committed to using business methods to create a just and sustainable world. Before business school he worked for a local community development agency and for the national Give US Your Poor project, helped rebuild a monastery in Mongolia and most recently spent the summer in Uganda designing a business that uses innovative clean technology to deliver electricity in rural areas. During his first year at business school he invited nine others to join him to address various social challenges, conditional upon each contributing $1,000 a year for ten years to those challenges.

- Phoebe Coburn, a fourteen-year-old girl from Jackson Hole, Wyoming, learned that there are hardly any books available for children to read in the Khumbu region of Nepal near Mount Everest. So she started collecting books, raising money and shipping the books to Nepal for the Magic Yeti Library for children. This is the first in a series of libraries she hopes to stock with books over the years ahead. Phoebe has even traveled to Nepal to help paint the library and catalogue the books.

In addition, there are many, many organizations already established by youth in the United States, Europe, Asia and elsewhere that are taking action. These include Global Youth in Action, Youth for Environmental Sanity, Youth Works, Youth Venture, PeaceJam, Generation Waking Up and the Energy Action Coalition, to name just a few. There are also online communities supporting youth interested in social entrepreneurship, such as the Youth Social Enterprise Initiative.

The Encore Generation

Something new and equally powerful is happening with men and women of retirement age who are addressing many of these challenges around the world. Unlike their grandparents, they can expect to live longer and stay relatively healthy and active for twenty or thirty years past retirement age. They have skills as a result of years of professional work, and may also have considerable financial resources. They know much more about the state of the world than did previous generations, are concerned and want to collaborate with others and come up with solutions.

In the United States, an organization called Civic Ventures awards "Purpose Prizes" each year to people over sixty who are taking on society's biggest challenges. Civic Ventures awards five prizes of $100,000 and ten of $10,000. As their website states, it is for "those with the passion and creativity to discover new opportunities, the experience to come up with practical solutions, and the determination to make a difference." Another organization, The Center for Global Service, also seeks to inspire and support seniors who want to play an active role in these areas.

While this is the age in which individuals young and old can make substantial contributions to create a more just and sustainable world, success will, to a large degree, require collaboration among a broad and diverse range of people and organizations with the necessary capabilities. The challenges are becoming so complex, often requiring financial, management and technical skills as well as experience and passion, that individuals and organizations need to pool their expertise. Establishing effective collaborations therefore will increasingly be critical for those who want to successfully tackle these challenges.

— CHAPTER 2 —

Becoming a Social Entrepreneur

What we need is an entrepreneurial society in which innovation and entrepreneurship are normal, steady, and continuous.

—Peter F. Drucker
Innovation and Entrepreneurship: Practice and Principles

M any who are concerned about the challenges of the twenty-first century do not know how to move from concern to action. They may feel overwhelmed or assume that they cannot make a difference.

While these feelings are understandable, today's world is filled with individuals no more capable than those reading this book who have stepped forward to develop initiatives for change. Some will join with other concerned citizens and take more modest and less time-consuming actions, such as committing to reduce their yearly consumption of energy. Some are called social entrepreneurs because they make it their life's work to tackle a major issue using unconventional initiatives to deliver health-care services to the rural poor in Africa, deliver mobile phone service to the poor in rural Asia or tackle some other issue they are passionate about.

First Steps

Whether you are aiming to become a social entrepreneur or simply want to take some meaningful action to address an issue that concerns you, the following are some practical steps that may help guide your journey:

Be clear on what you are passionate about.
You are undoubtedly concerned about a lot of things, but what are you truly passionate about: Teaching disadvantaged children in your neighborhood? Ending homelessness? Caring for battered women? Creating new hope for refugees in Sudan? Decreasing the impact of global warming? Improving market conditions for indigenous artisans? Helping resolve conflict in the Middle East? Something

else? If you are not passionate about what you choose, you won't commit to it fully, and you are likely to lose interest when life's other challenges give you the excuse to let your initiative slide.

Determine what skills you have that are relevant to the issue.
Passion is essential, but not enough. What skills or capabilities do you have that will help sustain and fulfill your passion? Do you have money to invest, or are you a great fundraiser? Do you have knowledge of the issue, or knowledge of the people and the culture where the work needs to be done? Do you have a network of friends and professional contacts you can draw upon? Do you have specific professional skills that will be required for the initiative to be successful, such as accounting, marketing, finance or production? Are you a good leader who can recruit and lead a team to help achieve your goals?

Consider whether you have the personality to be a social entrepreneur.
Not everyone has the disposition to be a social entrepreneur. Here are several important attributes:

- Great determination, coupled with a willingness to take risks, experiment and occasionally fail and have to start again. When Charlotte di Vita, one of the social entrepreneurs profiled in this book, asked Richard Branson for assistance, he asked her how many times she had failed, gotten up and tried to achieve her goals another way. He said he could not help her unless she had failed at least twice, reassessed what it would take to be successful and tried again.

- The ability to "boundary ride"—to imagine possibilities that are radically different from traditional approaches to the same problem. Muhammad Yunus of Bangladesh, the visionary behind microcredit lending, was a good example of "boundary riding" when he defied the prevailing view that one could not "bank on the poor." Yunus realized that many of the poor who had no collateral could still be reliable borrowers, and that banking on the poor was well worth the effort because it would address an important social challenge and could also become self-financing and possibly profitable.

Determine which of these three ways of being of service interests you most and would be a good fit, given your capabilities:

- Giving money to an organization that is addressing the issue.

- Working for an organization that interests you, as a volunteer or as a paid employee.

- Starting your own initiative by replicating an existing initiative, or developing your own.

These options are very different in terms of the financial resources, time and talent you may have to invest. One is not better than another and each has great value. For example, it may be wise to take on something relatively small and straightforward first, like going to www.GlobalCool.org, and developing a plan to reduce your personal carbon footprint over the next year by one ton. Or you may decide you want to become a volunteer at another environmental awareness building organization such as the Pachamama Alliance (profiled in Chapter 9). Or, you may decide you want to replicate the PlayPumps water system described in Chapter 3 to bring clean water to poverty-stricken areas of your own country. Social entrepreneurs, unlike those in competitive businesses, are usually willing to share their ideas with others who want to replicate them.

Log on to www.TacticsofHope.org.
This book provides examples of numerous initiatives that you might give money to, work for or replicate on your own. The personal stories of the social entrepreneurs profiled in these chapters provide valuable insights about potential obstacles you may face, and how to overcome them. We have also created a website to help you determine your next steps, direct you to other sources of information about the growing field of social entrepreneurship, help you identify other initiatives of interest and provide contact information with many of those with whom you may want to collaborate.

Take that first step.
Each of the profiles in the upcoming chapters has a section in which the social entrepreneurs share their own journey from concern and passion to action. A few did a great deal of research, consulted the experts and came up with a strategic plan as their first steps. Others just jumped right in and followed their instincts, taking one small step after another. Both approaches can work well, depending on the individual and the initiative. Procrastination does not work well.

Assessing Potential Initiatives

Let's assume you want to assess whether the challenges you are likely to face are manageable and what you might be able to accomplish if the initiatives were successful. To do this, you may want to take a look at the following characteristics that distinguish one initiative from another, and consider them as you look at the initiatives profiled in Chapters 3–9:

- **Replicability**
  Replicability refers to whether the project established in one locale can be replicated in another, by you or another entrepreneur. One example is the low-tech PlayPumps: when children play on a merry-go-round attached to a pump, water from underground wells is drawn into a 2,500-liter tank, providing rural villagers in sub-Saharan Africa access to clean drinking water. Another is Liza Kimbo's Child and Family Wellness health clinics, which she created to deliver basic health-care services in rural Kenya. Another is Agung Prana's restoration of the coral reefs adjacent to his ecotourism resort in northern Bali, using a simple technology and significant community involvement. In all these cases, the approach can be replicated in other parts of the world by others with the passion, determination and skills to do so.

- **Scalability**
  Scaling an initiative means extending its scope beyond the local region in which it was initially conceived to include thousands more people in a much broader geographic scope. This is certainly true in the case of Kiva, which has grown exponentially around the world by building human connections through the Internet. GrameenPhone is another example of scaling, as is the Campaign for Female Education (CAMFED), Room to Read, RugMark Foundation, World of Good and the Pachamama Alliance.

- **Ease of entry**
  Will it be easy to get your initiative up and running, or are there bureaucratic and other barriers that you will have to overcome? Since telecommunications service in Bangladesh is controlled and licensed by the government, GrameenPhone could not move forward without obtaining the government's permission, which was a long, costly and painful process. Mark Hanis had no such obstacles to overcome

when he took steps to raise awareness about the genocide in Darfur. Conversely, Karen Tse, a Chinese-American lawyer, is working tirelessly to help prisoners who have been locked away, sometimes for decades, by government officials who often use their prisons to torture and stifle those who criticize the government. She often has to deal with government officials who deny their prisoners any fundamental rights. In addition, she has to raise money for a cause that much of the world has little understanding of or interest in. Without Karen's passion, determination and tenacity, most people would look at these barriers and feel that they were just too big to tackle.

- **Immediacy of results**
  We'd all like to create initiatives that will have an immediate, positive impact. Public interest and good results have come fairly quickly to organizations like Room to Read and Kiva. By contrast, other organizations—such as Search for Common Ground, which works on ethnic and religious conflict resolution—know very well that it may take years for their efforts to lead to concrete results. Nina Smith of RugMark Foundation is a great example of how a social entrepreneur asserts the immediacy of her results. Nina is certain that RugMark's goal of ending child labor in the carpet industry is absolutely possible to achieve, and it should take no more than ten years. This compelling and realistic goal helps fuel the passion of her staff.

- **Public support**
  The more the public is aware of an issue and can relate to it, the easier it will be to raise the necessary funds. Karen Tse of International Bridges to Justice and Sasha Chanoff of Mapendo have the courage to tackle two issues that have little support around the world—prisoner rights and the protections of refugees who do not have international agency protection.

- **Long-term financial sustainability**
  Will the initiative have to rely each year on funds you will have to raise or provide yourself, or can you think of ways that it can be financially self-sustaining? Once GrameenPhone had invested the capital required to assure the availability of satellite phone service and had sufficient inventory of mobile phones, Iqbal and his team could see that the income generated from those who rented or bought the

phones would soon translate into positive cash flow for the company. If an initiative can generate sufficient revenue to cover all costs and generate a profit, you may want to convert it to a for-profit entity as Iqbal did. Riders for Health, which you will read about in Chapter 3, generates considerable revenue to offset some of its costs, as does the Child and Family Wellness Shops, RugMark Foundation, World of Good, 21st Century Leaders, Turquoise Mountain and the Coral Reef Restoration Project. On the other hand, Room to Read, the Campaign for Female Education, Mapendo, International Bridges to Justice, and the Pachamama Alliance rely almost entirely on funds raised from outside sources.

- **Startup requirements**
  Some initiatives require a lot of capital to be invested up front, while others do not. Iqbal's GrameenPhone initiative, for example, required a large amount, while Mark Hanis's Internet-based initiative to raise money and awareness to help stop the genocide in Darfur required a good idea, student energy and a well-crafted email to a few influential political leaders and journalists.

- **Internet intensity**
  The Internet is the underlying technology that enables some initiatives to operate, such as Mark Hanis's Genocide Intervention Network and Kiva.org's microcredit lending initiative. In many other initiatives, the Internet is critical to their organization's far-flung operations to assure prompt communications at low cost.

The three diagrams that follow provide an easy way to take the characteristics mentioned above into consideration as you explore the feasibility of any initiative. These diagrams provide the assessments made by each of the social entrepreneurs behind Room to Read, RugMark Foundation and the Idea Village initiatives highlighted in Chapters 4, 6 and 8, respectively.

Room to Read

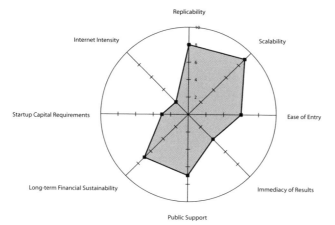

RugMark

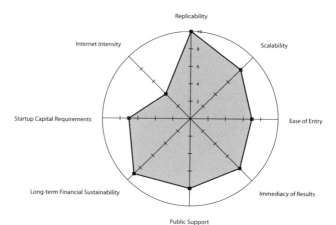

IDEA VILLAGE

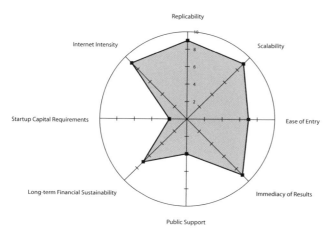

The source of the funds needed to get an initiative off the ground and then keep it in operation is one of the clearest ways of distinguishing one initiative from another. There are three funding possibilities: 1) fully funded by outside sources, 2) fully funded by internal operations and 3) funded through a combination, or hybrid, model of external and internal sources.

All of the initiatives profiled in Part II are plotted horizontally in the following diagram across this spectrum of funding options. Room to Read, CAMFED, International Bridges to Justice and Mapendo, for example, are among those that rely entirely on funds they raise from individuals, foundations and governments to continue their great work. At the other end of the spectrum are GrameenPhone, KIVA, 21st Century Leaders and several others that are already financially self-sufficient, or have the potential to reach financial self-sufficiency soon.

The diagram below plots vertically all of the initiatives profiled in the next chapters, as well as GrameenPhone and the Genocide Intervention Network based upon their relative ease of entry, one of the eight characteristics mentioned above. This may help you begin to distinguish between the various social entrepreneurial initiatives as you read about them in the next five chapters. And there are several other questions you may want to keep in mind as you explore what makes each of them so successful, in addition to replicability, scalability, funding requirements, ease of entry and the other characteristics discussed above. For example, to what extent is their success a function of listening deeply to and working closely with the communities where the initiative operates? How important has it been to work with national or local government officials? And have the social entrepreneurs sought to collaborate with other organizations with complementary skills they lack, or are their initiatives quite self-contained?

The chapters in Part II of this book are organized by issue. The introduction to each chapter provides statistics suggesting the gravity of the problem. What follows are descriptions of individual social entrepreneurs who have come up with powerful initiatives that are making a difference in addressing these challenges. Given your own particular interests, you may want to explore some profiles more than others. The websites of all the initiatives mentioned can be found in Part III as well as at www.TacticsofHope.org.

FUNDS

| From Donors | Hybrid | From Operations |

| Fewer Barriers | | |

E
A
S
E

O
F

E
N
T
R
Y

| Substantial Barriers | | |

- Genocide Intervention Network
- Room to Read
  - The Idea Village
  - Kiva
  - Pachamama Alliance
  - Philippine Youth Employment Network
  - Fundación San Miguel Arcangel
  - Next Level Foundation School
  - Child and Family Wellness Shops
- The Ella Baker Center
  - Committee for Democracy in Information Technology
  - World of Good
  - Riders for Health
- Campaign for Female Education
  - RugMark
  - Saúde Criança Renascer
  - Coral Reef Restoration Project
- International Committee of the Red Cross, Orthopedic Center
  - Trade plus Aid
- Search for Common Ground
  - PlayPumps
  - GrameenPhone
  - Roots of Peace
  - Turquoise Mountain
- Partners in Health
- International Bridges to Justice
- Mapendo International

Substantial Barriers and
Fully Funded From Operations

PART II

SOCIAL ENTREPRENEURS

CHAPTER 3

Health

Health-care systems in many developing countries are in crisis. Scott Hillstrom, the founder of CFWshops, an organization profiled with social entrepreneur Liza Kimbo later in this chapter, has said that part of what inspired him to tackle health issues in Africa was learning that 9 million children die each year from a lack of medicine that costs less than a cup of coffee.

In Africa alone, 25,000 children die every day—from diarrhea, malaria, malnourishment, poor sanitation or diseases inherited from birth—due to an inability to pay for life-saving medicines that cost the same as pocket change for most individuals in Europe and North America.

The lack of clean water compounds this devastating crisis in Africa. Clean water is of course the most fundamental element of good health. The developing world's access to clean water is inhumanely low: more than 1 billion people, half of whom live in sub-Saharan Africa, do not have access to clean drinking water. Lack of clean water causes or contributes to 80% of all sickness in the world. Children miss school days from such sicknesses. Women and girls in many developing countries walk an average of five miles to the nearest water source. Perhaps most strikingly, a child dies every fifteen seconds from a water-related illness. It did not used to be this way, but human activity is causing water resources to dry up as water tables drop.

Health and access to clean water are not isolated issues. They affect our ability to contribute to our community, and how we learn, work and produce. Health is intertwined with issues of poverty, education and citizenship.

There are many other social entrepreneurs taking a lead in improving human health worldwide. The Bill & Melinda Gates Foundation is the world-leading NGO in this arena. There are countless others doing good work, but they frequently lack the financial resources necessary to leverage their impact. While five stories of socially entrepreneurial organizations are told below, there are many others not detailed in this chapter that have also achieved incredible results. Examples include:

- The Center for Attitudinal Healing
- Ethos Water, Starbucks
- Hedge Funds vs. Malaria

- The Institute for OneWorld Health
- KickStart
- VillageReach

In this chapter you will read five very distinct stories from the following social entrepreneurs who have created revolutionary solutions to local and global health challenges:

- **Vera Cordeiro**, a physician in Brazil who began by setting up a health clinic, working with destitute children and mothers out of a horse stable.

- **Paul Farmer**, a Harvard medical anthropologist and physician who began fighting to save lives after traveling to Haiti when he was eighteen.

- **Trevor Field and Paul Ristic**, two advertising specialists who introduced a new way of bringing fresh drinking water to rural populations in Africa.

- **Andrea and Barry Coleman**, a husband-and-wife team bringing better medical transportation services to the African continent based on a shared love of professional motorcycle riding.

- **Liza Kimbo**, a businesswoman in Kenya who helped create franchise medical clinics run by unemployed nurses who sell life-saving pharmaceutical drugs at affordable prices to families suffering from treatable diseases.

VERA CORDEIRO
Saúde Criança Renascer

Brazil

Vera Cordeiro began Saúde Criança Renascer, or the Children's Health Association, in 1991 as a new approach to medical care in Rio de Janeiro, Brazil, to fight poverty and ill health simultaneously. Through its signature five-point program of health, housing, income, education and citizenship, Renascer seeks to treat not only the immediate medical problem of an individual, but also the conditions that may have caused the ailment in the first place. As a clinical physician in the Psychosomatic Medicine

Department at Hospital da Lagoa in Rio, she was exposed to thousands of children who were readmitted several times a year for the same illnesses. Vera believes that the greatest systemic treatment is not a particular medicine for a particular illness, but rather a holistic approach to patients' overall health concerns, employment status and family needs. Since starting Renascer out of a horse stable in Rio, over the last seventeen years Vera has recruited an enormous network of volunteers, physicians, psychologists, teachers and community leaders to offer their expertise in one aspect of the five-point program. Taking one step

at a time, the entire network of Saúde Criança has so far reached 20,000 people, breaking a vicious cycle of poverty and social exclusion in Brazil. As an example of how one social entrepreneur can be tenacious enough to affect the lives of so many, Vera was recognized as "The Most Influential Woman of Brazil in the Health Area" by Forbes Brazil *in 2005, fourteen years after she started.*

VERA CORDEIRO—*Treating the Health of the Whole One by One*

> *Whatever steps we take, even if they are small,*
> *The most important thing is to rejoice*
> *and to celebrate in those small steps.*
> *Then they become powerful.*

> —Excerpt from a Buddhist poem

In Brazil, we work to break a vicious cycle known to all the poor and sick. I saw it, as everyone in my profession did. Pediatricians, surgeons, psychologists and social workers all see it. The cycle, especially for women and children, goes from poverty to illness to hospital admission to release to readmission. And then often, too quickly, to death.

Too many of the poor, especially children, are treated for their medical condition, but not their living health. Children are released from a hospital for a scientifically diagnosed medical ailment, and then they return to the *favelas* (slums) they came from, to a place not only without food, but also without hope. It was all so frustrating to see as a doctor. My patients were returning to the slums, the same poor environment that most likely created their sickness in the first place.

Beyond a patient's medical diagnosis, we consider his or her overall condition in life. Every volunteer and employee at Renascer is trained to dig deeper to care for the whole person. We ask our patients where they live. What are their sources of income, if any? Have they had an education? Are they engaged in their community? These five areas—health, income, housing, education and citizenship—are all equally critical to those who suffer most from the misery of being so poor. It is a social, spiritual and medical diagnosis. It is true that I am a trained physician and that I have been trained to work in a hospital. But I believe deeply that to cure someone from the favelas, you must cure the whole person by providing the individual with dignity.

We started just by listening to patients' needs. Basic health was at the top of that list. To sustain health, though, children and families said that they needed income, housing, employment and proper health education. So we set to work applying for grants, and asking for companies to support our cause. We enlisted anyone who could provide a service: doctors, family care planners, homebuilders, teachers and administrative volunteers. Then, in those communities that were worst off, we began encouraging mothers to meet in groups, discuss their worries and challenges, and bond together to help each other. We also began creating dialogue workshops between those mothers and women from wealthier families. This is a fundamental pillar of encouraging citizenship through social inclusion.

Many have doubted this approach. Especially when we started, they said our work was too vast and not focused enough. Those who say such things do not understand our methodology. It is not too much to treat someone as a whole person. That is how we started, and that is how we continue to work, by treating one child, one family, at a time.

Muhammad Yunus, who won a Nobel Prize for helping millions in his home country of Bangladesh, began by giving a microloan to one woman. Like him, we started by treating and assisting just one family in a horse shed next to a hospital in Rio de Janeiro. The horse stable was our starting point, and I promised our few volunteers at that time that we would succeed by applauding every little success. Here we are sixteen years later and we've helped over 11,000 people, and the entire network around Saúde Criança has reached nearly 20,000 people. The government's ministry of health, which is used to treating people just for a medical disease or just for their poverty, is now looking to integrate all five areas of human health into its new plans.

In 1991, I remember wanting to begin Renascer because I saw my home country as two separate worlds. One world was the side that could work, eat, communicate and live properly; the other could not even do simple things like eat and walk. At home, I was a part of the world that had many material things and nice vacations. As a doctor in the psychosomatic department, though, I was a part of the other world. Or at least I witnessed it. I saw kids dying not only within their bodies, but also within their minds. So many children were suffering, from leukemia or other forms of cancer, infectious disease, HIV or starvation. It was never solely the physical manifestations of their sickness that affected me. It was also the psychological effects my patients were showing from a basic lack of hope.

So to raise money, I started by raffling things from my home. I sold things that were just "pleasures," everything from my own children's clothes they didn't really need to pieces of furniture and decorations that my husband and I had collected over the years. It was all very liberating to do that. I don't believe in the true effectiveness of a social organization that moves too fast. Sometimes people talk so much about accomplishing enormous goals like ending poverty or sickness. It's OK to think big, but you must walk slowly, one step at a time, in order to move forward everyday, because you must pass through the pains and obstacles and failures. This is a part of the process of succeeding: to overcome challenges to find truth in your vision and your ability to achieve what you set out to do before you learn how hard it might be.

We faced so many "no's" when we started. I sent out 117 letters applying for financial support and grants all over the world. It was frustrating to be turned down for every one of them in different languages: Portuguese, English, French, Spanish and even Swedish, which I thought was funny because I couldn't read it. But while thinking big and looking for financial backing, we were really just focused on celebrating the small victories with limited money to help each family that came to us. First, it was treating one family in a horse stable, then two families. Despite our setbacks, I was committed both in mind and heart to create a DNA formula for comprehensive health care that could be adopted for programs near each public hospital in our region.

The biggest breakthroughs came when we began to develop a fast-growing partnership network. Ashoka, Avina, Skoll, Schwab and now PATH have played the biggest role in our growth. Bill Drayton, the founder and head of Ashoka, recognized our work as social entrepreneurship from his first contact with us, and then helped Ashoka put us in contact with his old management consulting firm called McKinsey & Co. McKinsey is one of the corporate partners that aided us so much by giving us 5,000 hours pro bono to conduct proper measurement to see if our comprehensive approach to integrated health was really working. After much analysis, the tests proved without a doubt how much of a difference we really were having in people's lives and well-being. On a family-by-family basis, we were improving their housing situation, their ability to generate income, their community participation and their education as to what was possible in Rio.

To say that we treat the whole person does not mean that we have endless resources to buy everyone housing and provide them all with jobs and an education. With our current budget of about $1 million a year, that would not be possible for the hundreds of people who walk through our doors. Our comprehensive way to see a person or family comes down to communicating—from trained physician to individual patient—that to make themselves "healthy," we can provide the assistance, medication, care and support, but they are the true owners of their own family action plan to successfully establish lives of dignity and good health. Moreover, because we cannot go very deep into any one of our five areas given our limited financial resources, we strive all the time to build partnerships with those organizations specialized in areas deeper than we are. I think that this comprehensive approach is catching on. Last year, we won an award from UBS Visionaries. I asked Maximilian Martin, who presented the award, what he felt was important in our work. He said without hesitation that it was our integrative and holistic approach.

RENASCER'S MODEL—*An Integral Approach to Health*

Vera has underlined the core of Renascer's program from the beginning, as based on a "Family Action Plan" concerning five areas necessary to the proper well-being of a patient: health, housing, income, education and citizenship. Beyond just providing services for a patient, Renascer, meaning "rebirth" in Portuguese, trains volunteers and technical staff to work with individual families one-on-one to break a cycle known to any hospital treating patients who float between misery, illness, hospital admission, release, readmission and death. Fighting against this cycle, Renascer helps the individual families who most need help to create a coauthored action plan, in which the family becomes the owner of their own recovery and reintegration into society. The approach, which considers every patient holistically beyond their medical ill, is designed to break a larger socioeconomic cycle of poverty and misery while constantly searching for creative solutions that may promote the reintegration of people excluded by the government or social status quo.

Within the Family Action Plan, Renascer pairs a mother or family with a trained volunteer caseworker to cover all five areas Vera mentions:

Health includes donation of basic and special food, medicines, orthopedic and breathing equipment as well as nutritional, psychological and social services.

Income generation includes training and guiding mothers to take on professionalization courses to learn administrative skills, or how to start businesses by opening kiosks selling food, clothing or discarded manufacturing materials. Renascer has provided "start-up" work kits on entrepreneurship and income generation for over 1,000 families.

Dr. Vera Cordeiro with an assisted child patient at Hospital da Lagoa, Rio de Janeiro, Brazil.

Housing includes the recruitment of volunteers and construction workers to rebuild domiciles in the favelas by fixing leaking pipes, strengthening roofs and walls and providing proper beds.

Education encourages families to seek out their own avenues for employment and community participation, as well as providing an outlet for guidance and moral support to which volunteers and those who have been helped in the past by Renascer can return to work and encourage newcomers.

Citizenship entails the discussion of legal issues, so that the rights of every patient are protected, and the completion of written documents so that every family member officially becomes a citizen. Renascer also helps to foster community ties by sponsoring workshops, bringing rich and poor people together to work for social inclusion.

The Family Action Plan is a constantly evolving process, executed by Renascer's well-trained support team of volunteers and professionals. If a family is particularly afflicted, it may be recommended for additional counseling by Renascer's Psychological Sector team as a part of the health area. Because members of Renascer are trained not to sit idly as in a government bureaucratic health system, physicians and volunteers do not delegate to third parties anything that they can conceivably do themselves right away. The creative instincts of every individual trained by Renascer are thus enhanced as an effective means to a dynamic model that can respond promptly to the concerns of its patients.

Renascer has substantially increased its visibility in Brazil by marketing and scaling its services. In her first years of operation, Vera was overwhelmed with requests from other areas of Brazil, not just in Rio de Janeiro. Many people had heard of her organization's services, as it was willing to work with those that even the state department had ignored in the past. Soon, she began spreading the word to a growing network of physicians, who convinced their hospitals how much they would save by adopting Renascer's approach to prevent admission and readmission for patients who were repeatedly treated for the same ailments. Renascer's programs now exist near fifteen different hospitals throughout the country, and at least ten new units are just getting started.

The organization has also leveraged its impact through corporate sponsorships and marketing. Chiquinho, a nickname for Francisco, a common name of many of the children Renascer assisted in its early projects, is a childlike illustrated figure designed to represent "new humanity." More than just a logo signifying an association with Renascer to the public in Brazil, Chiquinho is widely considered to represent a movement of mercy, solidarity, friendship, hope and persistence in the larger fight against poverty and social segregation. Moreover, many companies have adopted Chiquinho as a sponsored emblem to advertise their corporate social responsibility and partnership with Renascer. When buying a product from Renascer, people know they are contributing to the sustainability of its invaluable programs.

With growing support, and even donated services from McKinsey & Co., Johnson & Johnson, American Express, USB Financial, Ashoka, Avina, Skoll, and Schwab, among many others, Renascer has been widely recognized both domestically and internationally as an entrepreneurial leader in Brazil. Above all, it has been considered innovative for its replicable approach to tackling poverty and health simultaneously, with an ever-growing strategy to improve the social well-being of the entire country.

SAÚDE CRIANÇA RENASCER—BY THE NUMBERS

- A 2004 poll taken with a sample of 200 families indicated a reduction of 63% in hospital readmissions.
- Because of this reduction, the Lagoa Hospital in Rio, for example, saved more than R$338,000 (US$191,610) a year by adopting Renascer's programs.
- A 2005 research database developed with corporate sponsors indicated a 45% increase in the average annual income of Renascer's families from R$259 (US$147) to R$376 (US$213).
- More than 20,000 people have been supported by the Renascer network, more than half of them children.
- Renascer has offered more than 1,700 courses through its five areas of training.

- In addition to its fifteen existing centers, Renascer is planning to open ten to thirteen new centers by the end of 2008.
- Recently, Renascer has begun an endowment plan for sustainability, with the aim of raising US$5 million in upcoming years; it now has US$250,000 in that fund.

PAUL FARMER
Partners in Health

Haiti, Russia, Guatemala, Peru, the United States and Sub-Saharan Africa

In 1983, just before entering Harvard Medical School, where he is now a professor of medical anthropology, Paul Farmer helped to establish a community-based health project in Cange, Haiti, called Zanmi Lasante, or Partners in Health. With the aim of providing health assistance to a community of refugees, PIH has developed extensive programs in medical service for the desperately poor. PIH has slowly grown to include pilot projects in five additional countries profoundly affected by poverty, violence and epidemics of disease. Throughout its history, the guiding principles of PIH have been determined by the voice of the communities it serves rather than the ever-shifting demands of government policies and economics. Partnering with the public sector, PIH looks to improve community health infrastructure to: 1) care for its patients, 2) alleviate the root causes of disease in poor communities and 3) share lessons learned around the world. Beginning with funding from just a single donor and a handful of volunteers, PIH has since grown internationally to include over 4,000 employees, volunteers and community-based health workers.

PAUL FARMER'S DREAM—*"Sustainable" Health Programs*

In 2002, when President Clinton was starting his AIDS initiative, he asked PIH to help launch a rural health initiative in Africa, Rwanda, Lesotho and Malawi. We have now done that, but at the time we had to tell him we couldn't expand to Africa unless we had fully set into motion our projects in Haiti as best we could to ensure sustainability.

People talk a lot about sustainability. Over the years, we have become increasingly clear that no local community health program succeeds or endures without simultaneous efforts to alleviate poverty. Providing proper health care goes hand in hand with reducing extreme poverty.

It might seem counterintuitive that our community-based health programs are considered entrepreneurial or innovative. But given the predominance of top-down or vertical approaches to health care that seek to cure diseases

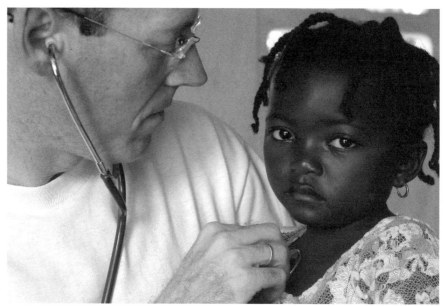
Dr. Farmer treats a young child in Haiti.

like AIDS by distributing funds and antiretroviral drugs to foreign state governments, it seems important to mention that the most effective and sustainable models work horizontally *with* local communities to understand their comprehensive needs.

An AIDS program must be tied to primary health care, prenatal care and pregnancy, vaccination clinics and educational programs to maximize its impact. We are thus partners not only with other nonprofit organizations who may enhance our reach, but also most importantly with the communities themselves. We ask the people in the communities we serve what ails them and then do whatever it takes to make them well, just as we would if they were a member of our own family.

In order to create local cultures that put value on caring for each other, it is critical that more financial incentives are integrated into the local workforce. One major problem globally is the mindset shared by many NGOs that community health workers should be volunteers. How can we pay ourselves but not the poor we work with who help us? They must be paid.

We just celebrated the first anniversary of PIH in Lesotho, which the prime minister attended. One community health worker gave a passionate plea, asking that community health work be more officially integrated into the economic infrastructure of the country, rather than volunteer based. The prime minister agreed, and I felt like cheering. It was a huge leap that I hope other African governments will take as well.

As we are now replicating our model in Lesotho and around the world, I am forty-seven years old, but still see Haiti as my true north, the inspiration for my life's work. Looking back at my decision to travel abroad at age eighteen, it certainly was the right thing to do, extending my view from the local to the international, as well as experiencing extreme poverty for the first time. I was there long enough to feel its texture, and that feeling, perhaps best described as indignation, gave me direction in my life.

Haiti taught me to extend my worldview, to see people less fortunate, to want to help them and to realize that even with limited resources, there is so much that one individual can do to effect positive change in areas like health and education. Another very critical lesson that Haiti offered, which took us some time to learn, is that no matter where an NGO or a social entrepreneur takes on their work—whether an inner-city American neighborhood or a developing country abroad—it is absolutely critical to include the public sector.

The Partners in Health Model—
Working to Treat the "Untreatable"

PIH has three main goals: 1) to care for patients, 2) to alleviate the root causes of disease in their communities and 3) to share lessons learned around the world. Through long-term collaborative efforts with international organizations like the Clinton Foundation and its local community partnerships, PIH brings the benefits of modern medical science to those most in need, while working to alleviate the crushing economic and social burdens of poverty that most exacerbate disease. PIH believes that health is a fundamental right, not a privilege, which it works to guarantee by building community-based programs in which neighbors care for each other.

In Rwanda, for example, Partners in Health has implemented its community-based approach so successfully that family members who took part in the chaos of the genocide against their fellow citizens are now helping to rebuild houses and new medical clinics for one another. The community health workers, or *accompagnateurs*, make up 98% of those PIH employs, to ensure that local programs are almost entirely sustained by the inhabitants themselves.

In its medical successes, Partners in Health has proven that allegedly "untreatable" diseases can be addressed effectively, even in poor settings. Until very recently, it was believed that neither multidrug-resistant tuberculosis (MDR TB) nor AIDS could be treated in disenfranchised urban or rural areas. PIH proved otherwise, developing a successful model of community-based care to treat MDR TB in the slums of Lima, Peru, and deliver antiretroviral therapy for AIDS in a squatter settlement in rural Haiti. National health authorities in both countries have now expanded these pilot projects significantly. Today, PIH has transplanted and adapted its model of care to the epicenter of the HIV pandemic in Africa, launching projects in Rwanda in 2005 and Lesotho in 2006. Elements of PIH's community-based approach have been disseminated to and adapted by other countries and programs throughout the world.

The five fundamental principles of PIH's work are the following:

1. Access to primary health care

A strong foundation of primary care is critical to fight diseases like AIDS. People seek care because they feel sick, not because they have a particular disease. When quality primary health care is accessible, the community develops new faith in the health system, which results in increased use of general medical services as well as services for more complex diseases. Therefore, PIH integrates infectious disease interventions within a wide range of basic health and social services.

2. Free health care and education for the poor

PIH works to ensure that cost does not prevent access to primary health care and education for the poor. The imposition of user fees has resulted in empty clinics and schools, especially in settings where the burden of poverty and disease are greatest. Because both health and education are fundamental routes to development, it is counterproductive and amoral to charge user fees for health care and education to those who need these services most and can afford them least.

3. Community partnerships

PIH doesn't tell the communities it serves what they need; the communities tell PIH. Health programs should involve community members at all levels of assessment, design, implementation and evaluation. Community health workers may be family members, friends or even patients who provide health education, refer people who are ill to a clinic or deliver medicines and social support to patients in their homes. Community health workers do not supplant the work of doctors or nurses; rather, they are a vital interface between the clinic and the community. In recognition of the critical role they play, they should be compensated for their work.

4. Addressing basic social and economic needs

Fighting disease in impoverished settings also means fighting the poverty at the root of poor health. Achieving good health outcomes requires attending to people's social and economic needs. Through community partners, PIH works to improve access to food, shelter, clean water, sanitation, education and economic opportunities.

5. Serving the poor through the public sector

A vital public sector is the best way to bring health care to the poor. While nongovernmental organizations have a valuable role to play in developing new approaches to treating disease, successful models must be implemented and expanded through the public sector to assure universal and sustained access. Rather than establish parallel systems, PIH works to strengthen and complement the existing public health infrastructure.

In 1987, PIH's project in rural Haiti aimed at providing assistance to a community of refugees. In the succeeding eighteen years, PIH grew slowly to include projects in five additional countries, and was invited by the community or government to provide services in areas profoundly affected by poverty, violence and epidemics of disease. Throughout its history, the guiding principles of PIH have been determined by the collective voice of the communities it serves rather than the ever-shifting demands of government policies and economics. Partnering with the public sector, however, PIH looks to improve community health infrastructure wherever there are inadequacies in services for the extreme poor.

PARTNERS IN HEALTH—BY THE NUMBERS

- Partners in Health began treating single families one at a time in Haiti; PIH now has built hospitals, clinics and schools, having received over 1 million patient visits in Haiti alone last year.
- PIH employs 4,000 people worldwide, and has expanded programs in eight other sites in Haiti, as well as programs in Lesotho, Rwanda, Mexico, the United States, Russia, Guatemala and Peru.
- More than 98% of those employed by PIH are members of the communities in which they work.
- Compared to other nonprofits working in the field of health, which on average budget 79% of their expenditures for program activities and 21% for administration and fundraising, PIH implements 94% of total expenditures on programs.
- In 2004, PIH was approached by the Rwandan Ministry of Health to adapt its model to a region of Africa where 5,500 people die each day, testing over 30,000 people and enrolling almost 700 on antiretroviral therapy in the first year of operations there.

TREVOR FIELD AND PAUL RISTIC
PlayPumps

Sub-Saharan Africa

The PlayPump water system is an ingenuous, simple, low-tech solution for developing countries, where thousands die every day from lack of clean drinking water. Roundabout Outdoor, and its non-profit partner, PlayPumps International, have adapted a water pump technology that doubles as a merry-go-round.

Children play and turn the merry-go-round, pumping clean water from deep in the ground to a storage container that is used for billboard advertising to generate revenue. The technology is replicable and scalable, as PlayPumps International plans to expand its operations with 4,000 new pumps to reach 10 million people across ten African countries by 2010. Trevor Field and Paul Ristic are the principles.

TREVOR FIELD'S SUCCESS—*The First PlayPump*

In 1989, while visiting an agricultural fair just outside of Johannesburg, South Africa, I came across a miniature model of a roundabout, or merry-go-round as it is often called, attached to a water pump. The inventor was a local farmer and borehole driller who had dreamed up the idea to keep children entertained while they watched his rigs at work out in the farmlands. I loved the idea and began a conversation with the farmer about how we could reproduce his invention on a bigger scale. He doubted that the model would ever be mass-produced unless we were able to attract significant outside investment. It seemed only natural to me, with my background in advertising sales, to subsidize the cost of his brilliant pump with advertising revenue, if we could only find a way of displaying billboards.

Since my selling background was in print media, I approached an outdoor advertising specialist named Paul Ristic. When he saw the PlayPump, as the inventor had named it, we formed a partnership on the spot. Together, we bought the original design and went to work adding a hand tap and a 660-gallon (2,500-liter) storage tank hoisted up on a steel tower to display a four-sided billboard space. We began marketing it to commercial branded consumer products as a unique way for them to reach rural communities. In particular we sought out ads that spoke to rural women, who still today are a largely untapped market.

Children playing on the PlayPump, pumping fresh water up to the tower storage tank.

With the original architect and Paul Ristic, both of whom had an invaluable wealth of knowledge in the engineering field, we spent six years refining the original design of the PlayPump water system into what it is today. We were not at first thinking about how the technology might have an effect on the global drinking water crisis. We approached the idea, rather, from an advertising perspective because that was our field of expertise. But when in one province of South Africa we noticed a complete shift in consumer buying patterns from one particular brand of bread to another, healthier variety, we realized that we could have the same positive impact with health messaging to influence behavior changes throughout the rural populations.

Our greatest success has been this realization that we could apply our professional expertise to make a significant social impact. We have since created an integrated approach to our new invention, providing clean drinking water, encouraging kids to play and enjoy themselves, uplifting rural women who would otherwise walk miles carrying buckets of often-contaminated water for their families to share and giving sponsors a platform to showcase brands associated with vital health and social messaging. I would like to think that our product is a temporary intervention in solving a problem that won't be around forever. I am hoping that as each African state becomes stronger they will be in a position to provide clean water to all their citizens in a sustainable manner. In the water industry, like so many others related to human health, individuals become dependent on resources that should be naturally available. We now face a crisis, which can be overcome by encouraging entrepreneurship, rather than dependency, to revolutionize distribution systems for basic human needs among the rural poor.

Paul Ristic's Contribution—*His Big Realization*

The impact of what we were doing struck me one day when we took our corporate sponsors to visit the PlayPump they had helped fund in rural South Africa. Within a year of receiving their new water system, the Thabong Primary School, under the leadership of Principal Cosby Thubela, had harvested the runoff water from our tap to irrigate a food garden. The food garden had been started from the donation of seeds from another corporate billboard sponsor, empowering two community members who were able to earn a living by selling the excess produce to other families in the area. Suddenly, I realized that we were affecting health, hygiene, food security, job creation and an entire school community simply by giving them access to clean water.

The two most important ways that individuals support PlayPumps is to raise awareness of the need and raise money to make the water systems available to more communities in more countries. A mere $6 provides one child with access to clean water for up to ten years, $36 provides for a family, $60 for ten people and $300 for a classroom of children for drinking and hand washing. The cost of an entire PlayPump system is $14,000, bringing clean water to 2,500 people for ten years.

How the Pumps Work

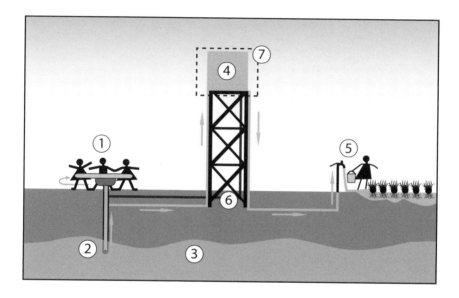

While children have fun (1) spinning on the PlayPump merry-go-round, clean water (2) is pumped from underground (3) into a 2,500-liter tank (4), standing seven meters above the ground. A simple tap (5) makes it easy for adults and children to draw water. Excess water is diverted from the storage tank back down into the borehole (6). The water storage tank (7) provides a rare opportunity to advertise in rural communities. All four sides of the tank are leased as billboards, with two sides for consumer advertising and the other two sides for health and educational messages. The revenue generated by this unique model pays for pump maintenance.

Working hand in hand with local governments and community leaders, the PlayPump system is introduced under a principle of community self-ownership from the beginning. Once a community has agreed that it wants a pump, a liaison is appointed. Roundabout Outdoor then trains a local crew to install and maintain the pump, giving jobs to local workers. Over the next three years, PlayPump water systems will be installed throughout sub-Saharan Africa, with the goal of reaching ten million people by 2010. In 2006, additional PlayPump systems were donated to communities in South Africa and pilot programs were initiated in Mozambique, Swaziland and Zambia. Expansion to Ethiopia, Kenya, Lesotho, Malawi, Tanzania and Uganda are ongoing.

PlayPumps—By The Numbers

- In all, 950 PlayPumps have been installed in four African countries to date; 700 of these have been in South Africa alone.
- Over 2 million people can access free, clean drinking water for the first time.
- Nearly one hundred jobs have been created through the PlayPump maintenance program.
- PlayPumps International plans to help install 4,000 pumps by 2010, in ten African countries, and at a cost of $60 million.
- PlayPumps International has raised $20 million to date for this initiative.
- One PlayPump costs $14,000 and includes equipment, installation, water quality testing, community liaison and ten years of maintenance.
- President Bill Clinton, First Lady Laura Bush and platinum-selling music artist Jay-Z have all endorsed PlayPumps in African communities.

 **Andrea and Barry Coleman**
Riders for Health

Africa

Riders for Health provides vehicle maintenance for health physicians to reach remote villages in Africa. Many African countries have only one health physician per 20,000 people and hospitals that cannot be reached by rural villagers in an emergency, if at all. One in fourteen women dies in childbirth, as opposed to one in five thousand in developed countries. Andrea and Barry Coleman, with world-renowned motorcycle Grand Prix champion Randy Mamola, founded Riders for Health to offer inexpensive transportation services to NGOs and health agencies in many African countries. The director of information and planning for the department of health in the Gambia said, "Without Riders, nothing would move. Our health programs would stop." Recognized as "Global health heroes in 2005" by Time *magazine, Riders for Health has the potential to scale its services across the entire African continent if it can continue to garner financial support.*

ANDREA COLEMAN—*A Love of Motorcycles*

My father was a motorcycle development engineer, a real independent thinker in the field. He devoted his life to making vehicles run better and faster. My mother's brother was a motorcycle racer, racing competitively before the Second World War. My mother, while somewhat interested in motorcycles, was an intellectual and artistic person, an avid reader with deep interest in poetry and art. So I really had a dual life as a young girl. I've always had a passion for motorcycle riding and loved watching it. The intricacies of engine design, gas flow and mechanics were fascinating to me. On the other hand, I fondly remember the colorful stories my mother told from British authors on Africa, particularly Rudyard Kipling. Between the two sides of my family, the knit and grit of motorcycle engines captured my romantic imagination as much as Africa did.

I became more and more interested while working in sports, first with the Chelsea Football Club doing funding and public relations, which I then did for motorcycle racing too. I raced for four years myself, but found my passion restricted by the small nature of the sport, as racers literally are confined to their circular tracks going round and round. My brother was a racer, and so was my first husband Tom. In 1979, when Tom died in a tragic accident on the raceway, I really opened my eyes to the health and safety issues of the sport, and what it means to be a rider.

Around that time, I had started working with one of the world's great motorcycle racers who, from an early age of fourteen, captured audiences in the European cycle scene. Randy Mamola, who is still considered one of the most exciting and talented riders of his generation after winning thirteen Grand Prix championships in his career, hired me to help with his public relations. While audiences all over Europe and the United States loved his style, the press found him impetuous, if not brash. Randy has always had an incredibly fabulous way of communicating, but often felt misunderstood as a young professional riding in foreign countries. As his public relations manager, I started bringing him to children's hospitals, which he immediately began to love as an activity that was so removed from motorcycles and racing.

As Randy's success took off, his travel schedule became more difficult to manage. A journalist for the *Guardian* newspaper named Barry Coleman, my future husband, grew immersed in Randy's story and began attracting an audience around the sport to the British newspaper for the first time, despite the doubts of the editing staff. Barry documented Randy's racing success, as well as his efforts off the track with children in hospitals. I was looking for creative ways to raise money in the motorcycle community, which we could donate to the nonprofit Save the Children under the Mamola team name. I was delighted to hear of a breakthrough when the organization invited Barry and Randy to visit its operations in Somalia. Randy became drawn to the idea of contributing international aid for starving and dying children, especially as these issues were covered in headlines extensively throughout the 1980s.

Randy came back from Somalia shocked by his inability to reach many of the villages due to poor transportation vehicles, broken road systems and a general lack of infrastructure. Vehicle upkeep is our everyday concern, and so when we pushed Save the Children on the issue, they invited us to take a look at another African country, the Gambia, where they had sent eighty-six motorcycles to their volunteers the year before. We arrived and only found twelve dead vehicles, a motorcycle graveyard for vehicles not eighteen months old with less than 15,000 kilometers on them! Using Randy's name to raise money and publicity, we began strategizing a more concerted effort around the problems he had seen.

Randy, Barry and I were all struck by the reality that pregnant women and sick children die every day trying to walk miles to a hospital while broken-down motorcycles sit unused along the sides of the road and in garages.

In one community, a young woman in the ministry approached me saying that she had been given a motorcycle to make family care visits. "After three months of my motorcycle doing a great job for me," she said, "it broke and nobody could fix it, so I was wheeling it around with no mechanic and no way to pay for it, so the ministry took it away." I finally was able to see the bike. It didn't work just because there was a bit of dirt in the carburetor!

In another instance I will never forget, we were heading to a site inspection and came across a man pushing a wheelbarrow, with his wife who lay crumpled in its wood-box frame undergoing unobstructed labor. Distraught and delirious, the man had been wheeling her for more than four hours as she carried their unborn child. We immediately transported her into our vehicle to get her to a hospital. She died from heavy blood loss before we could make it there.

Today in the twenty-first century where space travel, global networking and billion-dollar corporate budgets are commonplace, why do health workers in Africa have to walk ten miles over two days just to help a village get clean water and proper sanitation? Some pregnant women are at best sixty miles from the nearest hospital. So, what does it take to keep a rural village healthy? In our

A rider uses an Uhuru sidecar to transport a patient.

country, one in five thousand women dies in childbirth, and that's one too many. In Africa it's one in fourteen.

All that's needed to fix this problem is the resources that we in advanced countries already have in abundance. Thinking about such an easily identifiable gap between a problem and its clear solution, I never looked back after deciding I was going to do something about this. Riders for Health was born in 1996 out of a simple conviction to bring better health transportation to the African continent.

We started our first program in Lesotho, training our first employee, a health worker named Mohale Moshoeshoe, in the offices of Save the Children. With our training, Mohale maintained forty-eight motorcycles for six years without a single breakdown. Although under contract to us, the trained technicians are encouraged to take on new employees so as to become self-sustaining entrepreneurs developing their own mobile mechanic businesses in their respective communities.

Realizing that our model might be adaptable to larger countries, we replicated the approach in Zimbabwe under agreement with the Health Ministry. There, as in Lesotho, we established a training center, the Academy of Vehicle Management. The Academy provided teaching classrooms and tough terrain for simulating rural landscapes for students to practice and train in all kinds of poor conditions: sand, mud and thick brush. We extended our services to other NGOs, always with the promise that, "You put your vehicles in our system for us to take care of, and you go out into the country and do the great work you do."

While our service focuses solely and explicitly on medical transportation, we let doctors do what they are trained to do, the health care itself. Over time, we have proven that the core competence of our mechanic training is the key to our growth, as our model offers a systemic solution to the business of health transport for poor communities in any developing country.

In our efforts to set up shop in Zimbabwe, we learned a lot about our capabilities and lessons for the future, since we truly started with nothing. As we continue to have limits on our funding capitalization, which we constantly try to improve, we are also forced to demonstrate strict discipline in our ground operations. While we do charge a cost-per-kilometer amount for all bikes in service—which is significantly less than any corporate rental business—we are restricted to a funding model that relies on goodwill from philanthropists and donor-based giving from the motorcycle community in Europe and the United States. As our financial model remains restricted in this way, we are not yet able to initiate new programs in more countries. On the other hand, the very limits on our finances have been a blessing in the start-up phase, forcing us to scrutinize every business decision with careful accounting.

We stay focused on our vision with the knowledge that someday the health care organizations whose motorcycles we help maintain will continue their work without this kind of support. Our focus is on health transport, and our values in prioritizing this focus are myriad: entrepreneurship, quality care, innovation, collaboration, self-employment, training and local empowerment.

While recognizing the limitations of an ideal scenario, we feel that at the minimum every health clinic should be equipped with five motorcycles, one ambulance and two pickup trucks for delivery and distribution of heavier materials between hospitals and villages. Meanwhile, to find these villages, workers often rely on maps sewn together with cloth by local community women who know the land.

We hope someday to be able to extend our service capacity with GPS and mobile phones. We also hope to be able to rally more support from the motorcycle community through auctions, ticket sales and fundraisers. The motorcycle community is key to our success, and our efforts have introduced a new model of philanthropic entrepreneurship in the sport. As I hope the readers of this book may agree, you don't need to love motorcycle racing to care about health transport in developing countries. This is a universal issue, and Jenifer Mutedi, a young Zimbabwean woman who had never known that riding was an organized sport, is the best example of that.

A very intelligent and dedicated health worker, Jenifer was well trained by us and she quickly received a motorcycle from Riders for Health. In her coverage communities, which included 20,000 people she was responsible for, she set up some leadership groups and women's clubs to monitor progress. She encouraged parents to keep scorecards of their children's health, including how many times they had been immunized and treated over the year. The clubs also started sewing lessons and began growing gardens with fresh herbs and vegetables, which were often used to sustain the sick of their community who needed boosts for their immune systems.

After visiting Jenifer, I was so impressed with her local empowerment initiative that I wrote a report to *Motorcycle News* documenting her work. Despite all the lives that motorcycles sometimes claim from reckless driving or competitive racing, look at how motorcycles were saving lives for thousands in Africa! In an internationally sponsored awards ceremony for the magazine, Jenifer was flown to Britain—her first time outside Zimbabwe—to be honored. With poise she told a magnificently beautiful story about her experience with Riders for Health, speaking on behalf of what seemed like all of African womanhood. It was truly awe inspiring and humbling. After the ceremony, I asked her, "How did you do that?"

She smiled with confidence and reminded me, "Andrea, this is what I do every day."

Improving Transport Resource Management in Africa

For fifteen years, Riders for Health has been building a network of trained local technicians to improve the effective and efficient delivery system of life-saving medicines and care known as transport resource management (TRM). In all aspects of TRM in Africa, health workers do not have the incentive or the means to look after vehicles themselves, so Riders teams work on an outreach basis, meaning that technicians go to service the vehicles in the locations in which they run, the local communities. The Riders mechanics, as well as the health physicians whose vehicles they manage, all carry out daily maintenance and care for their own vehicles. Once a month, Riders' mechanics gather a group of physicians to replace spare parts and perform any specialized repairs.

Rates of malaria and deaths resulting from childbirth have significantly decreased compared to neighboring regions that Riders does not yet serve. The direct relationship between improved vehicle performance and health service is a simple yet powerfully transformative strategy for the continent at large.

Riders currently has three national programs in the Gambia, Zimbabwe and Nigeria, and two smaller initiatives working with NGOs in Kenya and Tanzania. In 2002, Riders and the Gambian government signed a historic and unprecedented agreement that outsourced all vehicle management, beginning with the Department of State for Health, to Riders. With this kind of momentum,

Riders is now helping nearly 11 million people receive basic health-care, who were before considered unreachable.

The organization is looking to replicate operations in many more countries, building on its core mission to encourage local Africans to take over the leadership and succession of the program throughout the continent.

RIDERS FOR HEALTH—BY THE NUMBERS

- Riders for Health employs fourteen people in Britain and 230 in Africa.
- Riders manages over 1,300 vehicles, including 500 vehicles in Zimbabwe alone.
- Riders maintains programs in the Gambia, Nigeria, Zimbabwe, Tanzania and Kenya, with planned operations to restart in Nigeria and Lesotho.
- Riders reaches 11 million people through its programs in Africa.
- It costs £10, or $20, for Riders to reach one hundred people in Africa.

LIZA KIMBO
Child and Family Wellness Shops (CFWshops)

Kenya

In her native home of Nairobi, Kenya, Liza Kimbo works to deliver health care services to the rural poor, calling upon the resources of a pool of otherwise unemployed nurses. As director of the Sustainable Healthcare Foundation, which operates the CFWshops to supply and sell basic pharmaceutical medicines at very low cost to rural people distant from hospital care, Liza has provided thousands of employment opportunities to nurses who were trained but unemployed by the government. With assistance from the organization's successful model approach, nurses have started sustainable, profitable and medically qualified CFWshops all over the country. With a background in health services, management and finance, Liza has helped grow the franchise model from its first eleven outlets to more than sixty, now serving 400,000 patients a year.

LIZA KIMBO—*Meeting Scott Hillstrom and Recruiting Nurses*

In the late 1990s, I was looking to establish a retail pharmacy business in Nairobi, because there was a terrible gap in the market for affordable drugs and health care. A large majority of our customers had lost many family members simply because they could not afford drugs from overseas.

I tried to get other pharmacists in the city to collaborate to help reduce the cost of medicines, but of course that was met with enormous resistance. And then I met Scott Hillstrom. He had borrowed a franchise model, in some ways similar to fast-food chains that lower prices by multiplying the number of outlets. Rather than unhealthy food, however, we deliver life-saving drugs to large populations in rural areas all over Kenya.

Immediately I saw the beauty of his idea, and the great potential to reach millions of people in need. Throughout the country, 50% of the population lives more than an hour walk from a public health facility. Individuals do not have much choice in the quality of products or providers, so they are forced to pay higher prices for basic medicines.

From my first meeting with Scott, I was committed to running a pilot for the franchise system. Scott, ever the powerful visionary, had clarity about the power of franchise businesses, and by the time I met him in 1999, he had already raised initial funding for the project. Together, we formed a local board, and I went out and recruited our very first batch of nurses, whom we called franchisees, to run the stores. The rural areas needed us most, so I relocated and moved closer to the franchisees outside Nairobi.

Early in our initiative, I went on a routine visit to one of our franchised outlets, which I was surprised to find closed. I was informed that the franchisee, James, had rushed off with a couple in need of urgent care. The couple had agreed to travel to the hospital as their child faced a life-threatening case of malaria. Because of James's swift action, he actually managed to save the child who had nearly died from lack of a medication that cost only 50¢. The family wept in gratitude. Many such stories motivate me to continue this important work of saving lives by providing such basic access to medicine.

The greatest challenge for me was entering the uncharted waters of establishing for-profit businesses in rural areas. I knew we were serving people who were poor, but at the same time I was convinced that "charity" was not going to build up a sustainable solution to their problems. We also had the challenge of getting qualified health workers with an entrepreneurial spirit, who could be sure to make their businesses successful. Finally, we were challenged to compete with cheap, poor quality or counterfeit drugs, and outlets run by unqualified people looking to make a dishonest profit. This systemic problem results from the infrastructure of drugs worldwide: it is an extremely unregulated market!

There are substantial costs to deliver the services that just cannot be met by the people we serve. The hybrid model of our for-profit, socially responsible business is useful in overcoming these challenges. We charge the full cost of the drugs and work hard to provide good quality generic drugs that are much less expensive

CFWshops in Nairobi, Kenya.

than branded products. We do not charge a full market price for consultation fees, though, and in many cases franchisees find that it is difficult to get clients to pay this at all.

We provide a lot of technical assistance from our head office and are heavily engaged in health communication and promotion of improved hygiene and practices to improve all health care in the communities we serve. All these are paid out of funds raised by the foundation attached to our businesses, which are the franchisees that run profitable businesses. We control the type of services and the products they sell, while assuring that they can make a good profit from reaching a large volume of clients seen. In this way, the motive of the franchisee to make a profit is controlled by the rules of the franchise system, such as control over prices, quality of products, services delivered, record keeping, outlet cleanliness and general presentation. All of these technical components serve our desire to reach as many people as possible in the rural communities.

The CFW Model—*Providing Affordable Health Care*

On average, the twenty poorest developing countries spend less than $33 per person each year on health care, compared to over $2,500 in the twenty most developed countries and $4,500 in the United States. Even a doubling of public health funding would fall short of meeting the need. While public funding will always be necessary, pharmaceutical reform in the developing world must continue to incorporate a sustainable, market-based model with effective incentives.

The CFWshops model, founded by The HealthStore Foundation, incorporates all the key elements of successful franchising: uniform systems and training, careful selection of locations and most importantly, strict controls on quality ensured through regular inspections. With its innovative model, CFWshops uses the combined buying power of the full network to obtain quality medicines at the lowest possible cost. With the ability to sell low-cost medicines, most CFWshops outlets are profitable.

The HealthStore Foundation has combined established microenterprise principles with proven franchise business practices to create a microfranchise business model called CFWshops. In this model, franchisees operate small drug shops or clinics strategically located to improve access to essential drugs. CFWshops clinics and shops enable trained health workers to operate their own businesses—treating common, basic diseases like malaria and diarrhea that cause 70–90% of illness and death in their communities—while following CFWshops' drug handling and distribution regulations calculated to ensure good practice.

To this end, the microfranchise business model operates with explicit goals in mind:

- To create a reliable supply of high quality, low-cost, essential drugs and to make them available to the people who need them when and where they are needed;

- To treat childhood infectious diseases in the communities where children live, thus reducing congestion in the health-care system so that scarce resources can be applied to others not so easily treated;

- To reduce under-five mortality rates, thus encouraging family planning and lower population growth rates;

- To discourage the development of drug-resistant microbes by the provision and appropriate use of adequate supplies of effective drugs; and

- To improve community health through educational and prevention activities.

The microfranchise business model engages participants in the health-care marketplace to create incentives for prescription drug providers to follow good practices for the handling and distribution of inexpensive medicines. Franchisees enjoy the benefit of owning a valuable profit-making business,

Mary, a franchise shop owner, monitors her patients' records.

which they maintain in compliance with CFWshops' drug handling and administration regulations.

The franchise model has delivered a wide variety of high quality, low-cost goods and services throughout the world, and has proven to be an effective method of mass distribution across a wide diversity of economic and cultural conditions. For any individual requesting to open a franchise, HealthStore requires up front a $200 deposit, a portion of which goes to the organization and a portion to the franchise's start-up costs. The individual usually also applies for about $1,000 in loans from CFWshops to cover the rest of the start-up and initial stocking costs.

The organization currently processes these loans in-house but is in the process of partnering with banks to take over the franchise financing. While CFWshops does not currently charge any membership fees to the franchises, it plans to start charging a $10-per-month operation fee beginning in 2008. The primary revenue comes from an average 15–20% margin earned on all products sold by the franchises.

Community health workers who own and operate a CFWshops outlet make a living selling the competitively priced drugs. All franchises receive an operating manual complete with policies, procedures and forms constituting a turnkey management system which if followed enables franchisees to conduct business and provide necessary compliance reports. The network operates two types of outlets: basic drug shops operated by community health workers, and clinics operated by nurses who provide a deeper list of essential medicines as well as basic primary care. As the franchisor, CFWshops can revoke a franchisee's right to operate an outlet if the franchisee fails to comply with the franchise rules and standards. CFWshops targets primarily lower or middle-income women and children subsisting on agriculture, although people of all ages and incomes are treated. CFWshops outlets are located at market centers in agricultural areas of around 5,000 people.

The CFWshops franchise-operating model provides training for all franchisees on how to diagnose common diseases, infections and illnesses. Base training is then backed up with continuing education on clinical skills and management practices. All products come only from reputable suppliers, and their quality is ensured through rigorous supply-chain standards and record keeping. The centralized operation of CFWshops compiles the vital health statistics of all patients, as well as the financial performance for each CFWshops outlet.

The franchisees' for-profit business is sustainable in the long term. In fact, as these franchise managers become more established, they generate higher volumes of medicines to prescribe and sell, which generate surplus revenue above all operating costs. However, because no individual is turned down for medicine, even if they cannot afford the treatment for which they were prescribed, the CFWshops does incur sunk costs, which it makes up for through targeted public fundraising by its U.S. founder, The HealthStore Foundation, and the operating Kenyan NGO, Sustainable Healthcare Foundation. Utilizing funds from both its franchise profits and its donor base, CFWshops is focused on the expansion of outlets into new regions.

CFWSHOPS—BY THE NUMBERS

- More than 1 million patients have been treated since 2000.
- The CFWshops network has more than quadrupled to 65 franchise locations, treating over 40,000 patients per month.
- In 2004, the CFWshops network treated 177,256 patients and in 2005, the number of patients treated nearly tripled, reaching 435,527.
- Treatments cost less than $1: the average transaction cost is 50¢. It typically costs 60¢ for medicines, and between 20¢ and 30¢ for a consultation with a nurse.
- By 2011, 225 clinics will be established serving over 1.5 million patients per year.
- The Ministry of Health for Kenya has incorporated the CFWshops network in its National Malaria Strategy.

CHAPTER 4

Education

There are 770 million adults in the world who cannot read or write, and two-thirds of them are women. Moreover, 30% of children living in rural areas of developing countries are not enrolled in school. Demonstrating just how interrelated health and education are with poverty, thousands of children miss school everyday simply because they are sick from water-related diseases, which of course stem from their extreme conditions of poverty in the first place.

Primary school education is critical as the starting block for every society's youth. Imagine if all the primary school-age children in New York, Paris, London, San Francisco, Tokyo, Boston, Sydney and Rome could not attend school for an entire year. That figure would be less than the number of children in the developing world who remain out of school from poor health and poverty.

Proper education, like health, is compounded by gender and socioeconomic inequality, where females are not given the same opportunities as males. It has become incredibly clear that female education is directly tied to fertility and mortality rates: a mother who is better educated will have fewer children. An educated mother is less prone to disease. She will live longer, as will her children, meaning that the improvement of female education will lead to the economic development of any society, in any part of the world.

Issues of education are also increasingly tied to the development of new technologies. The digital divide further separates the haves from the have-nots, but also creates enormous opportunities to reach and connect children through computer software and the Internet.

In addition to the four social entrepreneurs and their initiatives profiled in this chapter, there are many more that you may want to take a look at by going to their websites. For example:

- The Afghan Institute of Learning
- Central Asian Institute and Greg Mortenson
- The Container School
- Equal Access
- Fundación Escuela Nueva

- The Island School
- Magic Yeti Library
- Teach a Man to Fish
- Teach for America

The four social entrepreneurs profiled in this chapter are the following:

- **John Wood**, a former Microsoft marketing executive who has applied his business instincts to fundraise enormous sums to build libraries and schools while providing girls' scholarships in Asia and Africa.

- **Ann Cotton**, who has created opportunities each year for over 400,000 girls living lives of extreme poverty in sub-Saharan Africa to get an education.

- **Taddy Blecher**, an actuary and management consultant, who founded the first free university of higher education in South Africa.

- **Rodrigo Baggio**, a technology consultant who recycles computers for teaching purposes to bridge the digital divide for poor children in Brazil.

JOHN WOOD
Room to Read

Asia and Africa

John Wood, former Microsoft executive, founded Room to Read in 1998 to publish local books, fill libraries and construct new schools in the Himalayan Mountains. It all stemmed from a promise John made to a school headmaster while he was backpacking in rural Nepal that he would return with books for children to read. He did return a year later with 3,000 books to fill the school's empty library. In his memoir, Leaving Microsoft to Change the World, *John explains, "Did it really matter how many copies of Windows we sold in Taiwan this month when there were millions of children without access to books?" Scaling Room to Read over the last seven years since its founding, John has applied the rigor of business to improve systems of education, implementing an innovative and expansive growth model that will provide 10 million children the enduring opportunity of reading and learning by the year 2020.*

JOHN WOOD'S JOURNEY—
Leaving Microsoft to Build Libraries and Schools

Like many lifelong passions, my love of reading started at a very young age. Growing up, I constantly pressed my parents for new books to read and even used to ask them for a later bedtime so I could read more. We didn't have a lot of money, so I spent most of my time at the library in town, voraciously devouring any books I could get my hands on. I never realized how lucky I was. It's natural to be surrounded by endless books and libraries as a kid, right?

In the 1990s, as director of marketing and business development at Microsoft in Asia conducting million-dollar deals in air-conditioned conference rooms on the fortieth floor of a business office in Hong Kong, I began realizing the unethical and amoral nature of my first-world corporate lifestyle, living among the top 1% of the wealthy in the world. Everything was taken care of: the chauffeurs, gardeners, assistants, maids and all-expense-paid trips with five-star hotel rooms.

In what was really an eye-opening occurrence, I decided to take some time off to spend in rural Cambodia, and saw children in empty classrooms with no books and dilapidated schools that the Khmer Rouge regime had burned and destroyed. It was a situation for which someone clearly needed to take action—yet it seemed to me that few people were willing to fill the educational vacuum of Cambodia's youth.

The same shock hit me again on my first trip to Nepal, as I hiked through the Himalayas and came across community after community with dilapidated, over-crowded schools and empty libraries without books.

On a very small scale, I thought I could do something about the problem just by being there. It was 1997 in Vietnam, for example, and I met a kid named Vu who was passionate about learning about computers. The cost, or barrier to his goal, was only $10 a month. So I offered him the money, but he refused, being too proud to accept charity from a foreigner. So I tore a page out of my journal and proceeded to create a "Scholarship Award Certificate," saying that Bill Gates had endowed me with the power to award and endorse scholarships to promising young Vietnamese students. I called it the "Microsoft Computer and Reading Fellowship."

When I gave this to Vu, he had tears in his eyes. "If you believe in me, then I must be smart, and I will make you proud. I will send you reports every month, and you will be proud of your friend Vu when he gets straight As."

Vu did get great grades, and then went on to university (this time it cost me only a few hundred dollars a year) to study French, Japanese and English. He then became an engineer for the Vietnamese Railway and is now studying for his masters in computer science. As our first student, Vu was a success story, and the inspiration for Room to Read took off from there. If an initial grant of $20 could do this much good, what might be possible if I could raise millions?

Scaling massively was my top priority. The numbers are staggering, and depressing. Nearly 800 million people in the world are illiterate, and two-thirds are women. If that many women had four children each, which is not uncommon in the developing world, that equals 2 billion children growing up with an illiterate mother. Perhaps most egregious of all, 100 million children of primary school age are not enrolled in any school.

How can we let this happen? What chance do these kids have to break the cycle of poverty if they don't get educated? This strikes an emotional chord in my own consciousness. What if my own mother, grandmother and older sister had been illiterate and unable to read to me as a child? They were the strong women in my family who contributed enormously to my education and curiosity. Had they not been there to teach me growing up, I probably wouldn't have ended up in a nice Microsoft office making a lot of money.

Room to Read started with much more of an emotional motivation than an intellectual one, although both have played an important role in my journey. Calculating results through numbers is critical to measuring growth and documenting our performance to our investors. But these performance metrics are only as relevant as the people we serve, namely women and children who have no access to books or schooling.

The NGO sector often doesn't think enough in business terms. Too many organizations don't track or present their results proudly. We try to bring a business philosophy to Room to Read with a balanced eye on both the social and financial bottom line. So when we raise funds, we put our numbers in human terms. The $225,000 we raised in one night of fundraising in Tokyo, for example, could mean over 200,000 local language children's books that we self-publish. Or it could mean 900 girls receive comprehensive educational scholarships. We provide the link between the quantitative and the qualitative, while allowing our investors to decide how to allocate their funds, whether for books, scholarships, libraries or even entire schools. When a school in Nepal can be built for only $15,000, there is simply no excuse for us not to go big!

I've talked to a lot of business people who want to follow their passion but don't know how. It seems for most, there are two common problems that stand in the way: one is that too many people make the mistake of thinking that whatever they do next they have to do for the rest of their lives; and the other is getting

John Wood reading to children at the opening of a new Room to Read library in Colombo, Sri Lanka.

caught up in the trap of thinking that they have to receive permission to follow their dream. I can't tell you how many times I've heard otherwise rational business executives say, "I want to do this, but my spouse doesn't think it's a good idea," "I have kids so I don't have the time," or "my parents think it's silly."

Stop asking for permission. It's your life, and your life only. After deciding what is important to you, you can get clear about your vision and encourage others to rally behind you. So take that risk. It may ultimately be the most rewarding decision of your life. And if it doesn't work, you can always go back to what you were doing, and at least this way you'll never have to wonder about "what might have been" or what you could have done.

I also try to empathize with people whose ideas are not well received by friends and family or experts. I tell them that people used to think I was crazy, but now it's hard to say that, since we've opened over 400 schools and 5,000 bilingual libraries. There's a great Chinese proverb on this point: "Those who say it cannot be done should not spend time criticizing those who are actually doing it."

Big thinking is key to our model. In the charity and NGO world, there is often this scarcity mentality where people are afraid there's not enough funding out there. If there's anything I've learned from my days at Microsoft, it's that there is certainly enough wealth in this world; you just have to find it. At many fundraising events, I've often heard people say to the audience, "Even if you can only give $5 that's OK." No! While that comes across as gracious and humble, it in fact signals to potential investors that the organization is afraid to ask for money or apologizing for it.

Don't talk your donors down; talk them up. We have never lived in an era of greater wealth creation than in this modern world, and all of us who do this work need to challenge people to invest in the future of the world. Knowing that you have money passively sitting in a bank account is not nearly as fulfilling as being in a village the day its school opens or watching local residents draw water from their new well. We need tens of thousands of people to each create these small victories, and collectively the impact will be *huge.*

Among our investor community, I constantly repeat the same facts, as if I'm approaching my company board with a business opportunity that cannot be missed. "There are 800 million people in the developing world who are illiterate," I tell them. "Think big with me, that's 800 million individuals we have the privilege of educating. And every day we miss is a day we can't get back. Children's brains will either develop, or they won't. The most magnificent machine in the history of the world, the human brain, is at risk here. Do we want to leave a legacy, or don't we?"

Many people ask what advice I have to entrepreneurs starting their own organization. I can think of three steps:

1. Hire logistical support early on in the venture.

2. Think big, focus maniacally on results and celebrate small victories when you achieve them.

3. Find someone local who is well qualified to run operations. We were fortunate to find Dinesh Shrestha, a Nepalese businessman who has been entirely dedicated to our vision in Asia. Indigenous partnerships are essential; local organizations may be much better than you can ever hope to be at meeting needs in their part of the world.

The worst mistake a start-up social entrepreneur can make is talking yourself into not growing. Every success we have had since our inception is a step toward our ultimate goal. For us, this means lifelong education for 10 million children across the developing world. What do you want to accomplish? Think big, and then go do it.

THE ROOM TO READ MODEL—*Staying Focused while Scaling*

Founding Room to Read, John Wood wove corporate business practices with his inspiring vision to provide educational access to 10 million children in the developing world. His novel approach to nonprofit management includes the following:

- Scalable, measured, sustainable results
- Low overhead, allowing maximum investment per dollar in educational infrastructure
- Challenge grants fostering community ownership and sustainability
- Strong local staff and partnerships creating culturally relevant programs

Room to Read began working with rural communities in Nepal in 2000 to build schools and establish libraries. The organization's geographic reach expanded rapidly as significant needs and opportunities were identified in Vietnam, Cambodia and India between 2001 and 2003. The Asian tsunami in December 2004 provided a catalyst for entry into Sri Lanka, which had severe need for rebuilding schools. In 2006, Room to Read expanded to South Africa and is currently setting up operations in Zambia.

Room to Read has developed a holistic, multipronged approach under the following programs:

School Room: partnering to build bright, well-constructed schools.

Reading Room: establishing bilingual libraries and filling them with donated English books and self-published local language books, creating a colorful space with posters, games, furniture and flooring.

Local Language Publishing: sourcing new content from indigenous writers and illustrators to publish high-quality local language children's books.

Computer and Language Room: establishing labs to provide students with vocational skills and employment access.

Room to Grow Girls' Scholarship: funding long-term, comprehensive scholarships for young girls who would otherwise not have access to an education; includes school fees and supplies, medical expenses and local female mentors.

ROOM TO READ—BY THE NUMBERS

- By the end of 2007, Room to Read will have impacted the lives of over 1.5 million children through its education programs.
- Room to Read has built over 400 schools.

- It has established 5,200 bilingual Reading Rooms.
- It has self-published 250 local language children's titles, representing over 2 million books.
- It has donated more than 1.6 million English language children's books.
- It receives funding for over 4,000 long-term girls' scholarships.
- It has established 136 computer and language labs.

ANN COTTON
Campaign for Female Education (CAMFED)

Africa

Ann Cotton's on-the-ground exposure to extreme poverty in Zimbabwe in 1991 changed her life and, in doing so, the futures of hundreds of thousands of young girls in Africa. During that trip, Ann saw clearly the link between the lack of female education and extreme poverty. Since then, Ann and her team have built an organization that currently provides educational opportunities to over 400,000 girls each year in rural villages in sub-Saharan Africa. CAMFED works in partnership with local communities and ministries of education, using an approach that seeks to systemically break the cycle of poverty.

ANN COTTON—
Changing the Culture of Poverty by Educating Young Women

I was brought up in Wales. My father was a teacher and was the first member of his family to go to university through a scholarship. This was undoubtedly one of the reasons why he encouraged me to take education so seriously. I was also influenced by my Welsh grandmother, who had to leave school at age twelve to care for her father, who had been brain-damaged in a coal-mining accident. My interest in education caused me early in my career to establish a center in London for girls who were excluded from receiving an education within the existing school system.

After some years bringing up three young children, I decided to get an MA in human rights and education, a decision that brought me in 1991 to the remote Nyaminyami District of western Zimbabwe to study why so few girls went to school. My intention was to study the problem, not to get directly involved in the solutions, but what I witnessed in that village changed my life forever.

I had never before witnessed the depth of poverty I witnessed in Zimbabwe, and I was initially shocked by what I saw. I was also deeply disturbed by the level of insecurity the young girls had to deal with every day. I realized that the high levels of maternal and child mortality were both caused by women's vulnerability and their lack of access to education. I found that most parents wanted their daughters to go to school but they did not have the funds to pay for them to do so. In most cases the parents used their scarce resources to educate their sons rather than their daughters because boys had the best chance of securing paid work in the future. My realization was contrary to the broadly held notion that cultural resistance was the main reason for low female school attendance.

On one of my walks between villages, I met two teenage sisters, Cecilia and Makarita. They had bussed and walked sixty miles to attend the Mola Secondary School because the costs were much lower at Mola than at schools near their home. Yet these two young girls told me that they did not know whether their parents would have enough money for them to return to school the next term. As I lay awake at night fearful that scorpions were about to fall upon me from the thatched roof above, I realized that the girls were trapped. I also realized that what kept the cycle of poverty in place was not a poverty of culture but the culture of poverty. My passion was ignited, and my mind started to explore how I could help these girls and their friends get an education. My interest in educational theory was replaced by a new commitment to work with local populations to come up with and implement educational solutions that would work in their environments.

Back in England in 1992, my first effort to raise money to enable young girls like Cecilia and Makarita to go to school was making and selling cakes and sandwiches with friends at the local market. Before long I had raised enough money to pay for thirty-two girls in Zimbabwe to go to school for a year.

Right from the start, our approach was to set aside preconceived notions of what the challenges and the solutions were and to listen carefully to the needs and suggestions of the local villagers. They suggested, for example, that the scholarship money should go directly to the schools rather than to the families of the recipients. They recommended that CAMFED only hire locals to run the CAMFED offices rather than rely on expatriates. They stressed the importance of transparency so that everyone knew who was making what decisions and how educational funds were being allocated. They joined us at meetings with the Ministry of Education at the national and district levels to support the initiative and assure its effective implementation.

It has now been fifteen years since CAMFED was founded and I still feel energized by our work. What satisfies me most is seeing the change in others, such as when I meet a girl who received an education because of CAMFED and is now doing wonderful things she would not otherwise have had the opportunity to do.

Children in a CAMFED partner school in Zimbabwe.

My advice to others who want to get involved in any social effort is first and foremost for them to find their passion, to get to a point where they have no choice, where they have to act, have to get involved. One has to care enough to let go of fear, to care enough to risk failure and look upon not trying as failure. And listen always, and most carefully, to those experiencing the problem you want to try to solve.

THE CAMFED MODEL—
A Bottom-Up Collaborative Approach

> *To educate girls is to reduce poverty. No other policy is as likely to raise economic productivity, lower infant and maternal mortality, improve nutrition and promote health—including the prevention of HIV/AIDS.*

—Kofi Annan,
Former UN Secretary General

CAMFED now is in the midst of seeking to bring about systemic change in the education of young girls in Africa. Ann has turned CAMFED into a charitable organization that is making it possible for 427,000 young people in Zimbabwe,

Ghana, Zambia and Tanzania to receive an education. Most are girls, although some orphan boys are also supported. Boards of trustees are active at each branch, supported by an international advisory board.

CAMFED's model brings transformative benefits not only to the young girls who they help educate but also to the well-being of their families and communities. A virtuous cycle is set in motion, whereby girls are supported through childhood education and post-school years to become leaders who are in a position to break the cycle of poverty during their own lifetime as well as during the lives of future generations.

The following are some of the most important principles guiding CAMFED's approach:

A clear, powerful and inspiring vision: CAMFED's vision is of a world in which every child is educated, protected, respected, valued and grows up to turn the tide of poverty.

A focus on systemic change: The young women who have completed their education become the drivers of change in their local communities. They have all experienced a degree of vulnerability that is terrifying. Yet they have been able to transform their experiences of pain, exclusion and poverty into power—through education. As a result, the young women have the capacity to inspire other young girls who are facing the same problems they faced.

A bottom-up collaborative approach: CAMFED's approach centers on the needs of the students and their communities.

Staff in each country recruited locally: Staff includes locals and young women who have already benefited from CAMFED's approach.

Close working relationships with the Ministries of Education in each country: Ann notes that this often makes it possible for CAMFED to influence the work of the ministries nationwide.

Transparency: Ann points out that the problem of poverty is often not that there is no money in the system, but that the money does not come down to the poor. For this reason, CAMFED makes sure that the community knows who makes the decisions regarding the allocation of CAMFED funds and what decisions they have made. Since the young girls have no power themselves to get an education, she points out how important it is to understand how power in the educational system is used—and abused.

Replicability: To bring about systemic change, the approach has to be replicable in many diverse cultures. Skeptics told CAMFED that its success in Zimbabwe could not be replicated in Ghana because the predominantly Muslim communities in the north would not welcome CAMFED's approach. This proved not to be true. Another much bigger organization tried to replicate CAMFED's model but failed because they used a top-down approach, rather than CAMFED's bottom-up, community-driven approach.

Results-driven: By constantly focusing on and measuring results, CAMFED seeks to increase its cost-effectiveness. In 1996, for example, CAMFED devised a community-driven solution that would provide safe accommodations for girls near schools, but outside each school's perimeter. Since the girls were not staying at the school, they were charged the lower day student rate. This approach has been replicated in three countries.

A long-term commitment to those CAMFED seeks to educate: Since the poor families that CAMFED serves cannot pay for the continuing education of their children, CAMFED makes a commitment through each child's high school graduation. In addition, CAMFED has created programs to support girls following their education, such as their "Seed Money Scheme" that provides small-scale grants to young women as they leave school to enable them to start small businesses. Coupled with this is a training program to provide the girls with knowledge of financial planning and management.

Work to assure that employees and partners share CAMFED's vision and values.

CAMFED—By The Numbers

- Currently, CAMFED has fifty-four staff members, who in turn mobilize thousands of volunteers.
- By 2010, CAMFED's plan will achieve the following:

- Provide 800,000 years of education to girls and vulnerable boys from poor families in seven countries in sub-Saharan Africa.
- Train 20,000 young educated women in business and leadership skills to catalyze social and economic progress in the seven countries.
- Map the levers of change that achieve and sustain girls' education in partnership with three international research agencies and seven African academies.
- Partner with government departments to deliver best practices in girls' education and achieve gender equality in ten countries in sub-Saharan Africa.
- Advocate for urgent international action and transparency in spending on girls' education.

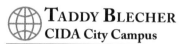 TADDY BLECHER
CIDA City Campus

South Africa

Taddy Blecher's vision of creating the first virtually free institution of higher education in South Africa has reinvented an entire method of education that is replicable, scalable and ultimately sustainable in any developing country. Students come from squatter camps and townships, and graduate with an accredited degree in business administration. In its unique approach of offering holistic, relevant, technology-enriched tertiary education at very low cost, Blecher's CIDA City Campus has blossomed under his stewardship, an impressive sign of hope in the economic and social transformation of the African subcontinent.

TADDY BLECHER—*From Actuary to Visionary, Creating Educational Opportunities for the Poor in South Africa*

We never took "no" for an answer. CIDA (Community and Individual Development Association) City Campus had an incalculable number of challenges from beginning to end in this process. Starting a school of higher education from scratch did not come about without its obstacles and extreme difficulties. It took six appeals to become accredited by the government. We had no money, books, computers, dormitories, classrooms, teaching qualifications or even students. But we did have the idea to start Africa's first virtually free university. We had the

Taddy with CIDA students, Johannesburg, South Africa.

idea to break paradigms, to take street kids and help them become chartered accountants and merchant bankers if they wanted to. We knew it was possible to create self-sufficiency through the students themselves, who could be trained to run a campus and take proud ownership of their own school by managing aspects of the institution and reaching large numbers in society through mentorship programs and outreach entrepreneurship.

We have come so far. In the mid-nineties CIDA's current directors ran Transcendental Meditation projects in township schools in South Africa to upgrade various levels of education. Through meditation, pass rates dramatically increased, and as a result, our impetus for starting an African tertiary education institution was launched with the simple focus of improving the country's approach to learning.

In the old South Africa, high school students would pass their final year with great effort but no prospects to further their education. They were stuck in a spiral cycle of poverty with no opportunities for employment. I remember thinking, "How is it that education in this country is such a dead end?" CIDA City Campus began in January of 2000 with the "aha" realization that anyone, no matter how poor or unprivileged, could succeed in our program.

Three years before the founding of CIDA, a veil fell from my eyes. I had been working for a consulting company and as an actuary, earning an incredible salary with all of the benefits I could ever need, except for personal spiritual fulfillment. It was in a large group of people in guided meditation that the veil fell and I suddenly realized I was free to do anything I wanted with my life. The only jailer was myself. I could live a much richer, fuller and more meaningful life serving others with every inch of my being. As I have heard from so many people, and as is indeed true for myself, it is in giving of myself to others that I feel blessed to receive so much more in return.

I believe resolutely in the innate potential of every human being. Poverty is a function of the fact that people with enough means have not been taught to solve problems effectively. If we nurture every person's talent, teach them how to create something from nothing, they can and will lead lives of dignity and empowerment. This shift in consciousness, no matter how destitute or poor one may be, is the key to addressing so many social ills from a systemic perspective.

As we are creating an advanced, financially focused, state-of-the-art learning site with worldwide acclaim, we have produced significant results for over 2,000 graduates to date in every area of education, including academic and business training, personal development, alumni success post-graduation, innovation, cost effectiveness, speed of learning, technology-enriched capacity, sport and culture, and grassroots societal transformation.

CIDA's Model—*Bridging Business and Education for Free*

CIDA City Campus was founded in 2000 in Johannesburg, South Africa. Its unique approach partners education with business. Its model incorporates professionals from the business world who teach pro bono, and combines technology with contact-based learning.

For example, the CIDA School of Investments capitalizes school programs through its sponsorships with JPMorgan, the Johannesburg Stock Exchange and Reuters, and has received hundreds of donated computers from Dell, while being bolstered by a consortia of South Africa's most notable tech organizations, including SAP Africa, Cisco Systems, SUN Microsystems, CompTIA and T-Systems SA.

Even the academic buildings themselves come from companies who believe in the CIDA City Campus method, such as the eleven-story space on Harrison Street in downtown Johannesburg that was renovated and donated by First National Bank. In all aspects of its mission statement, training, curricula design and public relations, the school is built around progressive business principles and partnerships.

CIDA provides a fully accredited, practical four-year Bachelor of Business Administration qualification that emphasizes entrepreneurship, business science and technology. Throughout the program, students run aspects of the campus and administration themselves, which gives them valuable hands-on experience, as well as pride in their own institution. Students are exposed to and study every major business discipline in an integrated way, covering forty subjects during the four-year academic track. Specialization includes information technology, finance, marketing, human resource management and entrepreneurship. The institution also engenders holistic skills development critical to creativity, self-confidence and reduction of stress, which it achieves through scientifically validated methods like counseling and meditation.

The Branson School of Entrepreneurship at CIDA is an example of the institution's larger educational philosophy. Named after Richard Branson, who was knighted in Britain for his service to entrepreneurship and social progress, the CIDA program provides an opportunity to financially disadvantaged students with skills in finance, accounting, technology and business development. The school thus seeks to encourage the dissemination of start-ups and microenterprises as an attractive and viable career by fostering mentorship programs for budding entrepreneurs in the early stages of their business ideas.

As the first and only free tertiary institution in sub-Saharan Africa for historically disadvantaged students, CIDA has achieved a practical model that converts youth seen as potential liabilities into leaders. The first graduates since 2004 are already in the workforce, and with more than $20 million in annual salaries and more than $700 million present value of earnings over the next forty years, CIDA is indeed making a difference. There are over 1,500 students currently studying on full scholarships worth over $6 million, chosen because they manifest the talent but not the financial means to attend university. CIDA is privately funded through local and international corporate sponsorships in the private sector and by foundations and charities in the United States and United Kingdom. CIDA's model is vital to creating broad-based economic development in Africa by generating exponential growth in highly trained leaders who will be trained to produce wealth and create sustainable businesses relevant to the African continent and its human and natural resources.

As the school's four founders—Richard Peycke, Thembinkosi Mhlongo, Mburu Gitonga and Taddy Blecher—attest, the sustainability of CIDA City Campus will be best brought about through indigenous leadership and a long-term financial plan. To this end, CIDA has established a newly unveiled endowment asset structure that will sustain the school from 2011 onwards, assuming current level of expenditure and planned student numbers for the Johannesburg campus. These strategies, which may be useful for any educational institution to adopt in their own financial planning, comprise the following:

CIDA Empowerment Fund (CEF): Conducts large-scale empowerment deals, usually for companies with more than R35 million (US$5.08 million) in annual turnover, providing a one-stop shop, broad-based black economic empowerment solution.

CIDA Investment Trust (CIT): Builds a group of strategically related businesses all united around cause-related marketing and social capital, using profits for good. Also, conducts smaller-scale empowerment deals, usually for companies with less than R35 million in annual turnover.

CCC Education Trust: Endowment Fund and Assets, including CIDA Diamond Fund, CIDA Alumni Fund, CIDA Properties, wills and bequests.

CIDA Diamond Fund: A part of the CCC Education Trust. An endowment focused on fundraising through wealthy individuals and organizations, to ensure cash availability to leverage deals in the CIDA Empowerment Fund and elsewhere to ensure that major potential investment portfolios can be built.

CIDA Ventures: Focused on making all CIDA campuses become financially self-sufficient (as opposed to sustainable through an endowment) through the creation of businesses that leverage the infrastructure and core competencies of the CIDA Education Group and produce an annual profit sufficient to cover all annual operating costs.

CIDA Seed: Part of the Branson School of Entrepreneurship, it provides venture financing to student businesses through the Branson School, as well as to CIDA Campus businesses and Branson School businesses on similar financial terms. The fund takes a percentage of all businesses it finances to build to something more significant over time.

CIDA is already so notably established because many world-renowned leaders and celebrities have visited it, including Oprah Winfrey, Richard Branson, the Dalai Lama, management expert Tom Peters, personal finance expert and author Suze Orman, Edward de Bono, supermodel Iman, the Lord Mayor of London, Michael Oliver and the conductor of the Boston philharmonic, Ben Zander. It was only a few years ago, however, that its first graduates entered the workforce, which suggests how much can be achieved in such a short time given the right people, passion and desire. As Taddy likes to say, inverting the common slogan that "It takes a village to raise a child," with proper education and with the right socially entrepreneurial instincts, "It takes a child to raise a village." CIDA's model is accordingly significant for a new Africa as it works to empower African students, families and communities in educationally driven opportunity.

- In South Africa the average costs to the country to educate a university student per year is around $5,500, and over $14,000 for a degree, but only very few of those who start university complete with a degree.

- Because of CIDA's financial planning, strong donor base and admirable mission statement, it costs CIDA around $1,000 per year for one student to be covered, collectively offering $6 million worth of scholarships.

- The integrated teaching system covers 7–9 hours per day, compared with the standard 3–4 hours, and 40–44 weeks per year, compared with the standard 34–39 weeks.

- There were over 1,500 students registered in CIDA programs in 2007, 52% of whom were women.

- There were 5,186 application forms requested and given out for the 2007 year, with an acceptance rate of 16% (one in seven).

- CIDA has served nearly 3,300 students who are now employed and collectively earning about $20 million in annual salaries.

 ## RODRIGO BAGGIO
Committee for Democracy in Information Technology (CDI)

Brazil

In founding the first Brazilian NGO committed to tackling the digital divide, Rodrigo Baggio has created a franchise model with the Committee for Democracy in Information Technology (CDI), in which communities receive donated computers to be used for lessons in finding employment, as well as social and civic engagement. Like so many entrepreneurs in this book, Rodrigo reaches people's hearts with dogged determination for results, taking only "yes" for an answer. Bill Drayton documented that when Rodrigo first began CDI, he managed to convince Japanese businesses and the Inter-American Development Bank to give him their used computers, then persuaded the Brazilian Air Force to fly the computers home, then won over customs officials to accept the imported machines when his country was blocking most computer products at the time. Having now graduated over 700,000 CDI students, Rodrigo's methods for fighting what he calls "digital apartheid" are being adopted globally.

Rodrigo with students from the Brazilian favelas.

RODRIGO BAGGIO—*Breaking Down the Digital Divide*

I've always had a deep passion for computers and social work. Growing up in Brazil, I would visit my father, who directed the Department of Information Management, at work during school holidays, and was fascinated by any of the new machines I could get my hands on. I got my first computer, a TK82, when I was twelve. Getting a computer at such a young age, I was affected by the reality of what I had when there were so many parents in my area who could not even afford school clothes for their kids. As my Methodist education inspired a strong desire for me to give back to the community, I started to volunteer at a young age, coming into contact with families of all social classes.

My first experience as a volunteer was with street children. It was a cultural and social shock to my insulated lifestyle. I remember thinking how much more I learned about the reality of my country working as a volunteer directly with people than I did at school. This early work with impoverished street boys redirected my life's path.

My professional career began in the business of learning new technologies. Self-educated with a love of computers from exposure to my father's work, I launched a consulting company and started teaching information technology in Rio de Janeiro private schools. I also worked for Accenture and managed IBM's Reinventing Education program in Brazil. But, pressed by a busy schedule, I had no time to dedicate to social projects, or so I felt. I felt empty in my daily routine;

it was a period of constant self-questioning, wondering where my corporate life would really lead me in five or even ten years. My goals seemed so measured by material comforts; I was truly lost. "Is there more to my desires than just a nice car and exotic vacations?" I often asked myself.

At the end of 1993, I had a dream in which I envisaged poor youth using computers as a means to discuss their reality and to solve their problems. I woke up deeply enthusiastic and curious about my dream. I realized then that my two vocations could coexist, using IT as a tool of social promotion and empowerment. My first step was the creation of a BBS, or Bulletin Board System, called Jovemlink (Younglink). The idea was to use a BBS to help promote dialogue between those in the *favelas*, or slums, and those from the more privileged neighborhoods within the city of Rio de Janeiro. The service had hundreds of users, but almost all of them were youth from the upper and middle class. The challenge, therefore, was to extend these technologies to the underprivileged communities, most of whom didn't have access to a computer.

In 1994, information technologies seemed poised on the dawn of a new age of limitless potential. Inequity was increasingly rampant, and it seemed clear to me that if new knowledge and technological accessibility skipped over poor communities, we would be exacerbating the differences between the rich and poor. Unwittingly, we were accelerating the creation of a new type of social disparity brought about through digital apartheid. Those who could buy and use the newest inventions did. Those who couldn't afford them began falling further and further behind. The very tools that were created to move our society forward were in fact widening the gap between the haves and have-nots.

During that time, a campaign called Computers for All started. It was a pioneer initiative in Brazil, which began collecting used computers to be donated to underprivileged communities. The initiative received great support, including the collaboration of several notable academic institutions. In July 1994, the impact of the campaign was evaluated, confirming that the computers were quickly being incorporated into the daily lives of the people using the community centers where they had been installed. Unfortunately, though, the study also revealed that most of the poor were frequently confused or frustrated by the machines' functions. Since the use of technology was not part of the local culture, few people knew how to use the computers to their fullest capacity.

This gap in the social and technological structures of my country brought me back to my dream. I took on the idea with full force, realizing my idea with the founding of the Information Technology and Citizens Rights Schools (ITCRS). Both my desire to help and the way in which I leveraged this ambition followed a completely unorthodox and unique strategy in my country: to ally technology and citizen rights promotion through the viewpoint, reflections and debates amongst the youth about the reality of their regional communities. This new vision was embryonic at the time, as nobody talked about digital inclusion. We had no model to copy, no example to follow.

Nevertheless, with our early efforts, we opened people's eyes to the fact that in big cities the underprivileged do not die from hunger, but rather from lack of hope and opportunity, leading them to crime, violence, drugs and sometimes death. In March of 1995, our first school was founded in Santa Marta, one of Rio de Janeiro's slums. In two years, we had begun a campaign to change our country's approach to digital education. With the hard work and donations of many, and with the approval of the local government, my dream began to be realized in founding the first Brazilian NGO of digital inclusion, the Committee for Democracy in Information Technology (CDI).

CDI relies on young people for talents they already display every day: organizational mobilizing, quick learning and entrepreneurship. Young students need very little encouragement to get excited by the opportunity to use technology. We simply channeled this excitement into efforts to mobilize job generation and investment in social projects. As students unveil the world surrounding them, they also discover alternative possibilities for how to use technology. This transformation is most achievable when the individual is empowered with community values while given control of technological tools they may then develop and explore on their own.

Several people have forever improved their lives by attending our schools. Last year, during a lecture by the Colombian sociologist Bernardo Toro in Rio, I was surprised and moved by a testimony from Ronaldo Monteiro, a former student of ITCRS at the Lemos de Brito Penitentiary. Ronaldo credited the radical changes in his life—from being a juvenile prison inmate with no prospect of social inclusion to becoming a young social entrepreneur—to the work that CDI helped him develop. During his time in prison, he attended the ITCRS to be trained as an educator. This was a singular turning point in his life, realizing through our program that he could change not only his future but also the future of others like him. Ronaldo learned how to conduct his own workshops on issues like recyclable goods, literacy and technology by helping to create a project called One Chance, which developed several permanent prison-training programs. As soon as he was able to leave prison, he established the Social and Cultural Integration Center, an NGO in Rio that teaches computer skills, entrepreneurship and information technology to poor community schools. Recently, he created an organization that offers these same lessons for a professional qualification exclusively for ex-inmates.

THE CDI MODEL—
Integrating Technology and Education for the Poor

CDI's objective is to promote access to information technology by disenfranchised audiences, using IT as a tool to stimulate active citizenship and entrepreneurship to foster political, social and economic development. CDI has overcome what some researchers call "the classic pilot syndrome" by successfully replicating its model in more than 840 different local contexts, including eight countries in Latin America and several CDI campuses in South Africa and Japan.

With over 700,000 graduates since 1995, CDI has grown rapidly in its approach to technology education, where the trained become trainers and the educated the educators. CDI schools are not run and governed by a grand administrative body; rather, they are funded, staffed and administered by their local community. This model is unique and highly economical as a strategy for education in cities with strong community ties.

Besides providing professional qualification in IT to its students, CDI's political-pedagogical proposal aims at promoting active citizenship. CDI affirms that information technology is an excellent tool to foster the development of successful citizens, because of the equality of opportunities and democracy that exist in web-based media.

As a whole, the main objectives of CDI's political-pedagogical proposal are the following:

- To provide qualification courses on the use of information and communication technologies (ICTs), allowing their social appropriation by communities;

- To foster awareness-raising and reflection by society;

- To favor the creation of a physical space in which discussions, participation and community actions can be carried out; and

- To enable the acquisition of useful knowledge, so that individuals and communities may exercise active citizenship, ensuring social, political and economic development.

CDI's team works jointly with the educators and coordinators of the community centers housing ITCRSs, qualifying them through readings, debates and certification workshops. As for their relationship with students, CDI emphasizes an educational starting point that extends beyond the classroom to holistic learning. Many tools are used to achieve this aim, such as debates, analysis of historic facts, statistical data, newspaper articles, books, poetry, music, research on the Internet and interviews with community members, but all lessons are related back to the everyday life of the students, educators and the community as a whole.

Through courses offered by CDI, computer tools such as word processors, electronic spreadsheets, database managers and Internet searches are used to aid research and to analyze and organize contents, allowing people to express their personal synthesis of reality. After twelve years, primarily in Latin America, CDI is examining the possibility of taking its model to poverty-stricken regions of Africa, Asia and Eastern Europe. The organization has also opened three fundraising offices in New York, Boston and London in order to advance the cause and mission of CDI. Moreover, it has established strategic partnerships with many other world-leading corporations and NGOs, including the Vale do Rio Doce Foundation, Philips, Accenture, Skoll Foundation, USAID, Inter-American Development Bank, Foundation Internationale Carrefour, Avina Foundation, Kellogg Foundation, Esso, UNESCO, The Brazilian Development Bank (BNDES), Cisco Systems and Microsoft.

CDI—By The Numbers

- Only 16.3% of homes in Brazil have access to computers, and only 11% are connected to the Internet.
- In all, 700,000 individuals have graduated from CDI's schools.
- CDI has received over 8,000 computer donations from international businesses and development banks.
- CDI has established 642 Brazilian Information Technology and Citizens Rights Schools (ITCRS) in 290 towns.
- About 200 international ITCRSs have spread in seventy-seven towns.

CHAPTER 5

Microcredit

While nearly all of the chapters in this book include examples of how extreme poverty compounds every other problem, this chapter focuses on the solution that most directly addresses the inability of the poor to borrow money to build small businesses with which to dig their way out of poverty: microcredit loans.

The Grameen Bank, which, along with its founder Muhammad Yunus, was awarded the Nobel Peace Prize in 2006, has been the model that has been copied by hundreds of other organizations around the world. The goal of microcredit institutions is to provide small loans, anywhere from $25 to $400 per loan, to poor individuals who do not qualify for loans from conventional banks that require collateral. Against the predictions of most critics, microcredit lending to the poor has achieved repayment rates that are nearly perfect all over the world, due to the strong core principles of incentive-based community trust.

While there are many subtle differences in approach adopted in different countries, the basic microcredit cycle is in fact quite simple. A microfinance institution (MFI) such as the Grameen Bank raises start-up capital and begins identifying individuals in a local community to whom to lend small amounts of money. In many cases, these loans are specified for women for two principle reasons: 1) women, much more so than men in patriarchal societies, repay loans at nearly a 100% rate, and 2) women who become financially independent have proven to be more committed to helping their children and general community. The MFI then gathers a group of five or ten women together in a principle of solidarity, by which they depend on one another to repay the loans at a low rate of interest. If an individual defaults, the other community members in that person's group cover the debt. The loan recipient then invests in materials, livestock, a cell phone or some such item that can generate income. In many rural communities, a borrower will buy a goat or a cow with the start-up loan and then sell the dairy products from the animal at market prices, slowly making a profit over time to repay the loan, receive new funds and expand the business.

By 2005, the Grameen Bank had reached 60,000 villages in Bangladesh through microcredit loans while providing financial services to more than 6 million poor families. In total, Grameen Bank had supplied over $5 billion in loans. Most impressively, within five years of their first microloan, over half of the individuals receiving microloans from the Grameen Bank had crossed the poverty line. Today there are over 158 institutions in more than forty countries utilizing the Grameen Bank microfinance methodology, which has become a major tool in the fight for global poverty alleviation.

The World Bank estimates that there are over 7,000 microfinance institutions reducing poverty through microcredit financing worldwide. Some of the microcredit initiatives that are not profiled in this chapter include the following:

- ACCION (Americans for Community Co-operation In Other Nations)
- Bonnie Clac
- BRAC (Bangladesh Rural Advancement Committee)
- FINCA (Foundation for International Community Assistance) International
- Grameen Foundation
- MicroCredit Entreprises
- SKS (Swayam Krishi Sangam) Microfinance
- Women's World Banking

In this chapter you will read three very distinct stories:

- **Matt and Jessica Flannery,** an American couple who wanted to start a profitable entrepreneurial business using the Internet to connect lenders in wealthy countries with low-income entrepreneurs in the developing world.

- **Marcelino San Miguel,** a businessman who founded the Dominican Republic's first credit bureau, the profits of which he used to provide microloans to the poorest women in his country.

- **Audrey Codera,** a young entrepreneur in the Philippines who began providing microcredit loans to alleviate poverty among the youth in her country.

MATT AND JESSICA FLANNERY
Kiva

Africa, Latin America, Asia, the Middle East and Eastern Europe

During the dot-com boom, Matt and Jessica Flannery were a young couple looking to start a business together that somehow could help others, but also was profitable. Despite the negative opinions from many "experts" as to why their idea would not work, Matt and Jessica created Kiva.org, leveraging the Internet to build human connections between lenders in the developed world and low-income entrepreneurs in developing countries. In just a few years, Kiva became a widely recognized success story among the solutions to global poverty, as it has connected tens of thousands of people around the world through web-based microcredit loans. Whether supporting a motor parts shop mechanic in Cambodia, a shoe store in Ecuador, or a peanut butter maker in Kenya, Kiva makes it possible for lenders with as little as $25 to choose where their money goes, and to track how that loan helps build an individual's business, or even in some cases an entire community.

JESSICA FLANNERY—*Loans that Change Lives*

My relationship with Matt is the most important relationship in my life. Neither of us are static beings. We have grown and developed together, and Kiva is a reflection of this. We really complement each other and carry each other—at times when I feel either down or overly optimistic, he remains practical, as he is such a good problem solver. His instincts for entrepreneurship really fit nicely with my desire to help individuals in Africa, after I returned from my first trip there working with an NGO called the Village Enterprise Fund (VEF).

Before Kiva had gotten under way, I was writing case studies about thirty different villagers in East Africa who were looking for seed funding. VEF granted $100 to the poorest of the poor who had promising new business ideas. I came back to Matt in California and excitedly told him all about the individuals I had met and worked with in Kenya, Uganda and Tanzania. It wasn't so much the business opportunity but the capacity to build new relationships that really compelled us to start Kiva.

Microfinance, contrary to big banks, is underlined by the impact of human relationships. Many said it would be too difficult to loan money to those in the developing world who don't have identification or can't even write their own name. To ensure accountability and participation, many young microfinance institutions and NGOs integrate grassroots leaders from the local population as much as possible, including field volunteer coordinators, teachers, faith leaders and businessmen and women. With their stewardship on the ground, they are able to administer extreme trust to leverage our impact with accountable results. This can be seen in the near-perfect repayment rate of successful microfinance programs worldwide, including Kiva.

For me, Kiva's approach to building human relationships through microfinance is not about having 200 names on my email list update or listserv, but about meeting another individual with a name and a face on the other side of the world. It is also about encountering that person throughout your everyday life—whether virtually, through your status updates between lender and loan recipient, or personally, as some lenders choose to visit their business partners. It has been tempting to get pulled away from this core notion at times. But the consistent reminder from our mission statement is the human aspect, which we return to every day. As opposed to a one-time donation with your name on a check that you may never see again, in creating a loan you build human relationships with an accountable return, both financially and personally.

MATT FLANNERY—
Overcoming the Skeptics

As a software developer, I had this theory that we could somehow turn Americans into business partners and supporters of these East African entrepreneurs that Jessica had met. In the beginning it was just our family, close friends and the names on our wedding list who helped to raise $3,000, which we then used to help kick-start seven businesses in Uganda. At that time, this was just a side project for me. We never had the intention of turning this "Kiva idea" into a real business.

But then I started getting calls from friends who wanted to follow up on the checks they had written. They even started doing their own research on the individuals we told them about. Our first real success story was a fish seller in Uganda named Elizabeth Omalla. "Hey did you hear?" one friend called to tell me, "Elizabeth sold twice more fish this week with the money we loaned to her!" Since Kiva began providing her loans, Elizabeth is now able to take her children to school, buy two cows and five goats and open a savings account.

Based on the excitement of the people who loaned and got involved in the very beginning, Kiva made me think about poverty in an entirely different way. It was the intellectual connection that intrigued me. When you lend to someone, you can connect with his or her business plan and share in its growth.

I was used to a different model of giving as "charity" to the underprivileged, sick or dying, creating a kind of benefactor or pity relationship to those in poverty. Visiting slums traveling abroad, I became overwhelmed with feelings of helplessness, that extreme poverty was so bad I could not possibly make a difference. For entrepreneurs, starting a business is all about small gains. This principle gave meaning to a fight against poverty that seemed to me, at times, impossible and hopeless.

By this point in 2004, we had become excited about our friends' interest but were discouraged by the opposite reaction we received from the "experts" to whom we pitched our idea. It seemed necessary for Jessica and me to succeed in order to get the approval of others. With our forty-page business plan in hand, we went to microfinance professionals, conferences at the UN, international lawyers and even the SEC. But each time we delivered our idea, we became lost in other people's reasons why our concept wouldn't work, which they argued with technical language about securitization, loan loss reserves and currency risk. They said our idea would not scale. They said the overhead would cripple the cash flow margin. And most of all, they made false pattern-matching comparisons to preexisting models, saying that Kiva was too much like other child sponsorship organizations. It was all very disheartening.

In the beginning of 2005, we put down our business plan and stopped asking the "experts." I quit my job and decided, at last, to join with Jessica in following our passion.

Our first seven businesses that we posted on our site, for a total of $3,500, included a goat herder, a fish monger, a cattle farmer and a restaurateur. Six months later every loan had been repaid, and these seven entrepreneurs became known as the "Dream Team," proving it was possible to lend to the poor over the Internet.

In the immediate period following the decision to quit my job and work full time to build Kiva, we learned more than we had in the entire previous year of asking others for help. As any entrepreneur will tell you, the very negativity from people saying we couldn't do it is what convinced us even more that we had to do it. So we did, and in putting the business plan aside and focusing on action, Kiva expanded rapidly, with the invaluable leadership of a few key people like Premal Shah, the former principal product manager at PayPal and cofounder of the Silicon Valley Microfinance Network, and Olana Hirsch Khan, who was a top-level officer at Google for six years. Incredibly, our core team was so committed to the concept of our mission that until November of 2005, six months after Premal and Olana came on board, we all worked unpaid with a handful of dedicated volunteers.

People lend, it seems, because they are drawn to the notion of being a bank themselves, able to lend to individuals of their choice, and getting to share in the success of someone else in need. Lenders come back to us every day echoing the words of our first family and friends who invested. They say how much more they receive in ways that the monetary amount they lend does not measure. Indeed, this is the true power of our original idea. Poverty can be eventually overcome by building human connections.

SELECT
an entrepreneur and make
a small loan (as little as $25)
using your credit card or PayPal

GET REPAID
within months as the business
succeeds. Once fully repaid,
withdraw your money or
LEND AGAIN!

KIVA
transfers funds to
overseas partners who
handle distribution and
collection of loan payments

WATCH
your entrepreneur's small
business grow via email
updates and the Kiva website

KIVA'S MODEL—
An Internet Platform that Generates Revenue and Social Capital

Based in San Francisco, California, the innovative Kiva model has in just a few years of operation established itself as the premier peer-to-peer microfinance site, allowing people from across the globe to fight poverty simply by logging on to a website, browsing businesses in need of funding, and making a loan. *Kiva* means "agreement" or "exchange" in Swahili. This is how it works:

Anoko Lawson-Savadoi, an entrepreneur's sewing business, Togo.

Logging on to the Kiva website, you will find people like Sum Kim Heng of Cambodia, who is seeking a loan of $1,000 to help purchase tools for his motorbike shop, and Margaret Antwiwaa, who needs just $550 to build up the inventory in her corner store in the Krobo District of Ghana. Sum and Margaret are borrowers of local lending institutions that have entered into partnership with Kiva to help raise debt capital to finance their operations.

Kiva facilitates its peer-to-peer lending relationships by means of field partners, or MFIs, in over forty countries across the globe. Organizations like Mercy Corps' Ariana Financial Services in Afghanistan, CREDIT (Cambodia Rural Economic Development Initiatives for Transformation) MFI in Cambodia, or Fundación San Miguel Arcangel in the Dominican Republic (which is also featured in this chapter) enter into institutional partnerships with Kiva in order to help raise 0% debt capital provided by individual lenders. Kiva currently has seventy partners, and is continuing to grow in Africa, Latin America, Asia, the Middle East and Eastern Europe.

Through its self-expanding network, Kiva is able to scale quickly to reach more borrowers in need while leaving day-to-day operations of microfinance, such as client screening, lending contracts, disbursements and repayment collections, to the MFIs. Meanwhile, potential lenders browse the site and decide themselves to which entrepreneur's operations they would like to provide seed money. Incredibly, in all of its programs Kiva has achieved a 98% repayment rate over the last two years. After a lender is repaid, they then can choose to relend to the same borrower, withdraw or loan to a different entrepreneur.

While Kiva.org is a non-profit 501(c)(3), it has implemented several existing or soon-to-be active income streams, which amount to a total portfolio size of about $13 million. Kiva raises about $50,000 a day and has helped to facilitate 20,000 loans to individual borrowers. Its revenues come from optional lending fees, which act as a kind of restaurant tip system volunteered by the lender: breakage, in which lenders choose not to accept the repayment sum; MFI fees, in which Kiva may charge the local institution a service charge or late fee on debt; interest on funds before they are transferred to or from the lenders and borrowers; and sales from merchandise, such as promotional pieces, clothing or educational materials. To date, Kiva has not yet implemented the latter of these five, but is in the process of incorporating such revenue streams into their system.

Kiva—By The Numbers

- Kiva's average individual loan size to borrowers is $642, and individuals can make direct loans to low-income entrepreneurs for as low as $25.
- Kiva facilitates loans to entrepreneurs in forty countries through seventy partner microfinance institutions.
- Kiva has helped 20,000 entrepreneurs in the developing world by facilitating loans of over $14 million.
- Kiva currently has a 99.75% loan repayment rate.
- Of Kiva's loan recipients, 73% are female.
- Kiva raises over $50,000 daily.
- Kiva has been featured on CNN, BBC, and the *Oprah Winfrey Show*, in the *New York Times* and *The Wall Street Journal*, and at the Clinton Global Initiative.

 ## Marcelino San Miguel
Fundación San Miguel Arcangel

Dominican Republic

Fundación San Miguel Arcangel, a "Grameen Foundation USA" Partner Organization among the Kiva-sponsored microfinance institutions, provides loans to the poor in the Dominican Republic, where in 2004, 58% of the population was living under the poverty line. Overcoming a culture of resistance, including the refusal of commercial

Low income female entrepreneurs paying off their monthly loans, San Cristobal province, Dominican Republic.

banks and the government to sponsor private microcredit initiatives, founder Marcelino San Miguel used the profits generated from selling his former company, the first credit bureau in the Dominican Republic, to initiate a highly successful lending program inspired by the Grameen Bank model.

Marcelino San Miguel—
Changing the Culture of Opportunity for the Poor

My father emigrated from Spain in 1917. He eventually did well for himself after initially working on the docks, first as a laborer unloading ships by hand, later as a delivery boy for an insurance company. Once he set to work on something, he never looked back. He saved and invested well and was able to provide us with food, education and a roof over our heads. Near the time of his death at ninety-seven years old, we had a conversation that shaped my own visions for making a difference in this world.

I asked him, "In your life would you have done anything differently or tried to do more of the same?"

He responded in his usual unruffled way, "No." Resting to reflect, he then said, "No, because at birth I was naked, and I had to earn everything from that moment on. Coming from very humble beginnings, I have learned much along the way, as will you, so take things as they come, making this world better in the end than as you found it." It has taken me a long time to realize what my father meant by that.

Marcelino San Miguel and Nobel laureate Muhammad Yunus work together to offer an innovative solution to global poverty through microcredit loans.

When I went to college, I studied physics. I quickly realized that professions in physics did not have a good "return on investment," so I switched to finance. But in finance, I faced another challenging realization. In the Dominican Republic, it's difficult to make financial endorsements or recommendations for individuals who don't have a financial track record. Under the Napoleonic legal code dating back to the eighteenth century, jurisprudence for our Dominican system mandates that it is illegal to give out personal credit information, except for criminal cases of financial concern. Many of the citizens needing financial support lack identification, a consistent address and a record.

In fact, about 30% of those we serve don't even "exist" as a matter of legal record, as they have no documents attesting to their birth and life. So there was certainly a need for some sort of institutionalized credit information source. This is how, against all odds, I founded my country's first credit bureau, which I eventually sold to one of the "Big Three" credit information organizations in the world, TransUnion, the American credit company based in Chicago. Gathering a database of information on as many individuals as possible, I quickly realized how a challenge can quickly become a great business opportunity, if you look carefully enough at how best to fix a system with an identifiable solution.

There are many challenges and problems in any society, but particularly in our developing world. For example, over the last week or so, when I was visiting our field programs, I saw a girl with a swollen belly licking a dirt floor out of starvation and delirium. In another village, drug lords harassed several of the local loan recipients, demanding to know why they were receiving money from us. In another, a family of six with four children under the age of eleven lost both parents: the father hung himself out of desperation and the mother died due to disease and lack of food. During our first days of doing business, we were robbed and shot at. And our government, despite the good intentions of many, is not helping. In fact, it has introduced new legislation making it next to impossible to lend money to any individual that doesn't have collateral or some sort of guarantee. Since the people we lend to are the poorest of the poor, who often cannot write their own name or even know how to spell it, they will be excluded from obtaining any kind of proper financial services.

The administrative bureaucracies of our government are endless, and outreach to the poor is limited, if not laughable. In the recent political election, one politician threw pocket change out of a helicopter showcasing his intentions to be "President for the Poor." The rhetoric would be fine, if they weren't making it so hard for us to do our job. If the government were to take over our foundation, which they would if given the opportunity, it would inevitably lose its self-sustaining capacity and falter due to insufficient resources and bad management. In turn, this would entice illegal loan sharks to raise interest rates above any level of sustenance capacity for the entrepreneurs to live on. It would also mishandle records, and worst of all, neglect outreach to women for community development. When we started, our goal was to provide loans to 10,000 people in five years. With the help of work tools developed by the the Consultative Group to Assist the Poor (CGAP), a consortium of thirty-three public and private development agencies working on microfinance, we determined that we needed $3 million to achieve our goal. Now, after two and a half years, we have reached over 12,000 women, each with an average of four children or dependents, and we have done this with an outstanding portfolio of US$2 million. Our average loan is a few hundred dollars, and our repayment rate is over 99%. Our market projections are accurate, our efficiency is tight, and our lending model is secured, not just by good records, but also by personal contact with the women we reach in their own communities. We are making a significant difference.

A great example of this is Linda, a woman who had nothing, living in a shack near the beach, cooking fish with oil that looked like tar from bad charcoal. Linda used our savings plan model to allow her capital to grow while achieving higher loan amounts from us over time. She invested in fresh oil, new pots and pans and even a newer building closer to tourists on the beach. After earning well with our seed loans, she eventually built rapport with the navy corps, who gave her a permit allowing her to set up business right on the beach's sand. Now she wants a loan of 50,000 pesos for finishing the roof of the restaurant, which I am happy to say is beyond our current level of service support. She has reached a level that enables her to obtain a loan from a commercial bank!

CREATING OPPORTUNITIES, NOT HANDOUTS

Marcelino San Miguel has always been a successful businessman. He founded CICLA (Credit Information Center for the Americas), the first reputable credit information bureau in the Dominican Republic. Meeting with the Grameen Foundation personnel for the first time in 2004, and drawing upon his background in financial credit information, Marcelino saw the need for a microlending model. He sold his investments in the bureau and was thus able to devote himself full time to the development of the nonprofit organization, Fundación San Miguel Arcangel (FSMA), which quickly generated revenue while empowering women to live self-sustaining lifestyles. In its first three years of work in the rural sector of the

San Cristóbal, Peravia, and Monte Plata Provinces around the capital city of Santo Domingo, the foundation was serving more than 12,000 women at an interest rate of 4%. Commercial loans at this level are not available.

As with his pioneering of CICLA, Marcelino's constant focus for FSMA is upward growth and scaling. The business plan calls for more than doubling, with 30,000 women receiving loans by 2010. Because of its tightly managed structure and efficiency, as much as 90% of funds go directly to financing the organization's portfolio. FSMA was operationally self-sufficient by mid-2007 as a result of the revenues coming from its interest payments.

In the San Cristóbal, Peravia, Santo Domingo and Monte Plasta Provinces and the other areas of the country in which FSMA works, loan groups comprise about twenty women divided into four groups of five, operating through a decentralized community-based organization. The foundation specifically looks for mothers of families who have demonstrated a desire to produce income to lead the centers. The center administrators organize their peers into self-proposed groups of motivated and creditworthy individuals under the principle of solidarity, as they each rely on one another to repay debts over time. Although each member of the group receives an individual loan, as FSMA does not require any formal guarantee or solvent cosigner, the group becomes the debt guarantor, responsible for on-time payments as a team. This tightly knit structure is enormously effective in maintaining a high level of trust and cooperation. By the end of 2006, when the foundation had over 4,500 members and a current portfolio of over $800,000, repayment rates were over 98% for all participants.

FSMA—By The Numbers

- By the end of 2007, FSMA had forty-eight employees and thirty loan officers.
- By the end of 2007, FSMA had more than 570 centers comprised of more than 2,400 women's groups.
- FSMA has had a total of more than 15,000 members since 2004, and currently has more than 12,000 active loan recipients.
- Its actual portfolio balance is more than RD$64 million (US$1.88 million), with more than RD$150 million (US$4.4 million) cash flow under management.
- FSMA has earned RD$30 million (US$885,000) in interest payment revenue since 2004.

AUDREY CODERA
The Philippine Youth Employment Network

The Philippines   **(PYEN)**

The Philippine Youth Employment Network (PYEN) is a premier nonprofit organization paired with an internally managed microfinance institution called YouthWorks, both of which share the same mission: to alleviate poverty by creating opportunities for entrepreneurial youth employment. "Youth" range from high school age to twenty-eight years old. Cofounder Audrey Codera has partnered with several major international youth empowerment initiatives to help promote PYEN's mission, including SAGE (which was highlighted in the introduction to this book), the International Labor Organization's Youth Employment Network and the Youth Employment Summit (YES) Campaign. Orchestrating a network of partners to collaborate on three shared goals, PYEN works on local, national and international fronts: 1) to conduct training, workshops and consulting for poor youth seeking profitable employment in the Philippines, 2) to offer microcredit loans at a 3% interest rate for entrepreneurial young individuals without substantial means to begin their own businesses and 3) to lobby policymakers and government legislators on behalf of youth empowerment, including the ability of young entrepreneurs to contribute significantly to their country's economic development.

AUDREY CODERA—*Empowering Youth Now*

There are many skeptics who say that youth are not trustworthy and do not deserve loans. I have had the privilege of watching PYEN grow with highly successful repayment rates. These youth are no different than the millions of others unemployed around the world. They are proving the skeptics wrong, and proving themselves to be key assets to international programs for economic development.

I am now in my late twenties, but when I was younger it really bothered me to hear people say, "Youth are the future!" It is true that youth will grow up to be adults responsible for contributing to their community or country in the future. It is limiting to think about youth potential, though, as simply relevant to a country's future growth and progress. Youth are not just important to the future. Youth are the present!

The importance of youth employment is not to be misunderstood as child labor. We empower working-age youths who, for lack of educational and professional opportunities, end up joining gangs, doing drugs or fighting. In the

PYEN high school student team with mentors.

areas where we work—as in many areas around the world where youth have no outlet to contribute their resources, ideas and creativity—the youth segment of the population becomes an underutilized resource, often damaging rather than contributing to the development of a community or country. At PYEN, we have shown that gainful youth employment not only leads to a starving family's survival, but also becomes a catalyst for economic growth, stability and security.

Meanwhile, there are 85 million unemployed youths around the world, at least twice more than the number of unemployed adults. The unemployment rate for youths is 15.8% in the Philippines alone, which means about 1.4 million are not working. An enormous majority of them, at least the ones we seek to help, may not even be in school, because their families are so poor.

I remember wanting to start a youth-based organization as my way of contributing to the progress of my country when I was in high school. At that time, working on social issues was just one of the activities I did while taking classes, playing sports and making friends. My family was never rich, though we were not poor. Once when I was very young, I remember a kid my age who knocked on our car window as we were driving to school. At that time it was illegal to give alms, but my mother handed me some money and instructed me to roll the window down and extend my hand with the small sum. I did, and the look of gratitude in the homeless child's eyes was memorable. That experience really stuck with me.

Our strategy works because we help young people become engaged in sustainable businesses. A stable income enables them to support themselves and their families, a first and necessary step to demonstrate to the greater society what they are truly capable of producing. The pilot project originally was located in the city slums of Napindan, but rapidly expanded to include more areas where people were demonstrating on their own accord a strong desire and commitment to take part in our programs.

The three pillars of our strategy include training and workshops for youth, microcredit loans for seed capital for those who use our training to start businesses, and advocacy and policy lobbying on the national level to raise awareness for youth entrepreneurship. Despite growing so fast, we have demonstrated a near 100% repayment rate, which means a profit to our investors.

When we first began in 2003, our investors were primarily family and friends. The uncollateralized start-up loans have been offered to youth between the ages of sixteen and twenty-four. Since our inception, we have built a concrete support system for budding entrepreneurs through toolkits, references, wellness programs, and capacity-building initiatives with international partner organizations, including the ASEAN (Association of Southeast Asian Nations) Meetings on Youth, the United Nations Development Programme (UNDP) on Millennium Goals, the League of Corporate Foundations Corporate Social Responsibility Initiatives and the World Summit on the Information Society. Beyond just being partners in our network, these organizations are in fact stakeholders in our mission, helping to make youth business opportunities available to many poor families.

There are two wonderful stories I'd like to share about PYEN's successes. One is of a single young person named Jeffrey Delgado, or "Ambo." The other is the SAGE team from Baras, a very poor area where high school kids are making a profit while engaging the local government through agriculture.

One of the most successful graduates of the program is Jeffrey "Ambo" Delgado, who finished his training when he was nineteen years old. At that time, he was in a gang and addicted to drugs while living with his family of five in a one-room, fifteen-square-foot lean-to home, with one bunk bed. With our training and a microcredit loan, Ambo set up a kiosk selling abandoned scrap materials from a nearby shipyard. He has now encouraged his family members to join the business, which has expanded into selling food to workers in the shipyard. Because of this opportunity, Ambo stopped taking illegal substances and stopped fighting in gang wars. He is an inspiration to his friends. In 2006, he completed a new-skills training in welding in 2006. His business has become a family venture, and his whole family looks healthier.

The second great success story is the Baras National High School, a poor public school that was the runner-up in last year's regional competition for SAGE, Students for the Advancement of Global Entrepreneurship. The team, most of whom do not speak English very well, began by convincing the local government to let them till soil in a previously unused lot of land near their school. The high school students had been considered "irrelevant" by the local government, because they were not yet voting age nor well educated. Despite their socioeconomic conditions, the students partnered with university mentors through SAGE and began developing the plot of land by producing and selling an organic fertilizer called vermicompost, also known as earthworm castings, which makes use of biodegradable waste like animal manure, vegetable and fruit peelings and rice straw. The production is technically and economically feasible, the product natural and environmentally friendly. Most impressively, the seven students taking part in the business are now earning a sustainable profit that amounts to more than I make through PYEN!

THE PYEN MODEL—*Integrating Young Adults into the Workforce*

PYEN's "Youth Multiversity" is a program of partners coordinated under PYEN, which makes available diverse experiential learning courses. Training includes basic entrepreneurial skills in self-reliance and innovative thinking, while offering more practical business teachings in marketing, accounting and management. To date, with a small staff of eight, PYEN has trained 200 underprivileged youth to be leaders in their communities.

PYEN conducts training at the local level and advocacy at the national policymaking level. Its partner institution, YouthWorks, is the entity that actually awards and tracks the microfinance funds. Together, they provide a dual approach to getting youth off the streets and focused on productive ideas that benefit others. PYEN urges its youth trainees to do this in a variety of ways, whether students want to start a new business or go into government leadership roles to raise awareness for youth employment opportunities.

As part of its policy work, PYEN has been successful in getting the topic of youth employment into many important forums. This includes for example the Philippines' Medium-Term Youth Development Plan in 2005, the ASEAN Ministerial Meeting on Youth Manila Declaration in 2003, the ASEAN Meeting on Youth-Initiated ICT (Information Communications Technology) Enterprise in 2007, the ILO (International Labor Organization) Regional Meeting on Priority Skills and Employability Among Youth in Asia Pacific Region, and the United Nations Development Programme for Sustainable Enterprise in 2006 and 2007. Meanwhile, more locally, PYEN pursued a needs and results-based National Action Plan on Youth Employment, which it unveiled by running eight local community consultations, four roundtable discussions, and five working sessions, all of which culminated in August of 2007 in a National Summit for Youth Employment, bringing together ideas that involved university students, mentors, nonprofits and private sector businesses with PYEN students.

PYEN—By The Numbers

- Roughly 85 million working-age youths around the world are unemployed, more than twice the number of unemployed adults; the unemployment rate for working-age youths is 15.8% in the Philippines, which means about 1.4 million youth are not working.
- PYEN has trained over 200 youth leaders through its programs.
- It has provided microfinance loans at 3% interest, 100% of which have been repaid in full.

CHAPTER 6

Fair Trade

According to the Fair Trade Federation, fair trade is "commerce with a commitment to developing equitable partnerships between marketers in highly industrialized nations and low-income producers in developing regions of the world." The seven key objectives of fair trade companies are to ensure the following:

1. Fair wages for small producers who cannot compete with multinational corporations and government subsidies;
2. Cooperative workplaces practicing gender equality;
3. Consumer awareness of where products come from and how they were made;
4. Environmental sustainability of production and distribution practices;
5. Technical support for small producers in their home countries;
6. Preservation and respect for local cultural identities; and
7. Greater public accountability for consumer purchasing decisions.

For thousands of years, business owners have utilized and in some cases exploited cheap labor wherever they could find it to keep their costs of production down, and it has been the disenfranchised populations with few financial options that have suffered from a lack of transparency and accountability. And in this era of rapid globalization, millions have been left behind by macroeconomic policies that ignore the factual realities of socioeconomic inequality in many poor countries.

To demonstrate a few recent trends directly related to free trade practices, in Africa today the average income per worker is 11% lower than it was in 1960, according to the World Bank. In the cotton industry alone, more than 12 million people in sub-Saharan Africa depend directly on the cultivation of the cotton crop for their livelihood, and yet the average small-scale producer earns less than $400 on an annual harvest due to competition from large-scale corporations. Similar discrepancies exist with most agriculture products, from coffee and oranges to corn and textile products like rugs and clothing. The exploitation of children for labor has been a major problem in developing countries with poor working standards. Child labor is a crime committed against nearly 220 million children, or one in seven children between the ages of five and seventeen around the world. According to the International Labor Organization, in 2006 an estimated 14% of children in India between five and fourteen were engaged in child labor activities. While conditions have improved over the last fifteen years, in 1995 there were 1 million child weavers working illegally in South Asia.

The Fair Trade Federation estimates that the number of people working for fair trade companies has increased substantially since 2000. Also, there are now twice as many for-profit fair trade companies as nonprofits.

The following are examples of fair trade initiatives that are not profiled in this chapter but may be of interest:

- Aid to Artisans
- BeadforLife
- The Crafts Center
- Fair Trade Federation
- The Fairtrade Labelling Organizations (FLO) International

The tactics that succeed best in running a fair trade organization are those that implement community-based solutions at the local level. The most sustainable practices are those that enable the indigenous populations to take responsibility for their own development.

In this chapter, you will read four very distinct stories from social entrepreneurs who have created revolutionary approaches to local and global fair trade initiatives:

- **Priya Haji,** who is creating U.S. market opportunities for the products of poor artisans from thirty-four developing countries.

- **Kailash Satyarthi and Nina Smith,** who are working to end child labor in the rug industry in South Asia.

- **Charlotte di Vita,** a "compassionate capitalist", whose concern for the impoverished prompted her to create several extraordinary ethical trading initiatives.

- **Rory Stewart,** who has created an initiative in Afghanistan to revive ancient Afghan crafts and rebuild the main bazaar in war-torn Kabul.

Africa, Asia, Latin America and the United States

Priya Haji is the cofounder and CEO of a for-profit company that distributes throughout the United States handcrafted products made by artisans in developing countries. Of World of Good's profits, 10% goes to its nonprofit foundation, which seeks to improve the standard of living of the artisans. This is a very scalable and replicable model using market forces and the profit motive to help alleviate global poverty and strengthen fair trade standards in the U.S. consumer market.

PRIYA HAJI—*Expanding a Family Legacy*

I guess you could say concern for global problems and social justice work is in my blood. My mother is from India, where her parents were part of Gandhi's movement for independence, and my father is from East Africa and was my example of a social entrepreneur. Both my parents are doctors; they came to the United States with their education and built a great life—not only raising my sister and me but six of my cousins too. My parents taught me that generosity is composed of a thousand small acts, not only the way you build your family, but in the way you build your work. And the most important thing my parents gave me was the confidence to believe that I could do anything I put my mind to accomplishing just like they had.

During my high school years, my aunt and my dad joined forces to create a free clinic to provide health care to the poor and uninsured. My aunt donated hotel rooms in her hotel, and my father gave his medical skills and time. I naively volunteered to be the one to organize the clinic—doing the incorporation papers, setting up the systems and creating an organization. None of the adults ever said that a sixteen-year-old couldn't do it, and I thought it seemed perfectly possible—so we did it. We called our initiative "Health for All." It now serves over 3,000 patients a year and is a significant free clinic associated with the Texas A&M medical school. Among the lessons I learned from this initial experience in addressing a social challenge was the importance of taking a first step. I also learned the value of getting others involved in your dream while also helping them to make it their own.

I went to Stanford University as an undergraduate and became very involved in volunteering in East Palo Alto, an adjacent community that was named the "murder capital of the country" at that time, largely due to economic divestment and the development of an underground economy based on drugs. In the midst of the circumstances there I also met some of the most inspiring people I have known in my life—leaders and activists who were recovering addicts who had changed their own lives and had a vision to rebuild the community from within. I learned so much about courage and strength from being mentored by David Lewis and Vicki Smothers, who were two of these leaders.

In 1992, David, Vicki and I co-founded Free at Last, the first community-driven initiative to build comprehensive services to address the addiction problems in the community, rather than just incarcerating people. We created a business plan for an organization with services ranging from a mobile health clinic and prison outreach programs to treatment facilities, residential care homes and affordable housing. We called the organization Free at Last because it represented the freedom of the community and families from addiction. I applied for an Echoing Green Fellowship and was awarded $15,000 toward our multi-million dollar business plan. And with those little resources we took a first step, opening a small drop-in center. The first day 100 people showed up. Over the course of six years we worked hard to build all the services we had originally dreamed of. Today, Free at Last serves 3,000 people a year in ten facilities with an annual budget of $2.5 million and a staff of sixty. One of the reasons we were successful was because we listened to what the community said they needed. If you want to solve a problem, you have to understand the perspective of those you are seeking to serve.

Once Free at Last was stable and I had finished college, I went to business school with the intention of figuring out how to create initiatives that harness the power of the market to create social change. In the back of my mind, I knew I wanted to create an initiative that would help alleviate poverty among women in some of the world's poorest countries.

With the additional knowledge I learned at business school, World of Good came into being. We seek to blend compassion and capitalism in ways that generate sustainable livelihoods for very poor women around the world, through access to fair trade markets for their products. I believe we are doing much more for these communities than just providing employment. Studies have shown that as income increases to more than $2 a day, there are quantifiable social impacts, including decreased infant mortality, longer life expectancy and lower health-care costs.

My dream would never have become a reality were it not for a whole team of people who share my dreams with me and make them real every day. I could not possibly have done this, or any of the other initiatives, alone.

THE WORLD OF GOOD MODEL—*Doing Good while Doing Well*

Before establishing World of Good Inc. in 2004, and its sister nonprofit foundation, The World of Good Development Organization, Priya went around the world looking at other programs that support fair

Weavers in a small village near Chinchero, Peru, practice a traditional form of backstrap weaving while watching over their Alpaca sheep. The women sell their woven goods in the local market and also seek out U.S. and European buyers in hopes of gaining additional income in the export market.

trade in artisan products. She found that considerable work was being done on the supply side to support individual producers and producer cooperatives, but little was being done on the market, or demand, side. She returned home clear that World of Good's greatest contribution would be to generate demand for ethically produced products from developing countries and to help strengthen international standards for these products.

She concluded that generating demand for these artisan products would require raising consumer awareness about the conditions of the impoverished artisans whose products they were considering buying. The message World of Good seeks to share with potential consumers is this: We are already changing the world with the things that we buy. How we change the world by how our dollar impacts others is what World of Good is trying to influence. When we buy products in a way that respects the people who made them, we are making a statement with our purchase.

After only three years, World of Good products are being sold in over 1,000 retail stores in the United States, including Whole Foods and other health-conscious food stores, large retail book stores and campus book stores. A member of the World of Good retail sales team comes to the retailer's store and provides a kiosk and merchandise in an all-in-one retailer package, with the price already on every item and labels ready to be scanned at the check-out counter. They even provide an online reordering system. World of Good is partnering with eBay, the Internet sales platform, to build the world's largest online marketplace for people and planet-positive products that connect consumers directly with artisans.

As with most start-ups, World of Good Inc. was initially funded by investments from friends and family, with additional funding coming from socially minded venture capitalists such as the Draper Richards Foundation and the Omidyar Network.

On the supply side, World of Good Inc. works with 142 artisan groups in thirty-four countries. In its efforts to assure that a significant percentage of the revenue from each sale goes to the person who made the product, World of Good seeks to reduce the number of intermediaries between the producer and the customer. This is similar to the disintermediation that eBay achieves by connecting buyers and sellers online, and what Kiva, the microcredit company profiled in Chapter 5, achieves by connecting lenders in one country with borrowers in developing countries that may be thousands of miles away. World of Good pays 50% in advance for all orders, works with cooperatives on production design and provides feedback so artisans can adapt to changing market demands.

THE WORLD OF GOOD DEVELOPMENT ORGANIZATION

Called the World of Good Development Organization, the foundation owns 5% of World of Good Inc. and receives 10% of its sister organization's profits. Thus, the more successful the for-profit, the more money the foundation has at its disposal to fund health and education projects in the artisan communities. In 2006, for example, the foundation provided funds to an artisan community in South Africa for a computer lab, medical equipment to a community in India and a water system in Guatemala. It also produced the Fair Trade Wage Guide, a free web-based tool that allows producers and buyers anywhere in the world to calculate a fair minimum wage for a product. By the end of 2006, over 650 products had been tested by one hundred groups in twenty-nine countries using the Fair Wage Guide.

WORLD OF GOOD—BY THE NUMBERS

- In 2006, World of Good sold products in 1,300 locations throughout the United States.
- Through all programs, it supports 142 artist groups in thirty-four countries.
- World of Good supports 5,680 artisans, who in turn have nearly 23,000 dependents.
- Since 2004, World of Good has sold over 1,000,000 handicrafts.
- Of the artists World of Good supports, 75% are women.

Nina Smith

KAILASH SATYARTHI AND NINA SMITH
RugMark Foundation

South Asia and the United States

The RugMark Foundation, a global fair trade nonprofit, is dedicated to eliminating child labor in South Asia's handmade rug industry. In India, Kailash Satyarthi first established RugMark in 1994, and Nina Smith launched its program five years later in the United States. Through their efforts, RugMark has leveraged its fair trade advocacy campaigns to influence consumers and carpet retailers in the world's biggest market to purchase and sell only those carpets that have been properly certified as child labor-free. A percentage of the sale price of certified rugs helps RugMark rescue and rehabilitate children they find in the factories. Nina and Kailash project that with just 15% of the U.S. market share for rugs, RugMark could achieve its goal and stop child labor in the South Asian rug industry by 2020.

KAILASH SATYARTHI—*His First Day of School*

My concern for children born into poverty started the morning of my first day of school. On the school steps was a little boy of my age who asked if he could repair my shoes. He was not a student at my school, and his father, a cobbler, was with him. I was confused and asked the father why his son could not go to school with me, to which he answered, "We were born to work. My son is doing what I did when I was his age and what my father did when he was a child. And we have no money to pay for school." My lifelong commitment to help young children get an education rather than being forced into labor started at that moment.

NINA SMITH—*Building the Market for Social Justice*

Like Kailash, the roots of my life's work also stem from childhood memories. My Grandmother Helen figures prominently; whenever we spent the Jewish Sabbath together, Helen took out the *Tzedakah* (charity) box, dropped in coins and delivered a short sermon about the importance of giving to others. *Tzedakah*

Child carpet weaver, India.

is much more than the act of financial giving, but rather a philosophy that also embodies social justice.

Helen's teachings stayed with me and crystallized in a specific way in the early 1990s. I was in an open market in Guatemala bargaining with a Quechua woman for her intricate hand-woven *huipile* (traditional woven blouse). I decided not to buy it. She followed me, begging me to buy the piece for mere pennies. I knew the price wouldn't cover materials, let alone her labor, and I was faced with a moral dilemma. If I paid the reduced price, I would be guilty of perpetuating the wage inequity that kept that woman in poverty. Market forces were making her poor, but I knew the same market forces in reverse could just as easily ensure her a fair wage.

That was the moment I knew I wanted to devote my life to closing the gap between low-income producers and the consumers who buy their products. My theory was that when given a choice, consumers would select a product made under fair and humane conditions. It wasn't long before I learned of the growing movement for fair trade.

I got involved. I volunteered with the Fair Trade Federation, worked in India with Tibetan refugee artisans, and also ran The Crafts Center, which assisted low-income artisans with market access. Then I learned of Kailash and RugMark. I was drawn to the simplicity of the RugMark approach. While experts debate the causes of child labor—extreme poverty, lack of education, caste discrimination—RugMark offers a simple action that any consumer can take: choose a certified child-labor-free rug and stop the market demand for exploitative labor.

Many people ask, "Why rugs? Why child labor?" The handmade rug industry has one of the highest incidences of child exploitation. Children aged four to fourteen are kidnapped or trafficked into debt bondage or forced labor, subject to malnutrition, impaired vision and deformities from sitting long hours in cramped loom sheds. The United States is the largest market for handmade rugs, selling approximately $1.1 billion annually.

The specificity of our work is part of what makes it achievable. RugMark engages consumers, retailers, designers and producers in a root cause solution to a social injustice while transforming an entire industry.

Children in a RugMark school.

RugMark's Model—*Ending Child Labor in the Rug Industry*

RugMark rugs are made on looms and in factories that are inspected independently for child labor. The rugs are certified with the RugMark® label, each with an individual number that can be traced through the supply chain back to the loom. A percentage of the sale of a certified rug helps fund child rescue and rehabilitation, as well as daycare, literacy, formal schooling and vocational training for children who might otherwise be coerced into labor.

Demand for child labor is so high in the countries where RugMark operates that desperate parents often sell their children into bondage, including child trafficking, commercial sexual exploitation, domestic work and the recruitment of children for armed conflict and drug trafficking. An estimated 14% of children in India between the ages of five and fourteen are engaged in child labor activities, including carpet production. Rugs are among South Asia's top export products and a high employment sector for the poor. Some people think it's better when all members of a family work, but child labor really makes poverty worse.

Child workers come cheaply and sometimes at no cost, driving down wages for adult laborers. Children who work forfeit an education that could help them achieve a higher standard of living as adults. If child exploitation is the norm in a country's principle industry, there is little chance to break the cycle of extreme poverty.

RugMark's strategy is replicable as a systemic approach to ending child labor. Kailash and Nina began by raising consumer awareness, and thus demand, for ethically made rugs. This sent a message down the supply chain that child labor would not be tolerated.

Inspectors, teachers, labor rights experts, loom owners, exporters, importers, designers and retailers work together to ensure that no child works on a RugMark rug. Connecting designers to manufacturers is an important step in the cross-continental business. To maintain the upkeep of the manufacturers' practices, RugMark inspectors make surprise visits to loom and spinning factories, monitoring an average of 64 looms a day, or more than 16,000 a year. If a child is found on a loom or in a factory, he or she is taken to a RugMark rehabilitation center and placed in school. More than 3,000 children attend school with RugMark support. RugMark's work is having a profound effect. Its certified rugs now represent 2% of the U.S. market. Roughly 30% of imports from Nepal carry the RugMark certification, already demonstrating major transformations within the industry in South Asia.

RugMark—By The Numbers

- Ending child labor would help the global economy. It would cost $760 billion to end child labor, but the economic benefits through increasing jobs and education would be seven times that—an estimated $5.1 trillion in additional wages where child labor currently is used.

- Experts estimate that child labor on South Asia's carpet looms has dropped from 1 million to 300,000 since the launch of RugMark in 1995.

- More than 3,000 children have been directly rescued and tens of thousands more deterred from exploitative labor by RugMark in just over a decade.

- There are currently 3,172 children attending school or vocational training with RugMark support.

- U.S. imports of certified rugs in 2006 were $9 million, or nearly 2% of the market. RugMark USA projects 15% market share as the tipping point to end child labor on an industry-wide basis.

Africa, Asia and Latin America

Charlotte di Vita has spent years with impoverished rural communities, working to create fair employment and training opportunities in Africa, Asia and South America. Founding the charity Trade plus Aid in 1997, she has always been a passionate believer in the power of ethical trading initiatives to effect real change in people's lives. Always the 'compassionate capitalist,' the same belief informs Charlotte's latest venture as a potent social entrepreneur, the Whatever It Takes Campaign, a unique charity artwork project. Charlotte has collected over 1,000 personal drawings and messages of hope from more than 600 world leaders and celebrities such as Archbishop Desmond Tutu, Snoop Dogg and George Clooney. These messages of hope for the new century are featured on ethically manufactured products, which are sold to raise funds for charitable causes chosen by each contributor.

CHARLOTTE'S JOURNEY

I grew up in Italy, where my father worked for British companies. My father was very skilled at turning around troubled companies and in empowering workers to envision and work together for a brighter future. From him, I learned empathy for the poor and how to empower them to become self-reliant, rather than the recipients of charity. By the time he died at fifty-two, when I was fifteen, my father had taught me a great deal about entrepreneurship and how to turn what others see as problems into opportunities. I will always remember picking up seashells and selling them on the beach, or lost golf balls in the dense forest near our local Lake Como golf course. I would cheekily offer to sell the lost balls back to the golfers in the clubhouse, and got away with it as a child! When my father heard about this, he encouraged me to find as many new ways as possible to generate income, and to structure the deal so that both the buyer and I would benefit.

Charlotte in Australia in 2002

My father also encouraged me to take risks and not to be afraid of failure. When years later I met Sir Richard Branson, the founder of Virgin Airlines, he asked me how many times I had failed and picked myself up again. He explained that he preferred to help entrepreneurs who push themselves and take risks, and have proven their abilities by pulling themselves out of failure at least twice. The theory, he explained, was that if you are a serial entrepreneur, it is likely because it is ingrained in your DNA. I think that is a quality I got from my father, but I also believe that everyone who wants to can develop these qualities and that it's not solely an ingrained characteristic. The more a social entrepreneur is willing to take a risk, the more successful we will be in tackling the world's social and environmental challenges together.

A turning point in my life occurred in 1992 when I became seriously ill with dysentery in a remote village in Ghana. The villagers nursed me back to good health, and in repayment I offered to buy seed for those who had lost their newly germinated crops in severe droughts, but they would not accept any money. Despite looking after me, they were a proud people, and would not accept my gift, seeing it as charity.

Instead, I offered them the last £800 of my traveling money if they would carve 800 wooden pendants in the shape of Ashanti goddesses. Back in England I sold these at local markets at a good profit and they became a fashionable accessory. I called the concept *Trade plus Aid*, and returned all of the net profit to help the community in Ghana. Eight years later, it was this Trade plus Aid concept for which I was made an MBE by Her Majesty Queen Elizabeth II.

By 1996 the sale of these and the many other handicrafts the communities produced for me had funded new seed and new seed stores for 6,000 small holding farms, feeding 25,000 people. The funds also paid for the building and equipping of three schools, the training of thirty-seven teachers, and schooling of 1,250 children. The Trade plus Aid concept was clearly making a difference and doing better and better each year, and those of us involved were enjoying every minute of it.

In 1997 we decided to register Trade plus Aid as a non-profit British charity. The charity did not need to accept donations from the public or governments as it received 100% of net profits from its trading initiatives. Trade plus Aid also helped poor communities to design exportable products and create employment opportunities under fair working conditions in many countries including Egypt, Ethiopia, Ghana, Kenya, India, Thailand, the Philippines, Belize, Brazil and Mexico.

To date, these trading initiatives have enabled over US$5.5 million to be returned to producer communities as payment for their handicrafts. In addition, more than $1.5 million has been donated to fund education, health care and microfinance projects in Africa, Asia and Latin America for impoverished communities that could not be directly assisted through ethical trade.

Poverty does not exist because there isn't enough money in the world. Poverty exists in part because there aren't enough people using their moneymaking skills creatively. Our trading initiatives mean more to the craftspeople than mere economic opportunity. They foster the fundamentals of self-esteem, education, health care and cultural continuity.

In 1997 I had also started a business of my own, which became the "Charlotte di Vita Collection" of miniature teapots and other enamel products. In a remote village in China, I found a talented craftsman familiar with seventeenth-century ena-

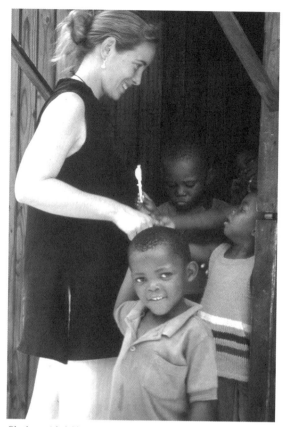

Charlotte with children who benefit from the Trade plus Aid program in Africa.

meling techniques. We convinced Chinese villagers from poor communities to produce hand-painted enamel miniature tea pots bearing the Charlotte di Vita brand name, which were snapped up by customers at Fortnum & Mason, Harrods, Saks Fifth Avenue and 2,500 retailers in all major global gift markets. This personal business allowed me to be financially self-sufficient, and also gave me the possibility of reinvesting 60% of my gross income into Trade plus Aid to further assist impoverished people in Asia, Africa and Latin America through poverty alleviation, education, and environmental initiatives. In 2003, as Goodwill Ambassador to the Nelson Mandela Children's Fund, I was among three dozen people invited to South Africa to attend a speech given by Mr. Nelson Mandela. Among those who came were former U.S. president Bill Clinton and Oprah Winfrey. When we gathered, Mr. Mandela challenged each of us to come up with our own idea over the next twenty-four hours that would positively impact the lives of millions of impoverished people around the world during our lifetimes. While tossing and turning that night it occurred to me that many celebrities would welcome the opportunity to have their messages of hope and their own designs on consumer products, so long as the proceeds were used to help create a more just and sustainable world. Thus was born the 21st Century Leaders initiative to which more than 660 well-known figures around the world have donated their art and messages of hope, and granted permission for us to reproduce them on our products. Those who have contributed include George Clooney, Archbishop Desmond Tutu, Snoop Dogg, Susan Sarandon, Liam Neeson, Sarah Ferguson Duchess of York, Sir Ben Kingsley, Samuel L. Jackson, Tom Stoppard, John Le Carre, Harry Belafonte, Whoopi Goldberg, David Bowie and Yoko Ono, among others.

My advice to readers interested in getting involved with the world's challenges consists of the following steps:

Get clear about what turns you on so much that you say, "Wow, I'd love to be doing that!" When someone says to me, "You never have any time for yourself," my reaction is that I am always doing what I love and, while I am doing these things for others, I am also doing all this for myself as well. I do not feel that I am sacrificing myself or my time. It's an honor to be involved, a privilege to be able to make a difference and to be doing what I love daily. Many people do not have such opportunities, and I am grateful for them.

Take one step at a time, no matter how small or seemingly inconsequential. You don't climb a mountain by looking at the summit from base camp and getting overwhelmed. You climb it by taking one step at a time and changing course as necessary along the way.

Tap into your courage and conviction and be willing to take some risk of failure. If you run into problems on the mountain and have to adjust your course, you have not failed; you have just learned a better route to the summit.

Develop a clear and powerful vision you are excited about and can easily communicate to others. This will help keep you inspired, guide you and enroll others.

CHARLOTTE'S 21ST CENTURY LEADER INITIATIVE

Charlotte's motto is to focus on things she is passionate about and leave everything else to others. And she is passionate about helping impoverished countries in Asia, Africa and Latin America, designing and manufacturing products to meet world quality and price standards, working with licensees and upscale retail chains who want quality products and engaging celebrities who support worthwhile causes. That is a lot, but she clearly feels comfortable in each of these unique environments.

Today, Charlotte has two full-time employees working from her loft in London, and she works with hundreds of others to achieve her objectives, including licensing partners in Europe, Japan and the United States such as VANS, Eastpak, Lee, UNIQLO, Dr. Hauschka, Virgin, Churchill China, Flame, Design House UK and Retro Sport.

To date, more than 600 politicians, sports stars, movie stars and other well-known figures have joined the 21st Century Leaders initiative. Each has received a kit containing all the materials needed to produce simple artwork. The invitation asks them to draw a simple self-portrait, and pen a message and a symbol of hope. While the celebrities technically hold the copyright, they give Charlotte the legal right to auction off the original and license the images for use on plates, mugs, shoes, T-shirts, wristbands, backpacks, cosmetics and other consumer products.

The product development, sales and marketing companies that 21st Century Leaders partners with know that celebrities and good causes help sell products. As a result, they are prepared to give the 21st Century Leaders charity significant royalty payments to gain exclusive access to the artwork and messages of the celebrities. The royalty payments are sent to the 21st Century Leaders program to be donated to charitable causes often chosen by the celebrity contributors. Charlotte finds that some celebrities know exactly what they would like to support, while others want Charlotte's help in researching options. The 21st Century Leaders program has already donated more than $1.5 million to various charities.

The program has also allowed Charlotte and the celebrity contributors to support the development of a biannual gala dinner with Reach Out To Asia, an educational charity based in Qatar and founded by Her Excellency Sheikha Mayassa Bint Hamad Al Thani. The first gala event, which Charlotte and the Reach Out To Asia team worked on together, was held on November 4, 2006 and that night raised a record $36 million to build schools in Asia. The next gala dinner is planned for November 2008, at which they hope to surpass their record.

Charlotte will not sign a license agreement with a product marketing company unless they can first demonstrate that their supply chain is meeting international social audit standards, which they can only do by undertaking a social audit of the manufacturing facilities they plan to use in Asia, Africa or Latin America. All 21st Century Leaders products read at the point of sale that they are "ethically produced."

The charity already has royalty agreements with eleven well-known product development and marketing companies, all of who have their own PR firms and sales teams promoting the products, thus relieving 21st Century Leaders of having to undertake this task.

- Funded the distribution of more than 1.2 million meals to impoverished families in Zambia; boosted water harvesting technologies in Sudan; increased medical resources in Mongolia; financed a first-aid medical station in Vietnam; and established two "Trust Banks" in East Timor to help stimulate the local economy.

- Funded agricultural improvement and seed stores and donated seed for 6,400 small holding farms in Ghana to feed 25,000 people.

- Built and renovated three schools in Ghana to allow 1,250 children to be educated.

- Assisted nearly two dozen countries by purchasing sustainably harvested rainforest products or handicrafts in Egypt, Ethiopia, the Philippines, Ghana, Kenya, China, India, Thailand, South Africa, Nepal, Peru, Belize, Guatemala, Brazil and Mexico.

- Collected more than 1,000 personal drawings and messages of hope from 660 world leaders and celebrities.

- Enabled over $5.5 million to be returned to producer communities as payment for their handicrafts.

- Donated over $1.5 million in licensing royalties to fund development projects in Africa, Asia and Latin America for impoverished communities that could not be directly assisted through ethical trade.

 **RORY STEWART**
Turquoise Mountain Foundation
Afghanistan

At thirty-four, British-born Rory Stewart has created Turquoise Mountain Foundation, a nonprofit organization that is rebuilding Murad Khane, the historic bazaar in Afghanistan, in order to help preserve the local culture and provide employment and vital income to the people of the region. He lives and works in Kabul, where his kinetic energy, creativity and determination are all contributing to his vision of helping revitalize

Afghanistan's traditional arts to regenerate the old city. His work achieves social objectives through the creation of institutions that will be financially self-sustaining.

RORY STEWART—*Finding His Passion*

I was born in Hong Kong, grew up in Malaysia, became a British army officer and joined the British foreign office where I worked in Indonesia, Yugoslavia and Afghanistan. I then took several years off and walked from Turkey to Bangladesh, across Iran, Pakistan, India and Nepal and then Afghanistan. My book, *The Places in Between*, is an account of the twenty-one month walk I took across central Afghanistan shortly after the Taliban were forced out. Among the wonders of the walk was the opportunity to stay in more than 500 homes listening to villagers talk about their lives and aspirations.

The idea for the Turquoise Mountain project initially came during my walk across central Afghanistan. By chance I heard of the "Lost City of the Turquoise Mountain" that was once one of the great capitals of a civilization stretching from Delhi to Baghdad. At the place where that city once flourished, I was saddened to see the great art and architecture of Afghanistan's rich cultural history being looted, and therefore lost to future generations.

When the Iraq war began and the British government became heavily engaged in the war and reconstruction efforts there, I was asked to become the deputy director of two provinces in southern Iraq to help organize the reconstruction. I had a budget of $10 million a month that we used to rebuild schools, hospitals, local bazaars, and on other infrastructure projects.

One day I was asked by some Iraqis what the coalition had done for them, to which I replied that we had rebuilt 240 of the 400 schools in the province as well as a number of clinics and hospitals. Somewhat to my surprise, these projects did not excite them the way our rebuilding of the bazaar in the town of Amara did. Even more exciting to them was a program we had created in the town of Nasiriyah to teach carpentry to 200 street children. Everyone loved this project. The politicians were competing to give speeches, and the Arab press could not get enough of it. From this experience I learned the importance of listening to the people you seek to serve rather than assume you know what they want or should want.

After my tour in Iraq I went to Afghanistan in 2005 on a fact-finding trip. I learned that the mayor of Kabul was planning to demolish the Murad Khane bazaar area near the city center. My reaction was that if Murad Khane could be rebuilt and turned back into the vibrant commercial center it once was, a significant Afghan cultural heritage site could be preserved, traditional Afghan arts and crafts reintroduced to the country, and employment and income generated for the people of Kabul.

It may have been a little crazy to think the situation could be turned around, but in three months that is exactly what the Turquoise Mountain Foundation did. There was a petition inviting us in, the major landlord had agreed to give us a lease and we had a presidential decree approving our work.

With regard to what it took to make this happen, I feel that it was a combination of an unquestioning faith in our goals and a great deal of luck. I suspect that if I had known at the outset all the challenges we would face, we might not have had the courage to start this project in the first place. In other words, sometimes the key to success is acting as though victory is guaranteed and ignoring the odds against you! I also came to realize the necessity of working closely with existing power holders and making compromises if you want to make rapid progress in a difficult environment.

With regard to what it takes to turn a vision such as this into reality, I feel that the ten years I have worked in the Islamic world, often with skilled but illiterate craftsmen, have given me confidence that I can work effectively with such people. I have learned to be more tolerant and more comfortable with uncertainty. You need to take risks and invest your entire energy in a project such as this. You also need to have a high tolerance for failure along the way.

You may wonder what I get out of this. At one level this a form of penance for what we didn't do in Iraq. In Iraq we wasted money on projects that were not appreciated by the people and will not last. I am also doing this in part because I want to prove to those people who don't believe the Afghanis can run anything that they indeed do have the capacity to undertake this project, rebuild their country and their national identity.

It is also my hope that four years from now Murad Khane will have been completely renovated and will be financially self-sustaining, as will the Center of Traditional Afghan Arts and Architecture that is also an integral part of our initiative. As soon as these conditions are met, the Turquoise Mountain Foundation should move on.

THE TURQUOISE MOUNTAIN PROJECT—
The Restoration of Afghan Arts and Crafts

Afghanistan was for centuries a trading capital on the Silk Road connecting East Asia and the Middle East, but has more recently been devastated by thirty years of foreign invasions and civil wars. It is a mountainous country sandwiched between Turkmenistan, Uzbekistan and Tajikistan to the north, Pakistan to the south and Iran to the east. The economy is in tatters, and the country's largest export is illegally grown opium. The second largest export industry is made up of

A building in Murad Khane undergoing restoration.

various traditional artistic crafts, including woodworking, ceramics, calligraphy and traditional architecture.

Rory and his Afghan and international partners at the Turquoise Mountain Foundation saw an opportunity in the midst of these challenges to rebuild the country's expertise in the artistic crafts and to use this expertise to regenerate the historic commercial center of Kabul. Their vision was to restore basic services, save historic buildings, create educational opportunities for children living in Murad Khane and construct a new bazaar and galleries for traditional craft businesses for sales domestically and internationally. Turquoise Mountain gained access to an old fort and converted it into the Center of Traditional Afghan Arts and Architecture, where some of the best craftsmen from various parts of the country are now working to reintroduce the traditional arts.

Turquoise Mountain is creating a model that is replicable and scalable not only in Afghanistan but in other countries with rich artistic traditions that are being lost. And, while the initial financing has come from private sources outside Afghanistan, the project has great potential for generating revenue and becoming self-financing. Turquoise Mountain has a very active development department that has already sold some of their crafted products to the Connaught Hotel in London, Kabul University and the American Embassy. It has a sophisticated website to generate international sales. It is planning to have a showroom in Murad Khane and to have an upscale restaurant there that will be attractive to foreign tourists. They are well aware that their products must meet stiff international price and quality standards and that they must not rely on goodwill purchases.

Turquoise Mountain—By The Numbers

- Turquoise Mountain built and made operational the Center of Traditional Afghan Arts and Architecture.
- It has an Afghan staff of 250, of which 70 are working in the traditional arts.
- It has prepared detailed site and building surveys of the Murad Khane area of Kabul.
- More than 920 cubic meters of rubbish have been removed from Murad Khane, some of it over two meters deep.
- Turquoise Mountain has repaired and reconstructed thirty houses in Murad Khane in partnership with their landlords and residents.
- Turquoise Mountain has an annual operating budget of $5 million.

CHAPTER 7

Human Rights and Social Justice

The term *human rights* is used and understood by many to have different meanings. According to the United Nations Universal Declaration of Human Rights, human rights implies the "basic rights and freedoms to which all humans are entitled," often held to include the right to life and liberty, freedom of thought and expression, and equality before the law. Like human rights, *social justice* can also have different meanings to different people. Regardless of definitions, however, human rights and social justice imply the basic freedoms to live a healthy, prosperous life in a fair and just society.

While societies and cultures differ in their interpretation and enforcement of the law, there are globally agreed-upon rights that transcend cultural differences. In 2005, according to the United Nations Millennium Goals Report, one out of every three people in an urban environment was living in slum conditions and lacked at least one of the basic conditions of decent housing: adequate sanitation, water supply, durable architecture or adequate living space for each inhabitant. In addition to the water crisis, which has been discussed throughout this book, the nondurability of housing is a major concern for millions of people in the developing world.

Even more fundamental is our basic human right to life. In the twentieth century, genocides resulted in the deaths, just to name a few, of 1 million Armenians, 6 million Jews, 1.8 million Cambodians, 200,000 Bosnians and 800,000 Rwandan Tutsis. Sadly, history is repeating itself today in the Darfur region of the Sudan where the death toll continues to climb, while hundreds of thousands of refugees have been displaced from their homes. Rape, murder and displacement can cause a country to collapse very quickly, thereby weakening the economic and social development of an entire region. Mass infringements on human rights are not an isolated challenge; they have global repercussions.

Even in countries that are economically stable, the rule of law is not always upheld, or even securely in place. While most people believe that torture is an issue that only the military have to be careful to avoid, by far the greatest amount of torture worldwide is in fact carried out by local police on ordinary citizens. International Bridges to Justice, which is profiled in this chapter, knew how seriously its services were needed in China, for example, where just a few years ago police station posters read: "Confess and the State will treat you with benevolence. Deny your guilt and face harsh punishment!" Unfortunately, such methods of interrogation are commonplace not only in many Asian countries, but across most developing countries as well.

Societies worldwide are working to overcome the technical and cultural barriers that stand in the way of proper human rights and social justice. In addition to the organizations and initiatives discussed here, there are thousands of others not detailed in this chapter that are achieving incredible results in issues of gender and racial equality, the right to suffrage, freedom of speech and other basic human rights. For example:

- Architecture for Humanity
- Delancey Street Foundation
- The Desmond Tutu Peace Foundation
- FORGE (Facilitating Opportunities for Refugee Growth and Empowerment)
- Free the Children
- Global Fund for Women
- Human Rights Watch
- Peace X Peace
- The United Religions Initiative
- Witness

In this chapter you will read three very distinct stories from these social entrepreneurs who have created innovative approaches to the age-old challenges of human rights and social justice:

- **Sasha Chanoff**, the grandson of Russian refugees, who has introduced new strategies in Africa for refugee and prisoner protection.

- **Karen Tse**, an American-born daughter of immigrants from Hong Kong, who has developed an initiative to end torture and to support criminal justice systems in countries that lack a proper legal infrastructure.

- **John Marks and Susan Collin Marks**, who help overcome deeply embedded hostilities among groups in Africa, the Middle East and elsewhere by pioneering creative uses of television, radio and the arts to find common ground.

SASHA CHANOFF
Mapendo International

Africa

As the grandson of Russian refugees, Sasha's identity is intertwined with his life's work, Mapendo International, a world-leading innovator in strategies for refugee protection. A lifeline for forgotten refugees, Mapendo identifies and protects people fleeing war and violence whose lives are in imminent danger and who fall outside existing aid efforts. Of the 8 million refugees worldwide, Mapendo is devising strategies at a scale to reach as many of the "forgotten ones" as possible.

SASHA CHANOFF—*Israel, Rose and Discovering His Life's Work*

In 1998, Rwanda and the Democratic Republic of Congo went to war. I was sent into the Congo's capital, Kinshasa, as a part of a rescue team to evacuate 113 Congolese Tutsis who were facing the threat of ethnic genocide and who had made it onto an evacuation list. BBC reported in August 1998 that a message from Congolese President Laurent Kabila was broadcast over the radio in Eastern Congo instructing that people "bring a machete, spear, arrow, hoe, spade, rake, nail, truncheon, electric iron, barbwire, stone and the like, dear listeners, to kill the . . . Tutsi." That was the kind of rhetoric that exploded against an entire ethnic group in 1998, and regrettably this kind of politically engineered ethnic violence is still going on today in the Congo.

The International Committee of the Red Cross created a protection center outside Kinshasa. About six months after the death camps had gotten started, the Red Cross managed to access a number of these camps and transfer survivors into this protection center. Tutsis who had gone into hiding in secret compartments, attics and hidden rooms heard about it and tried, often in vain, to reach the center. It was at this point that the U.S. government, in what was really an unprecedented move, decided to fund an evacuation team to rescue surviving Tutsis from the Congo and bring them to the United States via Benin and Cameroon, which had agreed to host the refugees while they underwent U.S. refugee resettlement processing. The United States then contracted the International Organization of Migration to go into the Congo to start evacuating Tutsi survivors.

My boss, David Derthick, was tasked to organize and launch the operation. I was sent in the last rescue mission. By that time, the Congolese president was publicly bowing to international pressure to free some of the victims, but the government reneged on its promises so often that it had practically sabotaged the entire process by the time our three-person team arrived. On this last evacuation, much of our job consisted of uniting families that had been separated or had

Mapendo rescues two orphaned Sudanese refugee girls from persecution and attacks in Kenya and reunites them with relatives in the United States Sasha Chanoff speaks with the girls in a Nairobi safe haven.

lost some of its members. One of these cases was Israel Ndeteba, a Tutsi under threat of murder from the government, as he had been a lawyer and activist in the country. Israel had spent thirteen months in the underground, getting news in hiding that his brothers and sisters were killed. After almost a year, he received word that his wife and two young children had made it to the protection center safely. My boss sent us, a team of three, to bring Israel and the others out.

I remember walking into the tent in the protection center for the first time, and seeing the hollow faces of people who had been hunted, imprisoned, attacked and tortured. There were so many people, many more than the 113 our team was supposed to bring back. My eyes were drawn to a woman, Rose Mapendo, holding two little bundles in her arms, twins that she had given birth to eight months earlier in a death camp. She had been imprisoned for sixteen months, and her twins weighed four pounds each at birth. Huddled around Rose in this tent were her seven other children, gaunt stick figures, and other Tutsi children orphaned during the war. In the tent were a total of thirty-two women, children and orphans whose husbands and fathers, we heard, had been executed already. They had come to the protection center only five days before our team had gotten there, and none of the thirty-two was on the list.

We had to strategize how to negotiate with a government that was murderous and untrustworthy. Our team delivered a clear and simple stance to the Congolese government officials with whom we had to work: we told them that our plane had 113 seats, our pre-approved internationally sponsored list had 113 individuals on it and that we did not have room for anybody else. Our plane actually had 126 seats, but we couldn't let anyone else know that. When we called our headquarters and explained that we had an additional thirty-two people who really needed to get out, the response was disturbingly explicit: "Leave them behind. Forget about it. It won't work. You could potentially sabotage the entire mission." The command was based on prior missions, during which the Congolese government used any change in plans to try to sabotage the entire evacuation. We were faced with an enormous dilemma.

Sheikha, a Kenyan woman who had overseen all the previous rescue missions, and I agreed with the senior rescue official sent in from Geneva who said, "We are the ones on the ground. We are a humanitarian organization. If we don't act, nobody will. We must make this decision ourselves." Going against our headquarters' orders, I spent a night changing the birth dates on our departure roster of every young child I could find, to make them appear to be two or younger, as kids under three were able to sit on their mothers' laps on the plane. This strategy created additional seats, which we filled with the thirty-two widows and orphans who weren't on the list. When we landed safely in Cameroon and received a military escort to the refugee camp, we witnessed the most heartfelt and moving scenes, as family members who never thought they would see each other again were reunited. I was elated to see these reunions, but the feeling was bittersweet. We had managed to get Rose, her twins and seven other children out, along with the others among the thirty-two widows and orphans who hadn't appeared on the list. But the man whose name appeared first on our list, Israel Ndeteba, had been held by the Congolese military, and was not allowed to board the plane. In the Cameroon camp, I watched as Israel's wife broke down with fear, disbelief and screams upon the news that her husband had not made it out, all too aware of what his absence most certainly meant. His wife and two young children would likely never see him again. The weight of that knowledge bore heavily on me.

We followed Israel's story intently over the next weeks and months. At first we didn't know if he was alive or dead. Then we heard that the Congolese government had tried to take him to a secret prison, where he would have been executed. But, with relief, we learned that our partners, the International Committee of the Red Cross, had managed to secure Israel back within the protection center. Six months passed and Israel finally managed to get out to Rwanda. I met him there and saw him off to the United States. Israel and his family were reunited after nearly two years of separation and constant threat of death in the Congo. Israel had survived, although most of his family had not.

This whole experience shaped how I began Mapendo in collaboration with a senior humanitarian aid official, Dr. Wagacha Burton, a Kenyan colleague. I would say we had a different view on refugee rights across Africa. Those with no rights deserved a voice and no one was acting to give them one. This was the beginning of my life's work, tuning into the dispossessed. These are African refugees who are not on any lists, not in the system of aid or protection, and who are desperate, in danger and voiceless.

MAPENDO'S MODEL—*Reaching Out to the Forgotten Ones*

Sasha Chanoff founded Mapendo International with Dr. John Wagacha Burton, a Kenyan doctor and senior humanitarian aid official. Named after Rose Mapendo, the woman who had been rescued during Chanoff's rescue mission to the Congo after giving birth to twins in prison, Mapendo means "great love" in Swahili. The organization, which devises and implements short- and long-term solutions for those like Rose who struggle to survive in the worst of conditions, is innovative in its efforts to address and solve the chronically unmet needs of hundreds of thousands of refugees. As Sasha says of the organization's approach, "We are out to help the forgotten ones." When Dr. Burton and Chanoff initiated Mapendo, there were no comprehensive programs to care for refugees who fall outside the existing system.

Among the 3-million-plus refugees in Africa, there are many hundreds of thousands who fall outside the existing aid network. Dr. Burton and Chanoff began their work in Nairobi, where there are more than 100,000 unassisted refugees. The most at risk have been abused, attacked, raped and sometimes sold into wedlock or a life of servitude.

Chanoff and Dr. Burton also recognized that any humanitarian aid organization must focus on local capacity in the country or region of operation. To this end, Mapendo not only employs and supports nationals in Kenya, but also has a long-term plan to build a health-care program that will provide service to refugee populations and simultaneously address Kenyan health-care concerns.

In countries that suffer under the burden of poverty, massive amounts of money flow in to supporting refugees that have arrived from neighboring countries. But these funds are often used in a crisis response manner—to keep refugees alive, without an eye to long-term change. Tens of millions of dollars a year are pumped into refugee camps from the top down; that is, from Western organizations with big grant money to provide critical support. But within these mechanics of aid, there is a distinct dearth of vision to change the status quo of refugees or to address local problems. With a fraction of the budget of most transnational organizations, Mapendo is nonetheless one of the top emerging refugee initiatives in the world, largely because of its approach to providing immediate protection to forgotten and at-risk refugees, and also for its long-term vision of building local capacity.

In their short-term operations, Mapendo identifies, saves and keeps refugees alive through their rescue and health initiatives.

In many cases, even these methods of "resettlement" are lacking in capacity and impact. For example, the U.S. government has exactly 70,000 slots for refugee immigrants available each year. Shockingly, every year tens of thousands go unfilled. In 2006, more than 30,000 slots went unfilled; in 2002, it was more than 40,000. With 8 million refugees worldwide, the United States is accepting more refugees than all other countries combined, and yet is not even reaching its promised capacity. Mapendo is most successful in its ability to leverage every given dollar to a specified return on investment (ROI) that is tangible and visible, going far beyond the same ROI touted by any humanitarian agency organized on a top-down model. Its advisory board has grown to include Rose Mapendo herself, as well as actors Susan Sarandon and Danny Glover; Dylan Leiner, the executive vice president of acquisitions and production at Sony Pictures Classics; and Julia Taft, the former assistant secretary of state in the second Clinton administration and the assistant administrator of the United Nations Development Programme and director of UNDP's Bureau of Crisis Prevention and Recovery. Richard Wayne, a managing director at Lehman Brothers who sits on Mapendo's board of directors, attributes Mapendo's successful model to its absolute financial transparency. Wayne is right to say that his hundreds of thousands of dollars in investment in Mapendo could not have been utilized any better. As supporters of Mapendo will tell you, Mapendo brings the best use of funds back to donors, not only with statistical results, but also with the story of a life saved.

MAPENDO—BY THE NUMBERS

- In its first two and a half years of operation, with resettlement projects to the United States, Mapendo has rescued over 1,000 refugees and launched a rescue resettlement mission to resettle 600 Congolese refugee massacre survivors who are in imminent danger.
- Mapendo has provided health assistance to 1,000 urban refugees without access to any care who live in the impoverished areas of Nairobi.
- In the coming few years Mapendo plans to launch rescue resettlement efforts for tens of thousands of refugees across Africa, as well as provide health assistance to tens of thousands of other at-risk refugees living in urban centers.

⊕ KAREN TSE
International Bridges To Justice (IBJ)

China, Cambodia, Vietnam, Burundi, Rwanda and Zimbabwe

Karen Tse, a former public defender and minister ordained at the Harvard Divinity School, was born and raised in Ohio by her parents, who had emigrated from Hong Kong in the early 1960s. With a sparkle in her eye, she emits effervescent energy with grounded appeal in the practical and often unglamorous work of the day to day. Since earning her law degree at UCLA and going on to become an established attorney at the UN, she has founded International Bridges to Justice (IBJ), which promotes systemic change by training public defenders on the local level in countries like China and Cambodia and thereby working with governments, and not against them. Her approach is innovative, as IBJ represents the first citizen-sector organization to work with China's criminal law bureaus under formal agreement. She has also set out to design a global initiative to support grassroots reform in criminal justice systems everywhere.

KAREN TSE—
Her Struggle to End Torture in the Twenty-First Century

I often reflect back on how different a place in history our world was when I was in law school twenty-five years ago. There were many dictatorships and mass ideological regimes that tortured citizens of their own country for petty crimes. Police brutalized victims for perceived crimes and without any evidence. Few individuals ever had the right to an attorney. Husbands and wives would go missing for years in prison with no explanation or trial. And in many countries such criminal investigation techniques were commonplace. Sadly, today torture continues to persist as the cheapest form of police investigation on the planet. The victims are ordinary citizens who get picked up by the police and are tortured for a confession, regardless of whether there is any evidence of their guilt.

In Sri Lanka, there was a woman who was tortured to give answers about her sister who had been accused of stealing something from the house where she had been a maid. Bloodied, she lied against her sister fearing she would lose her own life from the beating in the police station. In Cambodia, I walked into a prison and saw a four-year-old boy who was born into a jail cell for a crime his mother may or may not have committed years prior. Another mother in a Cambodian village said, "My husband was accused ten years ago, and since they couldn't find him, they took me, and I've been in prison for ten years." There was also the Indian lawyer who told us that in just a six-month period 1,600 individuals in his province had been taken, tortured, and had died in police custody, none of whom were granted an attorney. What so many people don't realize is that only a fraction of those tortured in the

Karen Tse with Cambodian prisoners.

world are political or military-related occurrences. The vast majority are everyday citizens.

Today, there are many more opportunities to take effective measures against citizen torture than when I was in law school. Much of the world is now moving toward democracy. There are 113 countries in the world that torture, but 93 have laws on the books regarding the right to an attorney. This legal progress has all occurred in the last twenty years. The sad truth, however, is that while many of these governments have the rule of law on paper, many do not abide by their promise. As I have met with some of the highest officials of governments, it is clear that the goodwill of that promise exists. But the necessary means to encourage these governments' commitment to the law is missing.

To change violent systems that have been in place for many decades requires not only local cooperation in law enforcement, but also a support system of citizens worldwide who are willing to stand up to say that torture is not an acceptable form of interrogation. People used to say that it would be impossible to end slavery in the nineteenth century or end apartheid in the twentieth century. People tell me it's impossible to end torture in the twenty-first century. They call me Pollyannaish, if not crazy. Like slavery and apartheid, torture is barbaric and wrong, but we haven't had the will just yet to come together as a world community to decide that. We will. This should be the single most important fact to realize for anyone committed to human rights: we can indeed make a difference to improving both local justice systems in developing countries, and the global movement to bring improved judicial infrastructures anywhere. And this will have a groundbreaking effect on citizens' rights around the world.

Not all defenders are courageous enough to stand up for citizens' rights. We support those who do, and strive to provide a safety infrastructure for those who are as yet unable. Until we, as a human rights community at large, can bring the technology of social networking, the expertise of trained justice professionals and the education of local governments together, the corrupt systems in place will persist. Torture will continue with little or no heed from the global community unless values and resources can be allocated to this important issue. Values are not abstract theories representing one person's moral compass; they are universally accepted truths as to what is acceptable and what is not, with regard to how a police officer or authority treats an accused victim before his or her trial.

We work top down and bottom up. IBJ signed a Memorandum of Understanding (MOU) with China, for example, that outlined not just a public face-lift, but actually a real implementation of reforms that greatly reduce the use of torture. This brought about the rights to due process for all citizens in the country. We didn't push any kind of moral justice argument on them. That would have won us a quick exit out the door. Rather, we worked hand in hand discussing how to better represent citizens' rights in police stations, which they agreed was an important issue.

Our vision, which we have begun in China, Vietnam and Cambodia, is to connect leaders in these local communities to public lawyers in the United States, for example, into a single values-driven global database online. Meanwhile, local implementation is critical.

At the grassroots level, we work to instill a shift of awareness in the minds of the police officers with whom we work. I base my own teaching, both as an attorney and as a Unitarian Universalist minister, on the power of transformative love. None of us is perfect, and nobody lives an angelic life. It is in our supportive efforts to transform misguided notions of power and rights that the due process of law will best be guaranteed.

Despite sounding idealistic, the capacity for human rights battles to succeed is because of the grunge work of everyday details: empowering defenders in local communities, building arraignment courts, encouraging corporate businesses to play their part in the countries in which they work and even writing and providing manuals for law systems in local provinces of developing countries. Although these should be viewed from a technical perspective, they all in fact stem from our power to transform something evil into something humane. This is the power of transformative love, and it guides all of my work to help rebuild outdated and often barbaric systems of law.

For the world at large, ending torture is more than just encouraging 113 countries to write their names down on a piece of paper saying that they believe in the due process of law. It takes judges, prosecutors, police officers, corporate leaders,

Karen and IBJ training one hundred lawyers in Jiangxi, China.

defenders, and mothers, fathers and children alike to step forward where there are abuses, and to reach out to those who are afraid to. Torture as a form of interrogation is not reliable, and it certainly is not just. Everyone who agrees to that can play a part in this movement. It will take slow and persistent effort to bring the international community together against those governments, police forces and systems of law that allow torture to continue. Our window of opportunity is now. We are on the cusp of deciding as a global community whether we will condone such basic affronts to our shared rights to live without the fear of being beaten for some senseless reason.

Have you ever built something backwards, starting from the end and working your way toward the beginning? I work in an unusual way, designing a solution that some call foolish and against all odds. But I believe it is entirely possible, and work backwards to achieve it. In this case, it is my conviction that torturing civilians, like slavery and apartheid, is absolutely possible to eradicate, in this century.

THE IBJ MODEL—*Working within the System to Change It*

International Bridges to Justice (IBJ), a nonprofit organization, has begun to build fairer and more effective criminal justice systems, starting in China, Vietnam and Cambodia, and is now expanding its activities to Africa and Latin America. Founded in 2000 as the collaborative result of interested lawyers, academics and business leaders, IBJ promotes the rule of law, good governance and equitable legal rights for all citizens by ensuring the effective implementation of existing criminal defense, justice and human rights legislation.

To this end, IBJ significantly supports and enhances criminal defender and governmental legal aid efforts in Asia and Africa to protect citizen rights and to implement existing criminal laws through providing training partnerships, legal and administrative structural support, and material assistance. In practical terms, this means training public defense lawyers; providing practical "how-to" manuals and website resources; mentoring individual defenders through specific cases; providing offices and equipment; organizing promotional campaigns aimed at ordinary citizens; and running awareness campaigns with prosecutors, judges and police. According to IBJ's website, fair and effective criminal justice systems require the following:

- A sufficient number of trained and available defenders
- Access to legal representation without delay
- A judicial environment which respects and embraces the role of public defenders
- International support to accomplish these aims

To further these goals, IBJ has adopted a three-pronged approach of creating partnerships at the local level, consent at the national level and agreement from the international citizen sector at large. To this last point, for example, following its successes in Asia, IBJ is now expanding its activities to other parts of the world, namely Africa, where program planning for legal aid support and advisement of rights campaigns in Zimbabwe, Rwanda and Burundi is just getting underway.

IBJ has recently launched a worldwide partnership program called Communities of Conscience aimed at building networks of support between legal professionals and everyday citizens, with the idea that exchange programs between legal professionals can empower criminal defense lawyers from developing countries. The Communities of Conscience stem from the basic tenets that peace is built on trust and solid relationships, and that through training and mentoring, lawyers who have before felt isolated in their countries may now construct their own Community of Conscience, with the support of a global database of like-minded individuals committed to changing the cultures of torture and violence in their countries.

At the time this book was being written, Karen Tse, despite receiving funds from Skoll, Ashoka, Echoing Green and the Open Society Institute, was uncertain as to the financial future of her organization. To ensure that IBJ sustains its objectives, Karen continues to innovate while looking for partners with whom to collaborate who may provide consulting, legal advice, fellowship sponsorship or business expertise. As Karen says, the window of opportunity is too timely to let pass.

- IBJ has trained over 10,000 defenders and produced a practical Defender Toolkit for use in China, Vietnam and Cambodia, increasing the chance that an accused person will have access to legal rights.
- More than half a million advisement of rights brochures promoting better public awareness of legal rights in China, Cambodia and Burundi have been distributed.
- IBJ has created bridges of support between developing and developed countries through its new and innovative Communities of Conscience training and mentoring programs.
- Programming has had a direct effect on amendments in the Criminal Procedure Code in China, which now allows defense counsel earlier access to clients, enabling more complete case investigation.
- IBJ has grown, with funding pending, to expand its programs into Africa, with the launch of the first advisement of rights campaign in Rwanda and Burundi.

John Marks and Susan Collin Marks
Search For Common Ground

Africa, the Middle East and Asia

John Marks and Susan Collin Marks are not only deeply committed to each other but also share a commitment to a world defined by what unites us rather than what separates us. This positive, visionary perspective guides everything that Search for Common Ground has been doing since John founded the organization in 1982. The nonprofit now has 375 employees operating out of sixteen field offices in Africa, Europe, the Middle East, Asia, and the United States. Search for Common Ground employs a comprehensive set of traditional techniques for conflict resolution, such as mediation, facilitation and back-channel negotiations. In addition, they have pioneered creative uses of television, radio, print journalism and the arts to help break down barriers between groups in seemingly perpetual conflict, such as the Palestinians and the Israelis.

John Marks—
From Protesting Against Something to Working for Something

In the late 1970s, I resigned from the U.S. diplomatic service in protest against the United States' invasion of Cambodia. Afterward, I coauthored a best-selling book about mind-control experiments entitled *Search for the Manchurian Candidate* that was highly critical of the CIA.

While I believe I had good reason to be unhappy about the course of American foreign policy during those years, I reached the point where I wanted to stop being defined by what I was *against* instead of what I was *for*. To this end, I went through a profound shift, starting in the late 1970s, in both my personal life and in my approach to world affairs.

The cold war between the United States and the Soviet Union was at its height, and I saw that I wanted to work to build bridges between East and West as an alternative to continual confrontation. My vision was to transform how the world deals with conflict—away from win-lose, you-or-me approaches, to win-win, you-and-me solutions. I had the audacity to think I could change the world, and that vision led me to establish Search for Common Ground.

I became a practitioner of "political aikido," which means that I accept the world as it is, while seeking to deflect and steer the energies of conflicting parties in ways that enable them to build on their commonalities. Because building trust and resolving conflict is almost always a prolonged process, I have also learned to defer satisfaction and/or receive it from sources other than the projects on which I am currently working.

I consider myself an "applied visionary," guided by a powerful sense of what is possible—while moving forward one step at a time. A pure vision may be what is called for if one wants to launch a new religion, but being able to advance in practical ways is more helpful if one wants to implement programs that will help resolve deeply imbedded conflicts. I believe it is important to combine this practicality with persistence. The image I like is that of a child's mechanical toy truck that runs into a piece of furniture, backs off, and finds another way around—but all the time keeps moving forward.

Susan Collin Marks—
Working toward Reconciliation in South Africa

I was brought up in South Africa, where my mother was one of the first members of The Black Sash, a women's human rights organization set up in 1955 to protest against the repressive apartheid regime. She took me to the black townships where I witnessed the poverty, pain and unjust treatment of blacks. My mother's courageous activism helped shape my own activism in South Africa during the years of transition from white minority apartheid rule to a multiracial democracy.

As a member of the Western Cape Regional Peace Committee, I mediated conflicts, intervened in bloody clashes in the streets, stood between heavily armed

Susan and John at a Common Ground Awards ceremony.

security forces and angry communities, facilitated multiple forums and meetings to resolve intercommunal violence and helped formulate national policy on community policing. During one particularly tense confrontation, I was shot in the leg while trying to mediate between opposing government and African National Congress (ANC) groups. During those years the differences that individuals can make became clear to me, despite the occasional perception that individuals are powerless.

For example, speaking about their transformation from an apartheid police force to a community policing service, I recall the South African police saying to several of us, "We could not have done this without you." I did not expect to hear that from them, but now realize that it was true. We did indeed make a difference.

The guiding principle in my work, then and now, is the compassion that derives from the African principle of *ubuntu*, the inter-connectedness of all human beings that embraces our common humanity. I seek to make it possible for people to rise to meet their greatest aspirations. That is one reason why I often remind myself and others of Gandhi's quote: "Be the change you want to see in the world." I chronicled the South African peace process—and the *ubuntu* spirit that defined it—in a book entitled *Watching the Wind: Conflict Resolution during South Africa's Transition to Democracy*. I seek to apply these experiences and principles in my everyday work for Search for Common Ground.

Golden Kids News reporter interviewing peers in Freetown. GKN is a radio news show produced by and for children at SFCG's Talking Drum Studios in Liberia, Sierra Leone and Côte d'Ivoire. It seeks to involve children and youth in national dialogue, conflict transformation and reconciliation.

JOHN AND SUSAN—*Joining Forces*

We believe that conflict is a normal part of human interaction, and that violence is only one in a range of possible responses. In our view, violent conflict is not inevitable. In fact, the opposite would seem to be true. The essence of our work at Search For Common Ground, therefore, is to transform how the world deals with conflict, from adversarial approaches toward cooperative solutions.

The challenge is not to try the impossible—to eliminate differences—but to learn how to manage them constructively and without violence. In our view, successful conflict resolution calls for a multilevel, societal approach that not only includes the intellect, but also touches people on a deeper, more personal level, reaching into the heart. Thus, while we have developed a diverse toolbox that includes traditional techniques for conflict resolution, we are also pioneers in the creative use of television, radio, print journalism and the arts—all effective channels for touching emotions. We have produced radio soap operas in ten countries, TV soaps in Nigeria, Egypt and Palestine, dramatic TV series for children in Macedonia and Cyprus, and peace songs and music videos in Angola, Macedonia and the Middle East. Because people create conflicts, we believe that people can resolve conflicts. We witnessed this in South Africa, where peaceful solutions seemed impossible, and we believe it is true everywhere.

One of the most extraordinary things that has occurred in recent years is the growing belief that individuals can make a difference in the world. In the past,

there was much more of a division between *leaders* and *followers*.
With regard to our advice for others interested in taking action:

- Only bite off chunks that you can deal with; take actions that are incrementally transformational.
- Hold to a larger vision but move forward by breaking things down into manageable pieces.

Using Tools to Find Common Ground

Headquartered in Washington, D.C., Search for Common Ground (SFCG) has 375 employees, a $20 million annual budget, and sixteen offices in Africa, Asia, the Middle East, Europe and the United States.

In addition to capacity-building work with governments and citizen groups, SFCG operates Common Ground Productions, a worldwide TV, radio and Internet production entity that has pioneered the use of media in conflict prevention; Partners in Humanity, an initiative that builds bridges between the Western and Islamic worlds; and the U.S.-Iran Project, dedicated to improving bilateral relations between those two countries.

SFCG's programs are firmly rooted in the societies they serve. There is no single operating model or prototype, because every conflict and every culture is unique. They identify countries, regions and specific conflicts amenable to their approach, and begin by building multiple partnerships with governments, civil society organizations, the business sector and international organizations.

SFCG builds local capacity and multi-stakeholder partnerships to do the work, so that each country can successfully manage its own conflicts. The basic operating strategy is to understand the differences and act on the commonalities. To do this, SFCG has developed and applies a diverse "toolbox of resolution techniques," ranging from mediation and facilitation to creative channels for helping people imagine peace and tolerance—radio, soap operas, sporting events, music videos and community organizing.

Burundi provides perhaps the best example of a country where the SFCG methodology has been applied across a whole society, and a model for the scale at which SFCG would like to work in all of the countries it serves. One year after genocidal attacks by the majority Hutu ethnic group killed some 800,000 Tutsis in neighboring Rwanda, SFCG opened its office in Burundi, a country with a similar history of political violence and demographics. SFCG operates Studio Ijambo radio, whose programs—news, drama, documentaries, discussion— examine all sides of the country's deeply imbedded conflict, highlighting issues that can unite rather than divide. This radio programming reaches 90% of the population. In addition, SFCG established a Women's Peace Center, which works with hundreds of women's associations and civil society organizations, sponsors projects to help former youth combatants reintegrate and help build a peaceable society, and promotes music, theater and dance events that bring Burundians from all sides together. It measures success in terms of people who identify themselves as Burundians first, rather than as members of an ethnic group.

In Macedonia, SFCG produced a *Sesame Street*-like television program, *Our Neighborhood*, whose ethnically diverse cast and inclusive language have won acceptance from all ethnic communities and several international awards. Survey research shows that children understand the message and use the model for thinking about conflicts in everyday life.

Another particularly creative and far-reaching program is the Middle East Consortium on Infectious Disease Surveillance. Recognizing that the time was not right to address an issue as sensitive as chemical and biological weapons, SFCG accomplished the same purpose by working with Israelis, Palestinians and their neighbors to set up a network for monitoring outbreaks of disease. Now officially sanctioned by the respective governments, the system overcomes barriers that cause crippling delays in sharing epidemiological information—the same information that would form the basis for recognizing a toxin released as an act of war or terrorism.

SFCG has helped citizens of conflict-ridden countries see possibilities for interethnic harmony by working with journalists to diminish inflammatory reporting and promote regional understanding in Africa and the Middle East, using sports exchanges ("wrestling diplomacy") to connect Iranians and Americans, and conducting regular policy forums and media events.

Devastated by 9/11, John and Susan moved to Jerusalem for several years where John wrote and produced the *Shape of the Future* documentary series, a four-part TV documentary examining the fears and aspirations of Israelis and Palestinians and showing how a settlement could address those concerns without threatening the national existence of either side. It was the first documentary ever broadcast simultaneously on Israeli and Palestinian TV.

SEARCH FOR COMMON GROUND—BY THE NUMBERS

- Search for Common Ground was established in 1982.
- It employs 375 individuals.
- It has an annual budget of $20 million.
- Sixteen field programs have been implemented on four continents.

CHAPTER 8

Disaster Relief and Rehabilitation

H uman responses to disaster have improved dramatically as communication networks have become more sophisticated worldwide. The Indian Ocean tsunami that struck much of Indonesia and Southeast Asia on December 25, 2004 demonstrated record results in global disaster response and relief funding. That being said, the number and frequency of disasters seem to increase faster than we are able to keep up with them. Due to environmental shifts in our atmosphere, heat waves, droughts and wildfire will only continue to occur more often. The number of Category 4 and 5 hurricanes, such as Hurricane Katrina, has almost doubled in the last thirty years.

Natural disasters like earthquakes, tornadoes, hurricanes, tsunamis and wildfires are often too powerful and unexpected for us to control, let alone prevent. Emergency responses, however, are not. Beyond natural disasters, though, man-made disasters are well within our abilities to limit and prevent, and social entrepreneurs are tackling them head-on in many parts of the world. For example, Roots of Peace (profiled in this chapter) is working to rid the world of land mines, which claim another victim, usually a child, every twenty-two minutes in a former war-torn area.

Henry Dunant, a Swiss banker with a big heart, witnessed mass human devastation during the Battle of Solferino in northern Italy and became the driving force in 1864 behind the establishment of the International Red Cross. He argued that those who are devastated by human conflict or natural disasters deserve to be helped, regardless of their politics or the conditions that led to their suffering. Fatima Guilani, the current head of the Afghan Red Crescent Society, is following in Dunant's footsteps and strives every day to do just that. The organization she runs is made up of 37,000 volunteers throughout the country carrying out many of the social service functions that national governments normally handle, such as disaster relief and rehabilitation. And due to thirty years of continuous war, Afghanistan does not have a national government with the resources or capabilities to deal with most of the victims of war and natural disasters, which means that the Afghan Red Crescent Society and its partner NGOs essentially are the social welfare system in the country.

Rehabilitation during and after disasters is often critical to a region's social and economic survival, particularly considering that governments too often fail to respond quickly or adequately. Among the hundreds of organizations taking on such great work are the following:

- CARE (Cooperative for Assistance and Relief Everywhere)
- International Federation of the Red Cross and Red Crescent Societies
- International Rescue Committee
- Oxfam
- World Relief

In addition to these well-established NGOs, social entrepreneurs, including the four profiled below, have stepped forward with some very unique and powerful initiatives:

- **Heidi and Gary Kühn**, a former housewife and businessman whose professional and family lives are now dedicated full-time to the eradication of land mines worldwide and the placement of agriculture seeds where those land mines were buried.

- **Alberto Cairo**, an Italian doctor who has devoted the past seventeen years to helping innocent victims of past wars "get back on their feet" and live productive lives despite their physical disabilities.

- **Tim Williamson**, a business consultant and financier who has created financial incentives demonstrating the power of entrepreneurs to rebuild the city of New Orleans after Hurricane Katrina.

- **Rosalind Jones Larkins**, a woman raised in the New Orleans projects whose strategy of education is designed to help women made destitute by Hurricane Katrina find employment.

⊕ HEIDI AND GARY KÜHN AND FAMILY
Roots of Peace

Afghanistan, Angola, Cambodia, Croatia and Iraq

Roots of Peace is a leading innovator in the global eradication of land mines, which maim and kill over 26,000 people worldwide every year, nearly half of them children. Its mission is to turn fields of death into prosperous farmlands, restoring community values and peace by helping former war-torn areas grow "from mines to vines." A cervical cancer survivor and mother of four, Heidi Kühn has united over 400 Californian

Heidi Kühn with an Afghan farmer who has worked with Roots of Peace to turn his field from mines to vines.

vintners to support her efforts. Gary, Heidi's husband, helped launch Adobe Acrobat after ten years of business leadership at IBM, and is now the executive behind the harvesting, distribution, and vineyard training programs. Together, through Roots of Peace, the Kühns have achieved incredible successes, including the removal of 100,000 land mines and unexploded ordnances, and the training of 10,000 farmers in Afghanistan alone. With completed and ongoing operations in Afghanistan, Croatia, Iraq, Angola and Cambodia, Roots of Peace replaces seeds of destruction with seeds of life.

HEIDI KÜHN—*From Swords to Plowshares*

As a mother of several children and a stay-at-home wife, I had no business plan, and certainly no 501(c)(3), but I did have a cause that I was passionate about—the removal of land mines that kill so many innocent people around the world. My grandmother's biblical words have always been etched in my soul: "Trust in the Lord with all thy heart . . . in all thy ways trust in Him, and He shall direct thy path." And that path has led me to a minefield.

To remove a land mine means not only to save a life, but also to give a family a vineyard, a community a soccer field and a nation its peace. When I got started, I was attracted to the dream of being there in Angola, Croatia, Afghanistan or Iraq when that last mine is removed. My work over the last seven years has only confirmed that our vision is absolutely possible.

It is a sacred process to free lands held hostage by mines. The mine is a symbol of hatred, a man-made instrument of war that does not discriminate in taking the life or limb of an innocent child, farmer or soccer player years after the war for which it was built has ended. A vine, by contrast, is a symbol of hope. It brings life and rebirth to dead soil, and hope and possibility to the farmer who grows it. Regardless of the color of a farmer's skin, the politics in his brain or the faith in his heart, the vine he plants will grow today like it did thousands of years ago. That for me is the promise of God in the universe transcending all faiths. As we go from mines to vines, our work is blessed with generational wisdom and respect for our collective roots of peace.

Love for our common roots is so hard for some people to feel in this modern world. There are so many more seeds we share than which separate us. When we plant pomegranates, the oldest fruits in the world, we reconnect with an ancient seed in its most pure and nascent form. Roots of Peace engages such practical work removing mines and planting vines, but in the bigger picture, we cultivate life and peace by planting a seed that has symbolic meaning to all faiths and religions. By extracting a land mine and planting a grape or any God-given seed in its place, we are demining both the soil and the soul.

There are those who say, "I hate my neighbor, the government or the person I ran into on the street." We cannot control hate, but so much of it is preventable. The hatred that lingers in war-torn countries may be alleviated by demining the soil, and so too the human heart, which suffers greatly when so many old land mines still explode today. We cannot go forward in peace when the sandals of a child or the boots of a farmer are not free to walk the earth for which they were made.

For New Year's at the turn of the millennium, I toured my first minefield. I had been working for three years from my basement in Marin, California, incubating a global vision for land mine removal in my heart and my home while raising four children. I was awake researching and making calls to the East Coast every morning at 4:00 AM. At 7:00 I was preparing bagged lunches and driving the kids to school, and by 9:00 I was back down in the basement at work while most of the other Marin moms were on the tennis court or golf course. After three years of work from home, in January 2000 I was finally taking my first steps in a Croatian minefield. This was just after the Balkan War, and Croatia was raw from its wounds.

To get there, I had approached Mr. and Mrs. Robert Mondavi, great vintners and humanitarians who live not an hour from my home, and asked them for help in funding a demining campaign in the rural region of Dragalic, Croatia. In giving to an unpublicized charity, Robert and Margrit demonstrated a profound respect for the grapevine, whether fermented or not, as a symbol of peace. I remember walking through the demined region and arriving at the local school for the presentation of the new fields.

There was a little boy who asked in translated Slavic in front of the group, "Mrs. Kühn, are you really from California?" He had seen the United States only via satellite dish. He paused after I nodded, then raised his chin. "Is it true that the children in California can hike mountains and run on beaches without the fear of land mines beneath their shoes?" I looked at him and nodded again, fighting back tears in front of the school's audience. "It must be heaven," he said, looking back down at his hands.

The grandmother of the young boy came up to me after the presentation. She was in traditional black and had beautiful, sad eyes with a haunting story behind their expressive stare. She gave me a Croatian handshake, one of those strong bone-crushing grips, and began her story through our translator: "I am thanking you on behalf of my grandchildren, for my life is now gone, but they are able to play and kick soccer balls and chase butterflies into the vineyards without having their feet removed." I respected her natural cadence, emotional in its reservation. "My dear husband of fifty years," she continued, "we had been through the war together, and we were poor with no pensions so we taught ourselves how to remove a mine in order to survive the cold winter. Nobody was there to help us, but we did it anyway. We had gotten all the mines out. Spring came and my husband turned on his tractor, that familiar sound. I was in the garden, and heard a sudden *boom*. Had the war started again? I walked into the backyard and saw the effects of a land mine. No woman in the world should have to pick up her husband in a hundred pieces." Stories like these make me carry on until that very last mine is gone.

In telling this story, I am reminded of my time with the UN Secretary General Kofi Annan. We were hosting an event together and he was walking me through the gardens of their New York headquarters on First Avenue in New York. I noticed a wall draped in ivy, the words beneath it covered by the vine. "With all due respect, sir," I said, "you have a wall of opportunity there." "I never thought of it that way," he replied. With his permission we helped build and cultivate the Roots of Peace Garden with the indigenous seeds of seventy different countries, planting them with budding hope that peace may grow as crops do, from the ground up. The ivy was eventually cleared, revealing the prophetic words of Isaiah, an Old Testament verse that had been agreed upon by Christians, Jews and Muslims alike. As we cultivated the garden, the wall's verse echoed in our thoughts:

They shall beat their swords into plowshares,
And their spears into pruning hooks;
Nation shall not lift up sword against nation,
Neither shall they learn war anymore.

Gary Kühn working in a former minefield, which Roots of Peace has successfully transformed into a vineyard.

GARY KÜHN—*From Computers to Agriculture*

I came on board Roots of Peace with a full-time corporate career at IBM to help the numbers and business side of the operations. For the first two and half years, I was making ten trips a year traveling and talking to local Afghan farmers to find the best crop regions in their countries. In 2002 and 2003, with a budget raised from our own contributions and from some very generous Napa Valley vintners, I spent more time setting up in Afghanistan than I did at home.

When I first got there, we couldn't get off the truck to put our foot down as there were so many mines. Red flags everywhere. You could actually see the unexploded ordnance sticking out of the ground. So at that time, we were entirely focused on mine clearance before we could even plant one crop. Everyone carried guns except us, and schools and soccer fields sat unused because nobody knew how to get these things out of the ground. We've since removed over 100,000 land mines and UXO (unexploded ordnance) in the country, allowing us to transition to the replanting process.

When I say replanting I mean a very specific approach to the crop market. These guys are growing apricots, grapes, pomegranates and almonds. We look at their specific varieties and then send marketing experts to do market analyses in Singapore, Dubai, Europe and America, and of course in the local markets too. We then look at when crops are ripening in Kandahar, Afghanistan, in one case, figuring out with whom they are competing and which are their best global markets to target. We come back to the farmer and determine a business plan for each one individually, depending on their crop specialty, telling them, for example: "In India, the monsoon season hits around July 1. At that same time in Kandahar grapes are ripening. The long green grape called Shmiles Khani, father of the Thompson's Seedless grape, sells for $2.23 a kilo in New Delhi versus the round green one called Girduk that sells for 70¢. Which one do you want to grow?" So, in our entire process we teach these farmers the concept of a pro forma income statement based on sound market proxies for maximizing yield and income.

A huge breakthrough in our fundraising came after two years of work, when we received a contract of $6 million over three years from USAID to support the grape industry in Afghanistan. Our growth accelerated, and we were able to expand our agricultural operations enormously by introducing refrigerator-packaged options for farmers to ship globally who before could only reach Pakistan. We've got teams in Kabul, Baharak, Mazar-e-Sharif, Kandahar, and Jalalabad. With other major funding from the European Union and private donations, we have helped make grapes the top legal crop of the country. The $6 million from USAID (United States Agency for International Development) has all gone to growing grapes in the region, but dollar for dollar these funds are multiplying their effect against poverty, starvation and illegal drugs.

As farmers' knowledge and profits increase, they multiply incomes beyond what they could make from the production of opium. Moreover, unlike drug crops, fruit crops allow farmers to be more independent in their market decisions. A typical poppy farmer would make about $1,200 a year. With grapes, farmers have gone from making $600 per year before our intervention to about $1,600 with our help. With vineyard trellising, which is a completely foreign idea to most indigenous farmers, who grow all their crops on the ground, many have been able to double their production and income.

The end game is sustainability for the indigenous farmer. The job is a real adventure being out there hand in hand with the rural farmers. It is the confirmation that we're doing something good when a normally reserved Afghan farmer smiles ear to ear, often a toothless grin, with his arm around his kids telling us how happy he is to be a grape farmer for his family again.

In thinking about critical success factors, the following several keys have given us a competitive advantage over other agricultural companies:

- We've really had to be a bull in negotiations. We're a compassionate bunch, but when you're dealing with rebuilding governments that are highly patriarchal and a country whose infrastructure has been destroyed, you have to be tenacious. Once these countries realize we really are there to help, they eventually cooperate, but it takes tough persistence to get started.

- Second, there have been times when foundations and national companies have waved money in our face with conditional clauses as to what we should grow and how. The power of our model is in the specificity of our target markets and production objectives. So it's crucial to stay grounded and focused on our business approach as we stay on track with what we know we can accomplish. It is sometimes the projects you do not accept that turn out to be the most beneficial to your targeted efforts.

- Last, the most critical factor to our success is the capacity to choose the right people to run operations. We've got some of the best European, Middle Eastern, African and South Asian experts working with us, many with PhDs in agriculture. From top to bottom, our operations staff of over 200 worldwide stays totally focused on our twofold approach for the indigenous farmer: implementation and income generation.

CHRISTIAN KÜHN, AGE 9

I know ten times more about the world than before Mom and Dad started working. I have traveled with them. It is really fun to go and see other kids who are my age playing soccer and running around. Sometimes I go to other schools and talk about my mom's work and the Roots of Peace Penny Campaign that my sister Kyleigh is so committed to. A lot of them get inspired and even go to speak to other classes about it. I really love to do it, because it's so fun to speak to my friends about this. One of my friends, *all* he wants to do is play video games, which gets frustrating, because I know how much he could do. I sometimes think about what could happen if people just took the time to listen and do this themselves. Sometimes I have to miss school, but I don't mind that too much.

TUCKER KÜHN, AGE 22

For a while it was just Mom working in the basement, then Dad joined to help, and now they've got a really good thing going helping to create so many jobs and better lives for other people. Dad took me to Afghanistan three summers ago and it was so different from what the media portrays. Yeah, there used to be land mines everywhere, and the country has had so much war, but some of the nicest and most gracious people I've ever met are in Afghanistan. Working face to face with them gave me new interest in the world.

After that experience I changed my major to politics, and Roots of Peace made my own education seem more important to me. A lot of people in my generation are all about their simulated video games, cars and new clothes. At school in San Diego, I saw so much materialism. It's cool now, though, because many of my friends have gotten involved too. Some are making films, volunteering in the office or doing art for Roots of Peace.

My parents are really my role models. Some people seem to think my mom is "out there" to come up with these dreams and visions. But you know what, she gets them done. She's brought our whole family together around this. That's what really matters.

THE ROOTS OF PEACE MODEL—
From Mines to Vines: Demine, Replant, Rebuild

Heidi Kühn and her family have united over 400 vintners of California to support her efforts. Jodi Williams, 1997 Nobel Peace Laureate for her own work removing land mines, has called Heidi "a worker of miracles . . . a powerful example of what an individual can do if they only will try."

The entire Kühn family represents an exemplary model in which every member is involved in the work and vision. Kyleigh, their daughter, has spoken at the UN about her leadership with the Roots of Peace Penny Campaign, an annual student-to-student initiative that collects pennies and spare change to convert minefields into sports fields and playgrounds. Their sons, Christian, Tucker and Brooks, have traveled with the programs and help daily in the office headquarters. Together, the Kühns are an example of what a family can do when they feel so deeply passionate about a shared vision of hope for others less fortunate.

With a staff of more than 200, Roots of Peace has trained more than 100,000 farmers in completed and ongoing operations in Croatia, Cambodia, Afghanistan, Angola and Iraq. Their model is replicable and scalable.

It costs only $3 to $30 to produce and plant a land mine, but up to $1,000 to remove one. Many mines are made of nonmetallic material, making them impossible to locate by metal detectors. Consequently, specially trained mine-sniffing dogs and other slow, costly methods are commonly used to map minefields.

The actual removal of the land mines is done using large remote-controlled flail tractors that systematically cover every inch of ground and can withstand the blast when a mine is detonated. In rocky areas, the removal is done by carefully probing and digging out the mine by hand, an extremely painstaking and dangerous practice.

A new, sophisticated technology known as global identification systems (GIS) is currently in development which has the potential to revolutionize the global demining effort. GIS uses software to identify and map minefields from space, eliminating the risk to human beings and dogs. Roots of Peace is partnered with Autodesk, a software company that is active in the development of GIS applications and committed to making them widely available for demining initiatives around the world.

The replanting process is both a symbol of renewal and an immediate catalyst for economic recovery. Almonds, grapes, cherries, pomegranates, walnuts and citrus represent crop alternatives to farmers who may otherwise produce poppy plants for drugs. Gary and his team focus on small rural farmers, who prove to be the best students. Farmers recognize that their families' livelihood is dependent on the efficiency and productivity of their work, demonstrating immediate turnaround yield after working with Roots of Peace. Farmers then independently establish small- and medium-size enterprises, ranging from commercial nurseries to full-size trellises, the produce of which they then package and distribute with sound market knowledge. In Eastern Afghanistan alone, Roots of Peace is helping farmers plant 900,000 fruit and nut trees in newly established orchards.

Roots of Peace upholds relationships with thousands of farmers to utilize market forces throughout the entire process, from cultivation of the vine through distribution, packaging and transport of the produce. In Cambodia, Angola, Croatia and Afghanistan, Gary and his team have taught illiterate farmers the essentials of business development, which the farmers then share with family members and rising management. These lessons include the concept of a pro forma statement based on profit-labor, input-output and supply-demand ratios. The farmers are also trained to achieve a consistent accountable bottom line. As vintners and orchard growers implement the recommendations from Roots of Peace, they then disseminate this information to their families and succeeding proprietors for the next generation of agricultural employment.

When Roots of Peace completes operations in a given country, farmers continue to be self-sufficient and prosper on their own, as they have been trained through cultivation, yield and distribution. Roots of Peace, however, does not earn great profit margins from this system as it now stands. The organization is currently dependent on aid donations and traditional fundraising. Roots of Peace has worked to diversify funding sources by working with development banks in Asia and Europe, but the key to sustainability is a hybrid business model powered by internally generated forms of income.

In Afghanistan, for example, the organization is in the process of establishing ten self-sustaining businesses, including one hundred hectares of pomegranate trees, and a juice operation that would bear the Roots of Peace name. As the company does not want to push any local farmer out of business, it is determining the efficacy of such a plan, and may opt for other forms of supply-side income generation, such as cardboard box manufacturing, and trucking and transport, all of which they would run by employing the local population.

ROOTS OF PEACE—BY THE NUMBERS

- Roots of Peace has helped remove 100,000 land mines or unexploded ordnances and trained 10,000 local farmers in Afghanistan alone.
- A typical poppy farmer would make about $1,200 a year; with grapes, farmers have gone from making $600 per year before working with Roots of Peace to about $1,600 after.
- It costs between $3 and $30 to place a land mine on the ground, and up to $1,000 to remove one.
- In the seven years of their work removing land mines, no one has been injured in their fields.
- Roots of Peace employs 200 people worldwide.
- It has ongoing operations in Asia, the Middle East and Africa, with an eventual plan to eradicate land mines completely from fields in any developing country.

ALBERTO CAIRO
International Committee of the Red Cross, Orthopedic Center
Afghanistan

Alberto Cairo moved to Afghanistan in 1990 to help land mine victims "get back on their feet." Seventeen years later, Alberto's greatest hope is that he will be able to "spend the next seventeen years doing the same thing, just doing it for more people and doing it better." His infectious laugh and gentle touch make him a favorite among his patients. Alberto's 300 staff members are all disabled former patients. They now have jobs, as well as dignity and empathy for those they now serve, making and fitting artificial limbs for over 2,000 other disabled people who come to the ICRC centers each year. They also help reintegrate patients into society by providing job training and microcredit loans.

ALBERTO CAIRO—*From Law in Milan to Physical Therapy in Kabul*

When I was growing up in northern Italy, my mother encouraged me to help those less fortunate than myself. I took this advice to heart and by chance became intrigued with physical therapy.

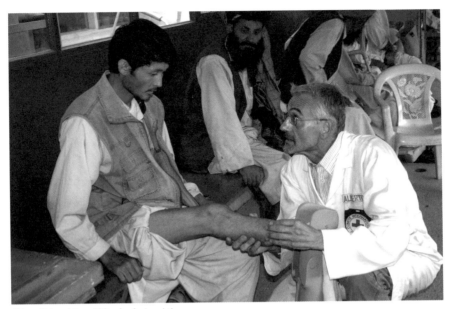

Alberto Cairo with an Afghan land mine victim.

I initially went to law school and started practicing law. But when I turned thirty, I asked myself whether I would rather be rich from practicing law or more satisfied by practicing physical therapy. For me the answer was easy. I quit my law practice, got a degree in physical therapy, and went to the Sudan to work with children who were victims of war. When the Sudanese government threw us out, I applied to the International Committee of the Red Cross to again work in Africa. Fifteen days before I was to leave, the ICRC asked if I would go to Afghanistan instead. I said yes, despite not knowing much about the country. When I asked about the climate so I would know what to bring with me, I was told it was like St. Moritz, Switzerland. When I arrived in Kabul I realized they must have been referring only to the altitude!

People ask, "Why do you stay here?" and "Don't you miss the theater, pizza and the other comforts of living in Italy?" My answer is always the same: When I first came here my motivation was primarily to respond to the needs of all the land mine victims in this country. But I soon realized that a deeper reason keeps me here: the joy I receive every day—more joy than anything I ever could have imagined.

I have stopped crying when patients come in with missing limbs or old wounds that have been left untreated for months or even years. I found crying depleted the energy I needed to help them get back on their feet. When someone crawls in here on his hands and knees with little hope for the future, I know that with our help he can walk out of here with a prosthesis and the possibility of a meaningful life. While my life here can be very hard, it is in giving of myself that I receive so much more in return.

We, as members of the same human race, must treat each patient's social and physical needs as a whole. All of our staff personnel are disabled. Imagine how much better you would feel when you realize that the staff member who greets you at the center has only one arm, the physical therapist who asks about your physical problem has no leg, the therapist who asks you about your future is missing both arms, and each of them gives you a big smile. We encourage disabled children to go to school. For those above school age, we provide vocational training. Our home-care program for those who cannot take care of themselves provides medical, economic, social and psychological rehabilitation. We also have a program for children with cerebral palsy.

Since 1997 we have offered microcredit loans of up to $600 for our patients to help them start their own businesses. The ICRC was at first reluctant to provide funds for microloans so I asked if I could use the money due to me for vacation days I had not taken. They permitted this and are now so pleased with the results that they provide all the funds. Our loans are interest free to the recipients, since this is a Muslim country in which charging interest is illegal. We started by providing loans to quadriplegics who seldom ventured outside. We provided them with small trolleys and a few goods to sell and it was a great success. We have a 95% repayment rate. Some of our disabled staff bicycle as much as sixty kilometers in a day checking on the progress of our microloan recipients.

We have had no problems with the different political regimes that have controlled Afghanistan over the past thirty years because they know we are doing something good for the people and have no political agenda. Everyone is welcome here. I recall one man who first came here with injuries caused while fighting the Russians. He later returned dressed as Taliban and more recently came to us dressed in Western clothes.

The ICRC Model—
Replacing Limbs and Rehabilitating the Victims

In 1988, the International Committee of the Red Cross created the ICRC orthopedic center in Kabul to provide artificial limbs to victims of war. This was badly needed then and remains so today due to the fighting that has engulfed the country continuously since the Soviets invaded in 1978. Afghan fighters known as the "mujahideen" fought the Soviets throughout the 1980s, and then each other in the civil war that followed, resulting in hundreds of thousands killed and maimed. In reaction to this anarchy and warlordism, the Taliban, a movement of religious fundamentalists and former mujahideen, emerged and ruled the country until the United States and its allies invaded in 2002.

Soon after Alberto arrived in 1990, he concluded that it was not appropriate for the orthopedic center to care only for those injured in war. In 1994 the facility opened its doors to anyone with a mobility handicap, whether from land mines, polio, tuberculosis, leprosy or any other cause. They also expanded their services to address their patients' nonphysical needs and geographically expanded their services to six centers across the country.

While the centers have been established as not-for-profit entities along the lines of many humanitarian organizations in the past, it is clear that they are constantly seeking innovative solutions to the challenges they face and going to scale up where possible. In addition, they are seeking to generate income where feasible. For example, they are manufacturing prostheses with local materials and currently providing them free to other health-care facilities in Afghanistan, but are considering selling them in Afghanistan and abroad.

ICRC—By The Numbers

- ICRC has six orthopedic centers in Afghanistan with 500 staff members, all of whom are disabled.
- ICRC has a total production capacity per month of 600 prostheses, 700 orthotics, 1,200 pairs of crutches and one hundred wheelchairs.
- The organization has registered 32,312 amputees since 1988.
- It has made 62,691 prostheses and provided 76,123 orthotics since 1988.
- Of amputees registered, 76% are victims of land mines.

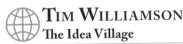

TIM WILLIAMSON
The Idea Village

New Orleans

Tim Williamson, a former Wall Street stockbroker, tells a before-and-after story of Hurricane Katrina in New Orleans, Louisiana. Between its inception in 2002 and September 2005, the Idea Village was the prominent nonprofit engine for entrepreneurship in the city of New Orleans, developing a database of over 600 local entrepreneurial businesses *that collectively employed more than 3,000 people and generated $150 million in revenue. Now, in the aftermath of Katrina, the Idea Village is helping to rebuild New Orleans, introducing an innovative approach to disaster relief that actively identifies and empowers entrepreneurs as the most fundamental pioneers of reconstruction.*

TIM WILLIAMSON—*Overcoming Disaster with Creativity*

It may sound strange to say, but Katrina actually accelerated our understanding of what could be accomplished by local entrepreneurs in Louisiana. I was called into the state capital, Baton Rouge, and met with the Southern Women's Action Network (SWAN), right after coming home from the storm. With $100,000 and a firm blessing from SWAN, we took to the streets, searching for, identifying and rewarding female entrepreneurs who were starting up business again. There was so much rubble and decay; you could still see the waterline stain from the floods twenty feet above your head on the second-story exterior walls. Spray-painted X-marks were everywhere on buildings and street signs, left by rescue teams to indicate survivors at every block corner. We all felt tattered, distraught and isolated from the rest of the country. Yet there was reason for extreme faith that we would resurrect urban life again. It came not from the government, but from the streets, the local entrepreneurs. One by one we found individuals who were giving reason for life, to begin again.

Creative destruction as an economic force is sometimes too difficult for people to internalize when they have lost so much, especially when the government has done so little to revitalize the well-being of families, neighborhoods and entire cities. Thousands of lives had been lost, buildings destroyed, homes demolished and families separated; the unimaginable had occurred. And yet, above all of the tragedy, in early September of that year, returning to New Orleans in the aftermath of the destruction, I became witness to an incredible display of hope not covered by the news. As I walked the streets still covered in the brown crust of floodwater, I found incredible displays of entrepreneurship, individuals who with pride and dignity were starting and reviving their businesses.

Back in 2000, the Idea Village was designed with the belief that entrepreneurship is the fundamental agent behind positive social and economic change. There were five of us guys in our thirties who came from business backgrounds in finance, advertising, Internet start-ups and venture capital. Since 1987, I had held several positions, working as a stockbroker in New York City, banking with Bear Stearns in Boston and even starting up several business ventures on my own in Atlanta and Pittsburgh, before coming back to New Orleans to oversee the initial launch of an Internet strategy group for Cox Interactive Media. Thinking back to my days as a Wall Street stockbroker in New York, the paychecks were great, but we were making money just to make it. Sure, we were helping our investors make the right financial decisions, but it was all about money. Ten years later in 2000, the five of us sat together at a bar in our hometown city, and on a napkin jotted down the vision that spawned the Idea Village: to make New Orleans a world-class city of innovation and entrepreneurship, a global incubator of fresh business ideas and social enterprise.

In the years before the hurricane, I remember how difficult it was to raise capital for a vision that had no track record. Every entrepreneur faces this challenge. In New Orleans, though, the task was especially difficult. This is a special city, and everyone who comes here attests to that. The culture. The music. The river. The food. The history. People aren't always able to put their finger on what it is that's so special about this place; they just feel it. But with such an old city of hundred-year-old traditions, there's always some resistance to entrepreneurial thinking. We were encouraging folks to innovate, to be vanguards, and that takes time to develop.

I remember, for example, one city leader with considerable financial and political influence whom we approached with our vision, but he resisted. I approached him a second time, but the response was again shaky. A third time I decided not to request that he fund our vision, but simply endorse our name. He was skeptical and unsure, questioning: "But what if it fails?"

This guy was too comfortable in his "leadership" seat, and his resistance to encourage positive innovation in a city that desperately needed to fight unemployment and crime was troubling. I came back and put a sign on the wall in our office that read, "But what if it fails?" Ask any entrepreneur that question and they'll come to materialize their vision with even more vim and vigor. And so, because we knew no one else was taking on new ways of thinking in business, we started the Idea Village, bringing together the nonprofit, for-profit and academic circles of this city with an unprecedented model.

We offered consulting, financial modeling and management consulting. Economic inclusion balanced with sound business principles was the core of our early mission, and it continues to be. The beauty of our programs is the diversity of individuals with whom we collaborate. With our revitalization plan, 95% of the entrepreneurs we funded right after the storm are still doing business. There's Chill the Barber and Kappa Horn, the first barber shop and restaurant to reopen just days after the storm, and the New Orleans Jazz Orchestra, Ticobeans Costa Rican Coffee and Debonair Clothier.

Our portfolio of entrepreneurs is as diverse as the city itself. We have taken on new technology and software firms, as well as online realty and gourmet food companies. With every entrepreneur, we demand that they not try to recreate their old business with the results they had before the storm, but encourage them to start anew with fresh perspective about what's possible now, after the storm.

The Idea Village breaks ground on its future New Orleans headquarters, which will become a central hub of entrepreneurship in the region.

We raised $500,000 in those early months after the storm. We called it the Pay-It-Forward Fund, lending start-up capital to individuals, who after succeeding with their business would repay the loan forward for the next entrepreneur to benefit from. The funds came from outside donors and investors who believed in and trusted us. Investors weren't sure where their funds would go if they gave to the government, considering FEMA's lackluster and uncoordinated strategies. They gave to us and the entrepreneurs we sought out because we were there working with people on the streets at a time when no one else seemed to be doing anything. I wondered what that civic leader must have been thinking when he said, "But what if it fails?" while we were making successful new businesses out of nothing.

You'll see it years from now when you read about how the world-class city of New Orleans recovered from the worst natural disaster in this country's history, using not the government's aid but free enterprise and innovation.

PROGRAMS AND KEYS TO STARTING A BUSINESS THE IDEA VILLAGE WAY

Since Hurricane Katrina, the Idea Village has designed a revitalization plan that includes several programs:

- The IV Business Relief Fund, which includes the Pay-It-Forward Fund that Tim mentions above, provides "triage" cash grants for businesses to restart operations, repay loans and pass on debt to the next entrepreneur needing start-up capital.

- The IDEAcorps, which brings together MBA students from Tulane University, community volunteers and professional consultants to develop case study approaches outside the classroom to local entrepreneurs.

- The IVNet, a database of contacts for all professionals to network, collaborate and consult.

- The "IV 100" Entrepreneurs, a group of one hundred companies, each with less than fifty jobs and $5 million in revenue, that the Idea Village identifies as the most promising entities for growth and expansion.

With all the entrepreneurs the Idea Village works with, and especially the "IV 100," Tim and his team manifest a strategy under the acronym ACE. The ACE objectives mean to *accelerate* the development of entrepreneurial ventures by *connecting* entrepreneurs to resources and facilitating the *execution* of their goals. In the post-Katrina New Orleans, or any city rebuilding from natural disaster, infrastructure is weak and slow, individuals are separated, and thus the ability to produce results is greatly impaired. ACE—Accelerate, Connect and Execute—while seemingly oversimplified in its catchiness, is in fact key to revitalization for any economic recovery process.

Among the "IV 100" that have benefited from the ACE program, here are just a few:

Hubig's Pies is a ninety-year-old manufacturing and distribution bakery serving all of southeast Louisiana, and portions of Texas, Louisiana and Alabama.

Loubat, founded in 1875, is a food service equipment, supplies and design company. This year Loubat would be celebrating 130 years in business, and would have an established client list of many well-known establishments: Antoine's, Galatoire's, Emeril's, Dickie Brennan Restaurants, Ralph Brennan Restaurants and Commander's Palace.

OffBeat, Inc. publishes *OffBeat* music magazine monthly, a music and culture publication distributed free in New Orleans, Baton Rouge, Lafayette and to subscribers around the world. OffBeat also publishes annually the "music bible," the Louisiana Music Directory, presents the "Best of the Beat" music awards and maintains websites for its publications, as well as a weekly newsletter.

IMDiversity.com was conceived by *The Black Collegian* magazine, which has provided African-American college students with valuable information on career and job opportunities since 1970. IMDiversity.com is dedicated to providing career and self-development information to all minorities, specifically African-Americans, Asian-Americans, Hispanic Americans, Native Americans and women. The goal of IMDiversity.com is to provide access to the largest database of equal opportunity employers committed to workplace diversity.

In talking about the "art of the start," the term any entrepreneur thinks of as his or her first steps in building a business, Tim Williamson notes several important ideas that have really helped the "IV 100" grow. According to Tim, above all the greatest challenge in seeking venture funding and getting a business off the ground is to choose the right core people with whom to collaborate. A company, like a social movement of systemic change, never starts by bringing in a ton of people in the front end, just the right people. There should be between three and seven individuals, each offering a unique skill set or business background, but all of whom share the same passion for the mission of the initial idea. The leader of that group must carefully and conscientiously walk the line between being the visionary and the executor. In other words, know when to lead from the front and when to push from the back. You may need to let other members of your team stand up and lead when they are best fit to do so; and in turn you should also be able to speak truthfully and trustfully for the group.

Trust is the most critical cohesive for any start-up venture. As Tim says, "Trust is the most important aspect of bringing any new entrepreneur closer to his or her collaborators, but it's certainly not an overnight thing; it takes enormous dialogue night and day." In order to drive a group forward, trust must take place through dialogue. Someone may look great on paper or on her resume, but unless you are truly able to trust her and understand her strengths and weaknesses, the vision may be compromised.

THE IDEA VILLAGE—BY THE NUMBERS

- From February 2002 up to the hurricane, the Idea Village developed a database of more than 600 local entrepreneurs who collectively employed over 3,000 people and generated $150 million in revenue.
- Since the hurricane, the Idea Village has raised over $700,000 to help develop businesses for 151 entrepreneurs.
- Roughly 95% of the companies it has worked with since just after the storm are still in business.

- Of the entrepreneurs funded by the Idea Village, 43% are minorities; 49% are female.
- In 2007, the Idea Village generated 951 jobs with 131 grants allocated to companies that collectively produced revenues over $62 million for the year.
- The Idea Village has been written about in *Forbes, Inc., Le Figaro, USA Today,* the *New York Times, Entrepreneur,* the *Times-Picayune* and the *Christian Science Monitor*, among others.

ROSALIND JONES LARKINS
Next Level Foundation School

New Orleans

One of the Idea Village's newest projects is the Next Level School, providing employment training and personal rehabilitation for women afflicted by extreme poverty after Hurricane Katrina. Rosalind Jones Larkins was born and raised in the projects of New Orleans, Louisiana. She is included in this chapter not as a social entrepreneur who has already achieved incredible results, but because her Next Level School has pioneered a promising approach to education that could be replicated in all inner-city environments. It heals the spirit for students, mostly women, who have very little hope and nowhere to turn, and provides them with career skills so they can find a pathway out of poverty. Rosalind has written a book entitled Quitting Is Not an Option, *about her own experiences growing up as the child of a single mother and an absent father, with accounts of repeated sexual abuse, rape, the murder of her first love and addiction to drugs while caring for two young girls. Having overcome such incredible hardships with remarkable resolve despite the many relatives and friends who gave up on her, she eventually became the first of her family ever to graduate from college. Rosalind has since earned a degree in law and started her own practice. Above her own success, however, she is included in this book as a new social entrepreneur striving to introduce a model that can be replicated for students, who like her at one time have no socioeconomic support system. They come to Rosalind's Next Level Foundation, LLC's proprietary school to get back on their feet.*

ROSALIND—*Quitting Is Not an Option*

Someone told me recently, "You need to start a nonprofit, because what you do is charity work," and I just didn't get that. I don't even really know what charity work is. I have a vision and passion to help people because I have been through so much hell in my life. People talk about being at the bottom of the barrel. Before I started to make some changes in my life, I was under the barrel looking up at the bottom.

I came from under the gutter, but you know what? I'm changing many more lives now than just my own. People ask me how I do this. I tell them the same thing I'll tell you: it comes from a burning realization inside that quitting was never an option.

We train individuals who, like me, come from nothing. Since Hurricane Katrina, too many people have been left stranded with no government assistance. They still live in trailers with no running water, children to care for, and no job.

One of my most recent graduates from the first class since the storm is Ashley, who has never had a job, because as an infant she was abandoned by her mother and so was never registered with a birth certificate or ID. Ashley, raised by her grandmother, is now a single mother herself. She often used to cry in class because she was unable to take care of her baby with proper food and clothing. She was jump-starting her car every morning to drive without a license across the river to get here. With love, hugs and encouragement, she graduated from Next Level as valedictorian of the office assistant class and attained her high school equivalency diploma. We applied for Ashley's birth certificate and got her an ID to secure employment, so she may now provide for her daughter.

Our building was restored fifteen months after Katrina. We had thirty people a day walking through our doors when we started. Like Ashley, they wanted us to help them get to the "next level." We treat every single student as a person with a story, not like so many big institutions do, viewing them as some number or statistic.

People come here because it's personal. We're compassionate and holistic in our approach. Unlike so many other institutions, this isn't a system where our students are numbers that get pumped out into an economy with degrees but no personal development. Those kinds of systems don't measure how many people fall through the cracks, because their successful outcome is the tuition they collect before the student is allowed to take a seat in the classroom. Our form of education recognizes every individual and opens up space for his or her personal story to be a part of the communal growth of the whole class. In opening up, our students are given a gift of healing, and the intellectual and practical teaching we provide follows from that. We give them a seat knowing they do not have the ability to pay. We measure Next Level's success by the success of its students.

The Next Level School doesn't just give a person a degree; it gives them a skill and a community in which that skill can develop as a part of a person's pathway out of poverty. Career development is a twofold process for everyone who comes to us. There's the personal side and the professional side. You teach a person to type, transcribe and take on a professional demeanor, and they can get a job just about anywhere. Such practical skills are taken for granted or ignored in typical classrooms, even though these are the most marketable forms of education to get someone into the workforce. The first few sessions are usually very emotional as these students share their personal hardships. With mentorship and training, we make students feel confident about their past shortcomings, and encourage them to leave it all behind so they can move onto higher platforms of personal *and* professional development. This is what we call the Next Level. When people make a decision to come here, they become students who learn to be at peace with their past while embracing educational training as the first step to moving forward.

Who am I to be different and to make change happen not only for myself, but for my children and other students' children? I might be little old Rosalind over here on Canal Street in New Orleans, but I believe so deeply in my mission. Nothing can deter me. With education you change a life. When you change a life, you change a generation. And when you change a generation, you change a society.

This city needs us. People here need an opportunity to rebuild their lives, even two years after the storm. My students live in trailer homes. They don't have clothes; they don't have money. The thing that keeps me going, that lets me know that Next Level has to go forward, is that we will change one life at a time. It's the small victories that make this worthwhile. The federal government has not given us a dime. The state hasn't either, because they say we have no track record. But will I let that be the deciding factor whether I really go forward in my vision and mission? No, I work to sustain Next Level with the insurance money for our home that was damaged in the storm and is still in need of repair. And it is worth every penny I don't receive back, because I wake up every day with the knowledge that it won't be the government or big institutions but the power and commitment of my husband and I that will get many more people back on their feet to rebuild their lives and this city. I am humbly blessed with the opportunity to do so and feely strongly that it is my purpose.

It's still month-to-month for Gregory and me, and we're treading new ground without really knowing for sure what's to come next. Sometimes there's that little voice on my shoulder that says, "Rosalind, you're silly to have given up your law practice that could have made you so much more money. You are struggling to fund the college education of your own daughters while providing an education for Next Level's students, who you don't even know." Everything I have is in Next Level, everything I've earned I've given away, and all that I have come through I bring here.

Rosalind works with a Next Level student in the classroom.

GETTING TO THE NEXT LEVEL

Next Level Foundation School offers programs of study that are designed to enable students to obtain an education through a comprehensive fast-track approach. Students who complete the program successfully will have received high-quality training from professionals in their respective fields. The student-instructor ratio in a class is a maximum of twenty students per instructor. Each graduate of Next Level is certified in a program of study that qualifies him or her to compete in the workforce as a paraprofessional and to qualify for career advancement. The academic programs are designed for individuals to gain skills that are transferable across industries.

In 2000, Rosalind incorporated Next Level as a for-profit LLC, which since the storm she has partnered with a nonprofit entity, Next Level Institute. While both components of her organization comprise the same mission statement and goals, the institute enables her to receive donations. Although she was not asking anyone for funding at the time this book was written—because she never saw her work as charity—she has, however, begun to receive consulting and potential financial support from another of our New Orleans social entrepreneurs, Tim Williamson of Idea Village, who is also profiled in this chapter.

Next Level is the only for-profit school in post-Katrina New Orleans. Regardless of its tax status, however, there is an enormous demand for Next Level's services among much of the urban poor, especially racial minorities, who are looking for employment but don't have the means.

What is more surprising is that Next Level has been repeatedly turned down for funding by federal and state governments alike. The need is there, her approach is progressive, but the models of education that have a "track record" are those that receive money. It is perhaps not surprising that when asking what differentiates Next Level from other educational institutions, top-level bureaucrats are not strongly persuaded by the school's focus on the "personal development" side of training. This is, ironically, the most forward-thinking and positive feature of the school's offerings, as it reaches out to those who are most neglected and marginalized in a city that is trying to rebuild itself.

To date, over 90% of the students who seek funding from the city to attend Next Level applications are denied or are awarded partial assistance. In an effort to help as many people as possible, Next Level must grant every student either a full or partial scholarship for tuition, books and uniforms. The ultimate goal is to acquire a building to expand its program offerings and services, including an in-house facility for women with children to provide a decent place to live and to provide the support they need to focus on achieving self-sufficiency. With education as its central mission, the facility would house a learning academy for the children while their mothers are attending class.

NEXT LEVEL—BY THE NUMBERS

- Next Level estimates that its students can earn at least four times more in income after their training than they did before enrolling.
- Next Level graduated sixteen students in its first class since Hurricane Katrina.

—————————— CHAPTER 9 ——————————

The Environment and the
Restoration of a Sustainable Planet

While each of us has our own health, education and socioeconomic concerns, there is only one planet we all share. It has provided life for billions of years. The frightening realization is that we are the only known species to have lived on earth in so destructive a way as to accelerate the likelihood of our own extinction. The earth has been talking back and we have not been listening.

According to the United Nations, Earth Watch and the Millennium Goals Campaign, since the beginning of the industrial age we have eliminated almost 70% of our forests, destroying 96 million hectares of forest cover in the 1990s alone. Desertification is potentially the most threatening ecosystem change, as more than two billion people, or one-third of the human population in 2000, live in these dry regions of the world and have insufficient water to sustain proper health and good life. Rainforests, considered to be the "lungs" of our planet's air supply, are in terrible danger. Forested areas totaling about 200 square kilometers, or an area twice the size of Paris, France, are cut down every day.

Our oceans suffer from similar damage. Currently, fishing practices are sustainable in only 22% of the world's waters, compared to 40% in 1975. Given current practices of ocean net dragging and overfishing, many species of fish will be extinct within forty years. Including life in the ocean, more than a million species worldwide could be driven to extinction by 2050 because of our use of resources at the expense of the planet's biodiversity.

Meanwhile, global demand for food is expected to double in the next fifty years, as urbanization increases and incomes rise. Economic growth has been given higher priority than have the consequences of its expansion on the environment.

For the world population, which is approaching 7 billion people, consumption and industrialization are increasing at rapid rates at a time when energy use and carbon emissions desperately need to be curtailed. Emissions of carbon dioxide rose from 23 to 29 billion metric tons between 1990 and 2004. Such drastic rises in carbon emissions, more popularly known as "global warming," have doubled the number of hurricanes during the past thirty years, and may soon result in a substantial rise in sea levels as shelf ice melts from Greenland and Antarctica.[2]

Despite conventional beliefs that developing countries are "inefficient" and thus contribute more carbon emissions, the plain and simple truth is that an

—————————————————————————————————————

[2] Statistics documented at www.climatecrisis.net

individual in sub-Saharan Africa, for example, accounts for less than one tenth of the carbon dioxide produced by the average person in the developed world.

While the oceans, forests, animals and climate are all individually subjected to our abusive patterns, it is the interconnectedness of such elements that we often fail to see as a comprehensive whole. For us, the water we drink, the food we eat and the air we breathe are free resources. The planet has provided all of this to sustain life for millennia, until now. In a recent documentary, *The 11th Hour,* produced and narrated by Leonardo DiCaprio, several experts shared an analogy of Earth as a single living organism. And no organism survives if it is infected and fighting itself for too long.

In his presentations on climate change, for which he recently won the Nobel Peace Prize, Al Gore has quoted the American author Upton Sinclair, who wrote in the early twentieth century that, "It is difficult to get a man to understand something, when his salary depends on his not understanding it." The social entrepreneurs who tell their stories in this chapter have all sought to address this primary concern, seeking to shift people's consciousness regarding habits of consumption, use and waste—whether on the individual or global scale. Paul Hawken, world-leading environmentalist, social entrepreneur and author of *Natural Capitalism* and *Blessed Unrest*, has written that if Earth is a single living organism in disharmony and in danger, then the countless organizations responding to the crisis globally are like white blood cells fighting to restore our planet's immune system to equilibrium. Wangari Maathai won the 2004 Nobel Peace Prize in large measure because she started a movement, The Green Belt Movement, led primarily by women, which plants trees to help restore biodiversity in her native Kenya. Hers is an excellent example of those life-saving white blood cells fighting to restore the planet's immune system.

In addition to the four social entrepreneurs listed here who are taking a lead in addressing the most pressing environmental challenges of our time, the following are a number of other organizations that you might also be interested in:

- Climate Crisis Coalition
- The Earth Charter Initiative
- Energy Action Coalition
- Eyak Preservation Council
- Global Footprint Network
- The Green Belt Movement
- "I Am Green," Facebook
- Quest for Global Healing
- (PRODUCT) RED
- Tesla Motors
- Whole Foods Market
- WildLife Works

- Women's Earth Alliance
- Youth for Environmental Sanity (YES)

In this chapter you will read about four very distinct initiatives addressing local and global environmental challenges:

Lynne and Bill Twist, a couple who, after traveling to the Amazonian rainforest, developed a program of "awakening" for individuals to realize how directly the industrial world has an effect on the natural world and indigenous cultures.

Van Jones, a brilliant speaker whose work incorporates environmental solutions with employment opportunities for the racially marginalized.

Agung Prana, who has engaged his local community and technology to restore coral reefs in Indonesia.

Andy Rossmeissl and Jake Whitcomb, two college students who created a credit card company that funds renewable energy projects and carbon offsets with every purchase.

LYNNE AND BILL TWIST
The Pachamama Alliance

Ecuador and the United States

As the march for private capital exploitation has decimated entire tribes in South America, the Achuar people, from deep in the Amazon region of Ecuador, have reached out to the modern world to help preserve their most ancient and sacred way of life. Bill and Lynne Twist, the founders of The Pachamama Alliance, have responded in kind, bringing skills and innovations from the developed world to join the Achuar in a larger process of rescue and preservation, contributing to the creation of a new global vision of equity and sustainability to be seen by both the northern and southern hemispheres in a common future.

LYNNE TWIST—*Awakening the Dreamer*

> *"If you are coming to help us, you are wasting your time. But if you are coming because your liberation is bound with ours . . . then let us work together."*
>
> —Indigenous elder, Amazon region

Lynne in the Ecuadorian rainforest.

In the process of moving from passion to action, from wanting to help preserve rainforests to sharing the deeply powerful vision of its peoples, I was moved by something outside of myself. As a mother, volunteer and full-time executive helping to run The Hunger Project, a global strategic organization committed to the sustainable end of world hunger, I had more on my plate than I could really manage. When invited to visit the Ecuadorian rainforests in the early 1990s, all of my commitments demanded that I could not leave, and yet I went anyway.

There were twelve of us that were allowed to enter and engage in the spiritual world of the Achuar in Ecuador. We were privileged to be in the company of these deeply private, unadulterated wisdom keepers. With no agenda of our own, we were awakened to the revelation of truths deeply rooted in the core of the human spirit. Despite local isolationism in the Amazon rainforest, these spiritual leaders revealed global truths with inexplicable accuracy and lucidity. Lifting the cloudy fog of unexamined assumptions in our Western preconceptions, the Achuar leaders gave us a gift of clarity. In order to protect the rainforests, we need not help *them* nor just work shoulder to shoulder in *their* land. Rather, if we really wanted to protect these lands permanently, as well as the future of indigenous cultures all over the world, we would need to "change the dream of the North" in the United States from where we had come. This is the dream of a modern world rooted in consumption, acquisition and private interest, and without regard for the natural world.

Upon returning from our trip to the Amazon, I grew terribly sick. I was largely bedridden, unable to work or complete the hundred responsibilities I felt I had to do. Despite my discomfort, however, it allowed me time to think. I thought of my past work, my identity as a wife, a mother and a nonprofit executive, and perhaps most importantly my deeply inspiring visit to Ecuador. In my state of illness, I was struck with the gift I had been given by the Achuar, the gift of clarity. With inexplicable conviction, I decided to quit my job and to share the story of the Achuar with as many others as I could reach. The Achuar had opened up their sacred space to us, and it manifested itself deep within my psyche as a life calling.

This calling developed from a basic insight that I could expand my work in the world through the core power of the human spirit. I realized there was no choice for me. I was determined to shift my global focus to incorporate the kind of spiritual and ecological harmony shared by an ancient people. The Achuar helped me do this, and it is in striving to honor this way of living and being that I awakened not only to the potential for personal transition, but also to global transformation.

The charitable relationship adopted by too many organizations and individuals is one of *us* helping *them*. This way of thinking is counterproductive. As the indigenous voices remind us, there are 6 billion ways to look at "everything," but there is only one "everything," and that is the planet we share as one whole. I don't believe in charity. I believe in alliances with coequal trust and partnerships. We are all a part of this vision, and we must therefore listen and respond to the living essence of the world, a newer and more just world that we can live in with honor and respect as we awaken to a new dream of shared coexistence.

BILL TWIST—*Shifting Peoples' Consciousness*

Although neither Lynne nor I had any special qualifications or expertise, and certainly not *the* answer for how to change the dream of the modern world, we responded anyway to an unshakable responsibility to listen to cultures that have much to teach.

The message of the indigenous peoples of the Amazon is that not only their rainforests, but in fact our entire society, are in danger. As we are bumping up against the limits of our evolutionary space, climatologists, anthropologists and demographers everywhere assert that we have a very limited time to change our course. We must work even harder for a new way of thinking, brought forth as a convergent awakening of environmental, social and spiritual consciousness.

The ethic of creation is at its best when it is given away. Our program grounds individuals in transformative possibility, which they may then lead for other groups of people. This is a continuous path of replicability. We encourage people to think about how they use their money, where their waste goes and how they may be able to live their lives with more intentional, sustainable decisions. The very act of intentionality in this process is critical to developing holistic worldviews that are materially conscious and spiritually fulfilling. As people's worldviews are likewise shifted to these awakenings, they replicate their insights elsewhere.

THE PACHAMAMA ALLIANCE MODEL—
From Environmental Awareness to Action

The Pachamama Alliance, a Quechua name referring to sacred space, time and universal community, concentrates its work in the Ecuadorian Amazon rainforest of 5 million acres, one of the most pristine and biodiverse ecosystems on earth. Empowering indigenous peoples to speak and stand for their own rights, the partnership affirms that those who have lived in harmony with their environment for centuries are also those best suited to preserve it.

The organization began its work at the request of the region's governing federations of indigenous people, including the Achuar, Shuar, Shiwiar, Zápara and Kichwa, to help strengthen the indigenous voice to represent itself in the vernacular of modern society. The Pachamama Alliance responded in kind, providing training to indigenous communities in the pragmatic language of negotiation, laws, plans, and finance.

In dialogue with the indigenous communities, The Pachamama Alliance embodies the earth-honoring wisdoms of ancient tradition while finding a place in the politics of state-sanctioned decision-making. The government of Ecuador, a country of nearly 14 million people, is increasingly determined to divide and sell its land to foreign private enterprise groups to compensate for its long-standing fiscal problems. While the Alliance recognizes that the long-term survival of the rainforests is deeply dependent on a shift in core values and worldview, the immediate needs for assistance in the region are much more practical.

There are four basic tenets to these efforts:

1. Mapping and territorial management includes training in Geographic Information Systems (GIS), so that the Alliance's indigenous partners can map their territories and establish accurate databases of sociographic information, which is an essential step toward legalizing territorial rights and developing long-term management plans for the lands and people.

2. Legal and collective rights advocacy includes training, consulting and mobilization on the local, national and international fronts, as the Alliance provides indigenous leaders with the tools to be their own advocates for legislative rights.

Bill playing the flute with an Achuar child.

3. Capacity building and organization includes planning, accounting and budgeting so that the indigenous federations have the skills necessary to coordinate community participation in health care, education and economic development projects.

4. Development of economic alternatives includes active research and education to create policy options that may greatly alleviate the country's external debt and offer substitutes for Ecuadorian oil drilling, such as through community-based ecotourism.

The Pachamama Alliance has offices in California and Ecuador, led by eight board directors and a full-time staff in both countries. Bill and Lynne Twist do not consider themselves creators, but rather assistants or "foundees" to the evolution of the Alliance's growth and development. In addition to the work they do in remote territories of Ecuador, their work in California includes running symposia, gatherings, fundraising events and a speakers' series.

The newest of these initiatives is the Awakening the Dreamer, Changing the Dream program that serves, in their words, "as a galvanizing space for individuals to explore the extraordinary possibilities inherent in a communion of technology with spirit." The initiative comprises speaker and roundtable talks, trips to Ecuador to one of South America's premier ecotourism sites in the Achuar territory, and educational training programs that individuals can replicate and lead in their own local communities. The capacity for replication is what gives the program its power. Between the summer and the end of 2007, newly trained facilitators led ten different symposia in cities throughout North America. While individual facilitators may direct a symposium in their own style, the symposia as a whole embody the central message of the Achuar people's shared wisdoms and insights.

The Pachamama Alliance is seeing promising results in Ecuador from its first steps in the creation of a Green Plan, including endorsement of the plan from the country's newly elected president, Rafael Correa. The initiative seeks to ensure sustainable development, cultural continuity, indigenous territorial rights and biodiversity conservation of the southern Amazon region in Pastaza and Morona Santiago provinces by assembling socioeconomic development options as alternatives to petroleum extraction and expansion. Several other elected government officials have expressed their commitment in public interviews to declaring a petroleum moratorium in favor of developing new and alternative socioeconomic options for the Amazon rainforest and its indigenous civilizations.

Income is entirely driven by the private contributions of foundations and a healthy donor support base. The majority of its funds go straight to program services.

The Pachamama Alliance—By The Numbers

- The Pachamama Alliance is fiscally extremely sound, allocating 81% of its 2006 expenses of $1,723,236 to its programs and services (7.5% to fundraising and the remaining 11.5% to general administration).

- More than 9,000 people have attended a symposium in the past two years, and 400 people are trained as facilitators. The symposium has been delivered in twelve countries.

- The Alliance has future plans to train more than 200 additional facilitators in the next two months alone, and with the number of symposia scheduled through the end of the year, more than 10,000 more people will have gone through a symposium (this is a conservative estimate).

- Recently, the government of Ecuador proposed a complete rewriting of the country's constitution, which the citizens voted for, and that process is under way. The Pachamama Alliance is hoping to provide input on wording that could ensure the rights of indigenous people and preservation of rainforest lands. The president of Ecuador has made a commitment to work to keep pristine rainforests lands intact.

- The Pachamama Alliance has worked with the Achuar Federation (NAE) in the Amazon to transfer Kapawi Ecolodge, located deep in the Amazon rainforest, to full ownership and management by the Achuar people. Currently, the lodge is owned and managed by a tour company, Canodros. The transfer of the hotel and all its assets to the Achuar took place on January 1, 2008.

VAN JONES
The Ella Baker Center

The United States

Van Jones is the cofounder of the Ella Baker Center based in Oakland, California, an organization that fights for social justice for underprivileged people throughout the United States. Integrating his upbringing in the 1970s as an African-American male from west Tennessee with a law degree from Yale University, Van is an impassioned force that commands attention. Winner of the 1998 Reebok Human Rights Award, and recognized as an Echoing Green and Ashoka fellow, Van has created an initiative to make sure that the new wave of environmentalism that is taking hold in the United States also benefits underprivileged Americans rather than excludes them. Van calls it "a movement for eco-justice, not eco-apartheid." In the next section, Van articulates his philosophy behind this new movement. The Ella Baker Center calls this new initiative the "Green-Collar Jobs Campaign" to create hundreds of new environmental employment opportunities in Oakland, California, while House Speaker Nancy Pelosi has adopted the philosophy for her national Green Jobs Act.

VAN—*Eco-Justice and the Green Wave*

The first wave of environmentalism was the movement to conserve the natural wealth and beauty of this continent, which the Native Americans had treasured and preserved for thousands of years. The second wave started with the 1963 publication of *Silent Spring* by Rachel Carson. That second wave was a movement to regulate the poison and pollution of the industrial age. It can count among its successes in the 1970s the passage of the federal Clean Air Act and the Clean Water Act, as well as the creation of the federal Environmental Protection Agency (EPA). Today we are seeing the start of a new wave—which I call the Green Wave. The Green Wave is not about conserving the beauty of our natural past or regulating the problems of our industrial present. It is about investment in the solutions of the future.

It is already a multi-billion dollar phenomenon, and it could open many doors for students, youth, the racially marginalized, the disenfranchised and people without money in this country.

People were stunned in 2005 when "clean and green tech" placed sixth among the big money industries in venture capital. People were blown away last year when clean tech then passed information technology on that list. Most venture capitalists, folks whose job it is to predict and bet on the biggest industries for investment, are saying to bet green. Why? Because green technology will be number one in just a few years. Just the clean energy sector alone grew from $40 billion to $170 billion in ten years. Now when you add in LOHAS, by which I mean Lifestyles of Health and Sustainability, which is everything from echinacea to yoga lessons to hybrid cars and solar panels, we are talking about a $230 billion segment of the U.S. economy that is growing nearly vertically. As the Green Wave takes hold, who is going to get that money?

Three different scenarios are within the realm of possibility, and I dedicate my life to accomplishing the latter of them:

1. Eco-apocalypse. If we stay on our current path, I believe we are heading toward a global environmental catastrophe. It will be caused by our commitment to a suicidal form of capitalism. Under our present economic system, we take a bunch of beautiful living things, destroy them, turn them into products, shrink-wrap them, use them, throw them away as trash and then continue to do this process as fast we can—over and over again. And just think: most corporations call this kind of activity "economic growth"! With a planet of nearly 7 billion people, such an outcome is what environmentalists call a dead planet. I believe we can avoid and avert this outcome. Enough people are waking up to the reality and taking action.

2. Eco-apartheid. Under an eco-apartheid scenario, the world would be divided into ecological haves and ecological have-nots. You say, "It's not possible, that's not going to happen, because

Van articulates the opportunities for and the importance of environmental entrepreneurship in the Green Wave.

environmentally minded individuals would not allow it to happen," but this environmental movement is actually one of the most racially segregated movements in our country's history.

Take for example my home in California's beautiful Bay Area. Come to Marin County and you will see solar panels, thousands of hybrid cars, yoga schools in every town and organic food at every grocery store. Marin is doing it right, a model to counties all over the country—no question. But then come across the bay just twenty minutes away, and visit some parts of Oakland. There you will find people who don't care about melting ice caps and polar bears in the Arctic. Some are having a hard time finding safe and decent housing. They live near the port, where dirty-fueled ships and trucks foul the air. There are no decent grocery stores close by, so parents have to serve their families food from corner liquor stores, which sometimes has been sitting under the heat lamp for two days. This is just one of so many similar cities in the country. We are already staring down the long barrel of eco-apartheid—a society divided by race, and divided by class.

We are fighting to reclaim a future that is different from that. Why? Everyone would agree that eco-apartheid is bad, unjust and immoral. Fine. Worse than that, though, eco-apartheid would not be an alternative to eco-apocalypse but in fact a speed bump on the way to eco-apocalypse.

3. Eco-equity. The green economy will only succeed if a majority of people, a diversity of individuals, play their part and are empowered to participate. If only the eco-elite participate, the environmental movement will fail. In California, people of color make up 55% of the population. The majority of them must live in green homes, have access to clean energy transportation and work in clean and green workplaces, using processes and making products that respect the earth. This is the dream. And it represents the third alternative, the only sane and survivable model: what we call eco-equity.

In 1963 Rachel Carson demonstrated that environmentalism is not just about creeks and critters, but also about people. Forty years later, we need to birth an environmental movement that has a social justice agenda providing eco-pathways out of poverty and green-collar job training programs for troubled youth. In Oakland, this is what we do at the Ella Baker Center. We create, fight for and celebrate opportunities at a time when crime and poverty are particularly bad in our city. Most people don't even realize how much needs to be done here. We have high rates of homicides, incarceration and drug abuse. In some parts of this city, when a child sees balloons and flowers, they often start crying—because they associate those things with funerals and sidewalk memorials. Above and beyond Oakland, though, eco-justice and the green economy should not be at the fringes or margins of our future planning. They now must be at the core of our national agenda. Likewise, the disenfranchised are not a "throw-away" population. This very segment of our society—people of color, disenfranchised youth and people without money—can and must play a key role in meeting our environmental challenges.

So many people from both political parties talk repeatedly about "taking America back, taking America back." The defilers of our planet, those corporations who have been polluting for years, are now talking about "green this, green that, and taking America back to green." We at the Ella Baker Center are working to build green-collar jobs as the pathway out of poverty for the people of our community. We fight for the green economy because we are fighting for our lives. So when they say, "Take America back, take America back," we will say together, "We are the next generation; this is our job; we will take America forward."

The Ella Baker Center and Its Fight for Social and Eco-Justice

"Give light . . . and people will find their way."

—Ella Baker

Van Jones cofounded the Ella Baker Center in 1996 with two others whose shared goal it was to tackle the justice and prison systems in California. The center was named after an African-American civil and human rights activist whose career spanned five decades beginning during the Great Depression. The Ella Baker Center works to break the cycle of violence that persists in low-income communities around the country, offering smart solutions and uplifting alternatives to violence and incarceration. Although social justice and environmental restoration seem to be quite different issues, Van argues that they should be linked. The most powerful initiatives will take advantage of the great employment opportunities of the latter to better address the former.

The Ella Baker Center has an initiative that does just that: the Green-Collar Jobs Campaign, formerly known as Reclaim the Future. The program, based in Oakland, California, creates opportunities in the green economy for the poor and people of color through policy advocacy and public outreach. It has successfully advocated for the City of Oakland to create an employment pipeline, the Green Jobs Corps. The program is working with high school, vocational and community colleges to train people in the green-collar work of the future, like retrofitting buildings that are leaking energy, solar panel installation, wastewater reclamation, organic food, materials reuse and recycling. The center adopted the following concrete policy proposals to launch its campaign:

1. A city council resolution to fund a "Green Economic Development Plan." Oakland needs and deserves an equitable and environmentally sustainable blueprint for its economic growth that considers things like job creation, energy production and energy use, transportation infrastructure, food, waste management and zoning. This resolution puts real money and staff in place to research and craft a "green jobs" economic development plan for Oakland. The plan would then go before City Council as a binding resolution later in 2007.

2. A citywide Green Jobs Corps. This resolution would fund and establish a collaborative effort among community-based organizations, unions, workforce development service providers and employers to train Oakland residents in green construction and retrofitting.

It would also employ Oakland residents on city-sponsored energy projects funded with energy company settlement money. On June 19, 2007, the Oakland City Council unanimously voted to fund the Green Jobs Corps starting with $250,000.

Van argues that the Ella Baker Center does not want people of color, and especially kids, just to be employees in the green economy. He also envisions that these individuals, with help, can be inventors, investors, owners and entrepreneurs as the movement takes hold. Van reminds us that it was not Governor Arnold Schwarzenegger alone who was responsible for the landmark Global Warming Solutions Act of California. Fabio Núñez, the young Latino speaker of the state legislature, was the key player behind the scenes.

In the big picture, as Van sees it, the Green Wave will spawn a coalition as powerful as FDR's New Deal coalition, which tackled the Great Depression. This kind of green-growth alliance would incorporate the best of the business, labor, and community organizations in the Bay Area, and over time in states across the country.

The eco-elite needs partners and opportunities, for both the short and long term, and a green-growth agenda with shared prosperity and broad social opportunities are key to its success.[3] The Ella Baker Center and Van Jones lead by example, showing us how we all have much to gain both socially and economically in the wealth of the Green Wave.

The Ella Baker Center—By The Numbers

- The Ella Baker Center has helped to cut the California youth prison population by nearly 40% since 2002, by advocating statewide for alternatives to incarceration.

- In 2007 the Ella Baker Center helped to convince Speaker Nancy Pelosi to champion the Green Jobs Act of 2007, which if signed into law will allocate $125 million a year to train 30,000 people in green-collar jobs.

- The Ella Baker Center has launched a national initiative called Green for All, which aims to lift 250,000 people out of poverty through federal support for green-collar job training and incentives for green employers.

---

[3] Some language in the last paragraph is borrowed from Van's words in his interview article, "A Van With a Plan," with David Roberts published on March 20, 2007 at www.Grist.org

AGUNG PRANA
Coral Reef Restoration Project

Bali and Indonesia

Agung Prana's coral restoration project near his ecotourism resort in North Bali has restored the coral reef, reintroduced fish critical to the local fishing community and substantially helped his business. If done with community support, it is an approach to the restoration of coral ecosystems that is replicable all over the world.

AGUNG PRANA—*His Spiritual Path*

I was born into a relatively poor family, dropped out of school, got a one-year tourism diploma and became a tour guide. I then learned some business skills by manufacturing Balinese products for export to the United States.

I have always been on a spiritual path, and in 1987 while at a temple in North Bali, I had a dream. In the dream a priest appeared and told me that I was to restore and look after "all the coins in the sea," which I took to mean the fish and the coral near the temple. To implement my dream I decided to start a community-based tourism facility nearby, focused on eco- and spiritual tourism.

I sold my only car, bought some land along the coast and built a very modest six-room hotel, using local labor and materials. Before I was finished in 1990, six Australians appeared on three motor bikes and asked to stay. I told them the rooms were not ready but they insisted. They gave me six one-dollar bills, which I still have in my holy shrine as a reminder of how far I've been able to come.

The beach was lovely, but most of the coral in front of my little ecotourist facilities had died due to overfishing as well as destructive and unsustainable fishing practices. In 1998 there was a worldwide El Niño that caused the waters to warm so much that the corals died, a phenomenon called bleaching. That was also the year of the Asian monetary crisis when the Indonesian rupiah collapsed and rice prices went up fivefold. Whole communities of desperate fishermen from neighboring islands—where their own fisheries had been exhausted by over-exploitation—targeted the reefs of Pemuteran in front of my small tourist facility, bringing with them destructive bombing and cyanide fishing techniques that caused further marine habitat destruction. After one reef was destroyed, they would move on to the next. The reefs in front of Pemuteran were destroyed very quickly and fishing and tourism collapsed.

Because of my dream, I decided to try to rebuild the coral, but I knew that I would not be successful without the full cooperation of the local community of Pemuteran. In particular, I knew I had to convince the fishermen that they should stop being fish hunters and become fish farmers. This was in fact a most time-consuming and difficult task, but eventually some of them agreed to give my idea a chance. Sponsored also by local dive shops, they created a community marine patrol to keep other fishermen away and give the coral reef time to recover.

I spent 90% of the income from the six rooms trying to restore the coral and work with the villagers, including helping to restore their temples. I took the villagers by bus around Bali to explain the successes and failures of other beach resorts and how valuable coral reefs are both for fishing and tourism—including scuba diving—and how unpleasant it is for tourists to have locals walking the beach hawking trinkets. I paid for entertainers to come to the village and before they performed I would speak about the importance of the environment. I spoke to the children in primary schools with the hope that they would speak to their parents. Now, whenever we receive an award for our coral restoration work, I make sure that the award is also given to the villagers.

When it became clear that the villagers wanted to work with me, I was approached by two coral reef experts. They told me that they had a technology that would rapidly grow coral, but that their efforts in other parts of the world had failed because of a lack of community involvement. It is now seven years after we started using their technology and the reef has been largely restored. I have built a small hotel resort with thirty rooms and built villas that I continue to sell and maintain for the owners. Now I retain 90% of the profit with the village receiving some from the resort and some from the dive shops.

Every night the bay is now filled with fishermen in small fishing boats, using kerosene lamps on their bows to attract the fish and nets with which to catch them. It is a romantic sight for the ecotourists that come from around the world to stay at Tamin Sari Resorts and Villas.

THE CORAL REEF RESTORATION PROJECT MODEL—
Engaging Community and Appropriate Technology

Dr. Thomas Goreau, a leading U.S. coral scientist and president of the Global Coral Reef Alliance, and Professor Wolf Hilbertz, a marine architect from Germany, came to Bali and spoke to Agung Prana and the Pemuteran community about an approach to coral restoration using mineral accretion technology. They said it would cause the coral in the bay adjacent to the village and resort to grow up to five times faster than if just left to nature and undisturbed by dynamite and cyanide.

They noted that coral is an animal, and when the algae leave the coral due to global warming or other factors, the coral goes into a state of starvation and bleaching occurs. They went on to explain that coral and shells use dissolved calcium carbonates and magnesium oxides in the sea to build their shells, and that this process could be speeded up by the use of their system.

Agung Prana at Taman Sari in North Bali.

They initially proposed building a coral arc nursery of two structures built out of locally available rebar that is used in all reinforced concrete structures. One was 12 meters long, 2 meters wide and 1.2 meters high. The second was formed in the shape of a horseshoe. Once they placed them in the water about 50 meters offshore, they connected each to a power source onshore by a cable delivering low levels of direct current to the structures. The electrical current rapidly formed a film of limestone on the structures, the first step to forming coral and reducing the stress to the coral caused by pollution. As the coral gradually attached itself to the bars and grew, small fish were attracted, which in turn attracted larger fish. Eventually even some dolphins have reappeared in the bay.

This initial experiment was very successful and over the next eight years thirty coral structures and four fish structures were built which eventually covered an area 200 meters long and two hectares wide. The Pemuteran Village Marine Protected Area is a "bottoms-up" program established and enforced under village law. The community marine patrol is the first in Indonesia and the coral restoration project is now the largest mineral accretion arc system in the world.

The local fishermen now collect 200–300 kilograms of fish a day near the shore as opposed to as little as 5 kilograms seven years before when they had to go 5 to 10 kilometers offshore. The bay now has a thriving scuba diving community that brings in revenue to the resort and employment to the villagers. Almost all those working at the resort come from the local community.

This successful experiment in North Bali is now being replicated in other coastal areas of Bali and other Indonesian islands. It has received many international environmental excellence awards, catching the attention of the Indonesian government.

CORAL REEF RESTORATION PROJECT—BY THE NUMBERS

- Indonesia's coral reefs account for 14% of the world's coral reefs.
- Only 6% of Indonesia's coral reefs are in healthy condition.
- Over half a kilometer of nearly barren coral area has been turned into a full reef of vibrant coral with an active fish population.
- The total out-of-pocket cost of the Pemuteran Coral Restoration Project is estimated to be $24,000, of which $19,000 has gone to electricity costs. This estimate does not include thousands of volunteer hours by the outside experts and by members of the local community.

Jake Whitcomb

 ## JAKE WHITCOMB AND ANDY ROSSMEISSL

Brighter Planet Visa®

The United States

Inspired by a forward-thinking Environmental Economics professor at Middlebury College in Vermont, Jake Whitcomb and Andy Rossmeissl turned a class project into a growing business. Together, they created the Brighter Planet Visa, a rewards-based credit card that provides the opportunity for consumers in the United States to contribute to renewable energy projects and fight global warming with every purchase. Over the next five years, the Brighter Planet Visa credit card will offset the effects of several million tons of carbon dioxide. This impact will be the equivalent to offsetting a coal plant's emissions for an entire year.

Andy Rossmeissl

Getting Started with a Class Project

We didn't know each other when we started taking "Environmental Economics" with Professor Jon Isham in the spring of 2005. Nevertheless, we both had the same motives for taking the course. We were both drawn to the class because it was about the environment and economics as complementary subjects. Twenty-five years ago, putting those two words together would have been contradictory, but now environmental concerns can often be solved best by implementing an economic lens.

Professor Isham, who had just finished co-authoring a book called *Ignition: What You Can Do to Fight Global Warming and Spark a Movement*, has always been practical and innovative in his approach to teaching. He cares less about the busy work of economics than he does about applying economic principles to real-world situations. Our class project, and eventually Brighter Planet, really began with a simple question that arose at an Isham family meal at Steve's Park Diner earlier that year in the small town of Middlebury. As the Ishams got up to leave and pay with a credit card, Professor Isham's father, who was paying for the meal, wondered how his consumer purchasing power could possibly contribute to the fight against global warming: "Wouldn't it be cool if my credit card could do this for me?" he ruminated. The idea for our class project was born.

Much of the course we took with Professor Isham focused on service learning. He encouraged each student to develop a business plan or project that moved beyond the classroom. When Professor Isham shared his father's idea with our class, a little light bulb went off in our heads. We would go on to find out just how bright it was.

THE "AHA!" MOMENT

Many entrepreneurs talk about some "Aha!" moment as if a bolt of lightning carrying a business idea struck them. In truth, it rarely happens that way. Our experience while we were developing our ideas for Brighter Planet during our coursework was that there were a series of calculable and tangible moments along the way—all important indications that we were on the right track, but never a lightning bolt.

The first time we really sat down with a spreadsheet to get a handle on the numbers, we came across an incredible coincidence. Using data from the Statistical Abstract of the United States, we found that in 2005 the average credit-card carrying American would spend about $12,000 with their credit cards. We also found that rewards programs direct about 1% of consumer purchases to rewards programs like mileage and shopping discounts.

Our next step was to look at the various prices for carbon offsets in markets internationally. Carbon offsets basically represent the right to claim credit for the environmental benefit of a project that reduces climate emissions. For example, new reusable energy project developers can pre-sell offsets as a way of funding their projects and making them a reality.

We then plugged these numbers into a rough Excel model. In a moment of jubilant coincidental calculation, we realized that our theoretical credit card and its rewards program would allow the average spender to offset his or her annual carbon footprint: about twenty-three tons.

Connecting consumer spending to carbon offsets in such a neat and concise way was indeed an "aha" moment as the numbers matched up, but an equally important piece of empirical evidence really resonated with our team. A Gallup poll from 2005 reported that 80% of Americans considered themselves environmentalists. The population of the United States at the time was roughly 300 million, which meant that there were 250 million environmentally concerned citizens who might be interested in our credit card. "Wow!" we thought, "that is a lot of customers."

BUILDING A COMPANY

We were faced with a major challenge. The opportunity for our business was great, but our resources were meager. Staying realistic about our needs and capacities during our development process was critical to our success. We had to learn how to ask, how to listen and how to build partnerships. Throughout, we stuck to our ideals and were driven by an unwavering conviction that we could tackle the climate crisis head on as we struggled with the pragmatic fundamentals of starting a business.

It would have been useful to have had two dozen skill sets while developing the class project into a real company, namely fundraising, legal, accounting, finance and credit card experience—it was truly a start-up! We had only two major, but ultimately crucial ones. In the first place, we knew how to ask for advice. Approaching potential advisors in the right way, we discovered, led to supportive partnerships and guidance. Second, we knew how to communicate clearly, and were able to describe our business model for carbon offsetting through a credit card rewards program to potential partners in an effective manner.

After getting some serious feedback from an organization called CERES, (Coalition for Environmentally Responsible Economics) a coalition of organizations that addresses sustainability problems with business solutions, CERES President Mindy Lubber joined our advisory board. With his help, we developed a seventy-five-page strategic business plan.

As we spread the word about our idea and how serious we were about launching Brighter Planet as a viable business, some key players provided critical advice and resources. Bill McKibben was one of the most inspiring. He is one of the most influential environmentalists in the country, and it was incredibly encouraging to get his approval for our concept. Peter Schiller, a veteran venture capitalist, taught us how to refine our business strategy. All dedicated environmentalists, these advisors were keen to help us because we put the environment first.

As our business model began to emerge, other critical players engaged with our idea. We were invited to the Clean Air-Cool Planet (CA-CP) conference in New York City, where we gave a presentation. We both remember feeling so out of place, but were excited to be representing Middlebury College, which received a Climate Champion Award. The other recipient of the award, Bank of America, would become one of our future partners.

At the CA-CP Conference, as was the case at other venues where we unveiled our idea, people engaged most with the personal story of how we transformed a class project into a viable business plan for tackling climate change, rather than with the technology, marketing materials, business plan or products we displayed.

With so much encouragement, we decided to make the sacrifices necessary to pursue our vision. We dropped summer work, quit jobs and moved back to Middlebury, where a local venture group called Fresh Tracks Capital provided a desk, a phone, internet access and their experienced minds to boot. A Middlebury alumni-backed fund offered a summer stipend for our work. We spent countless nights on the office sofa, housesat when we could and lived out of the back of a Volkswagen Jetta when no other options were available.

Our friends and family were our first investors. We started small. Pursued with persistence and passion, our first round of fundraising grossed $25,000 during the summer of 2006. We had been living on a shoestring, and this early capital made a tremendous difference. We stayed awake at night, haunted by a very sobering realization: we were now the fiduciaries responsible for our friends and family members' money.

At the end of 2006 we hired Patti Prairie as our CEO, which was a major step. Patti had held senior executive positions at IBM and American Express. She had also been an environmentalist for much of her life. We followed her stern strategic advice to the letter. In the months that followed, we teamed up with Bank of America, finalized our Carbon Offset Policy, and formed a partnership with *Native*Energy, the leading carbon offset provider and our neighbor in Vermont. We'd brought all the pieces of our vision together. The Brighter Planet Visa credit card from Bank of America was released at the end of 2007.

WHAT CLIMATE CHANGE REALLY MEANS FOR EACH OF US

It is now widely recognized that global warming is the biggest cross-civilization challenge our generation faces. We are approaching the limits of our environmental crisis, and we must act now. Many strategies for tackling this challenge demand significant changes in behavior. The Brighter Planet Visa credit card, on the other hand, empowers individuals to take an active role in tackling climate change by harnessing a program to consumers' existing purchasing power.

The capacity of our program to give people the ability to take measurable action in a struggle they are passionate about has been key to our business strategy. In 2005, the yellow "Livestrong" wristbands allowed people to use their purchasing power to make a pledge of solidarity to fight cancer under the Lance Armstrong Foundation. People are still wearing various color wristbands for many different causes today. The Brighter Planet Visa is even more powerful than a pledge or badge, though, because it allows one to take an active and ongoing role, connecting one's beliefs to a visible result—offseting one's carbon footprint.

The future of climate change is uncertain, and while many strategies for fighting global warming that produce significant results while demanding more drastic changes in infrastructure and lifestyle are well underway, the best strategies for the present are those that empower each of us to do something right now. Imagine walking through town, swiping your new card at the grocery store, purchasing a round of beers for your friends, or even just buying a new pair of shoes. Every time that card comes out of your wallet, you can feel good about having a positive effect on the environment.

THE FUTURE OF THE BRIGHTER PLANET CREDIT CARD

The biggest struggle in starting our own company was the very decision to make it our own. In the global markets of carbon trading, the critical elements of transparency and accountability might have been compromised had we gone to work for a global corporation. We wanted to remain independent. The future of the Brighter Planet Visa credit card will be in alignment with the central impulse that drove our class project from the very beginning: to show consumers what they can do. By showing consumers exactly which renewable energy projects and carbon offsets they contribute to, we make a global problem very tangible.

We plan to scale our business model in the years to come so that it continues to enable individuals to take part in future plans to improve the climate. We also plan to make these contributions more effective. By 2010 our goal—which we hope to achieve by encouraging the participation not only of consumers, but also of governments and corporations—is to offset several million tons of carbon every year. In just our first two months of operation, we had offset a thousand tons, so we feel very positive about our ability to live up to our projections.

HELPFUL ADVICE FOR COLLEGE ENTREPRENEURS

We were so ignorant when we started to plan Brighter Planet, and there is still so much we feel we have to learn. When we began, for instance, we didn't even know the job title of the person at the bank we were supposed to talk to about starting a credit card company, or even how to find office space! We just took one step at a time, following our passion for the environment and living by our conviction that with enough persistence we would eventually reach our goals.

It is easy to romanticize the experience of starting a business. The truth is, it's a complex and daunting process. In the first place, there are a lot of details to keep track of. In most cases, you will have to retain lawyers, secure health insurance for your employees and hire a bookkeeper. Finding the answers to the nuts and bolts questions are critical and tough.

It goes without saying that you'll have to remain committed in the face of all the challenges you will be presented with. There were times, for example, when we had to make a hundred phone calls to find one person who would say yes. You'll face a lot of rejections. Dedication is key.

While being determined is crucial, you'll also have to learn to be flexible. A successful business needs to adapt. Just make sure you are able to bend in such a way that you don't sacrifice your core mission.

Despite all these challenges, we can definitely say that it's worth it. For any of you readers who are considering starting your own business, we encourage you to go for it.

BRIGHTER PLANET VISA—BY THE NUMBERS

- The Brighter Planet Visa credit card was launched in August of 2006 with $25,000 in funding from friends and family.
- It plans to offset several million tons of carbon dioxide, or the equivalent of shutting down a coal plant for an entire year, by 2010.
- Roughly 60% of adults wish there was an easy way to stop global warming.

CHAPTER 10

Other Agents of Change: Intrapreneurs, Philanthropreneurs and Celebrities

To borrow a metaphor from Nobel Peace Prize Laureate Desmond Tutu, business, like a knife, or a religion, is neutral. How it is used determines whether a company adds to the world's challenges or helps solve them.

The illegal brick manufacturers in rural China, who are kidnapping children and forcing them to become slave laborers, are examples of businesses contributing to larger social problems of poverty and exploitation. The huge fishing trawlers that catch fifty tons of fish in two minutes by dragging nets the size of soccer fields across the ocean bottom is another example. These trawlers are not doing anything illegal, since political will and public awareness have not been sufficient to ban such activities. Nonetheless, the damage they cause to the ocean floor's ecosystem is enormous. They destroy 90% of what they catch, and are responsible for bringing numerous fish species to the brink of extinction. As a result of such fishing techniques, many fish populations that we have presumed to be in endless supply most likely will not exist when our children are adults.

But in this chapter, we'll see why other businesses are becoming forces for positive change.

HOW BUSINESS CAN MAKE A DIFFERENCE

Without question, businesses have created many of the social and environmental problems the world faces today. But it is also true that many of these challenges will not be solved without business playing a significant role in finding and implementing solutions to these problems. Multinational corporations attract the best management talent on the planet. They have access to huge amounts of capital, and they have built the most sophisticated, efficient and dynamic distribution systems across national and geographic borders. They are infused with the competitive drive to find innovative solutions where markets most demand them.

Enlightened Self-Interest and the Triple Bottom Line

Many corporations have come to realize that it is in their enlightened self-interest not to be seen as a contributor to a problem but rather as part of the solution. In 1989, at a conference in Hong Kong on social responsibility sponsored by *The WorldPaper*, almost all of the seventy businesspeople in attendance argued that such issues as human rights, social justice and the environment were not the concern of business. They often quoted economist Dr. Milton Friedman, who in 1972 stated "The business of business is business," which they took to mean that social and environmental challenges were indeed "none of their business."

While it remains true that the business of business *is* business, it is also clear that many of the world's most sophisticated corporations have gradually expanded their view of what they consider pertinent to the continued success of their "business." Since the mid-1980s, many multinational corporations have moved from corporate social responsibility (CSR) focused primarily on public relations and damage control to the current phase in which CSR is becoming a more integral part of their corporate strategy. Many use the term "triple bottom line" to refer to the corporate goals extending beyond pure business accounting to include social and environmental returns on investment, or "profits, people and planet."

An indication of the increased importance now being given to these issues is the emergence of numerous consulting firms and associations that research and infuse social ideas into corporate strategies. Examples include Interaction Associates, SustainAbility, AccountAbility, the Monitor Institute, International Business Leaders Forum, the Prince of Wales Business & Environment Programme, the World Business Council for Sustainable Development, Global Business Network and the World Business Academy, among others.

Corporations shift their priorities in response to legislation and pressure from their customers, employees and investors, in addition to their own forecasted assumptions about future trends that create opportunities or risks for their businesses. The following are several of the reasons behind the shift by corporations toward greater social and environmental responsibility.

The "Transparency" Argument

A few decades ago, if a large clothing company's products were manufactured by impoverished women or young children, or if a multinational oil company allowed toxic substances to destroy a rainforest or expose an indigenous tribe to cancer, few around the world would have heard of it or complained. Today, news organizations have twenty-four hour coverage and are looking for such stories, and television and Internet-based services such as Google, Yahoo and the *New York Times* online edition now spread such news around the world in seconds.

As a result, consumers and socially conscious investors are much more aware and take such abuses much more seriously than ever before when making their business decisions. In 1989, when the *Exxon Valdez* tanker spilled 11 million gallons of oil into Prince William Sound in Alaska, a pristine area I had kayaked in, it appeared that Exxon's safety precautions were poor, its response slow and its concern for the environment and the fishermen who relied on Prince William Sound for their livelihood, cavalier. Since that moment many of us have made a conscious choice to bypass every Exxon gas station. While it is obvious that the actions of one consumer or potential investor has little impact on a multinational corporation's bottom line, it suggests the power that greater transparency will have over corporate behavior in the future.

THE "FORTUNES AT THE BOTTOM OF THE PYRAMID" ARGUMENT

Professor C. K. Prahalad's book *The Fortune at the Bottom of the Pyramid: Eradicating Poverty Through Profits* gives many examples of businesses that have become extremely profitable by providing products and services to the poor. Muhammad Yunus, mentioned throughout this book, is an excellent example of Prahalad's argument. To reiterate, in 1983 Yunus founded the Grameen Bank in Bangladesh to provide small loans to poor villagers who did not have collateral. Since then, Grameen Bank has provided over $6 billion in loans, almost exclusively to women who began uplifting their communities as they added to their family's income. Grameen Bank has a repayment rate of 98%. The ownership of Grameen Bank is also revolutionary, with 94% of the shares in the hands of its borrowers. Yunus's microcredit revolution has since spread to nearly fifty countries and is an excellent example of how one initiative has enabled millions of impoverished people to get themselves out of poverty. Many of the social entrepreneurs highlighted in this book clearly believe in the "trickle-up" approach to empowerment and economic well-being.

Such approaches to empowerment for economic and social development are akin to the old adage, "Don't give me a fish, teach me how to fish." "Trickle-up" is a radical departure from the "trickle-down" approach formerly espoused by practitioners of international economic development.

The "Extreme Poor Will Hurt Your Business" Argument

There is another, more ominous reason why multinational companies need to be increasingly mindful of those living in extreme poverty as they build their global strategies. Professor Rosabeth Moss Kanter of the Harvard Business School, a former editor of the *Harvard Business Review*, wrote, "Radical extremists—and not just radical Islamists—are fanning the flames of discontent among poor people who feel left behind by global capitalism. We can write off each event as the actions of young hotheads or the violence of crackpots led by despots. But honestly, with the gap between rich and poor growing in many places, do sensible people really think that the poor and disfranchised will sit still and take it any longer? Affluent Latin Americans, like the well-to-do in Johannesburg, Paris or Miami, can barricade themselves in gated communities only so long before the violence hits home. If we don't care about helping the poor struggle out of poverty because it's the right thing to do or in the long-term interests of our nation, how about poverty reduction in the name of safety? For businesses, it's imperative to be seen as part of the solution, not part of the problem, or the backlash against free markets and trade will turn uglier."

The "It Will Be Good for Our Business" Argument

Many companies are engaged in practices that actively address the public's concerns and have gained great loyalty as a result. Patagonia, Life is Good, The Body Shop, Osh Kosh, Newman's Own, Zeiss, Aveda, Ben & Jerry's, and American Apparel have long been regarded as very socially and environmentally responsible companies. Whole Foods, the organic grocery chain, attracts customers who want to be sure that what they eat is organic and fresh. Investors are attracted to Whole Foods in part because of its fair trade products and corporate salary scheme. In a world in which the average large public company's CEO is paid 475 times as much as the average company employee, the total cash compensation of Whole Foods executives is capped at fourteen times that of the average employee team member. And CEO John Mackey has announced that he will continue to work, because he loves his job, for only $1 a year. Another example is Starbucks coffee, which recently established a distribution agreement with Ethos Water as part of its efforts to be a socially responsible company, helping to tackle the clean drinking water crisis in the developing world.

The "Our Best Employees Will Go Elsewhere" Argument

Employees of the multinationals, who have choices as to which company they work for, increasingly want to be comfortable with their company's business practices. Many potential employees are knocking on Google's door, for example, not only because the company is doing exciting, well-paying work, but also because Google is perceived to be a socially conscious company, particularly due to its creation of Google.org—a for-profit entity investing only in socially responsible activities.

Intrapreneurs are individual employees working to change a corporation's policies and practices from within, advocating new and improved ways to produce or market products. While many young people who are concerned about social and environmental issues tend to recoil at the thought of working for a multinational corporation, there is a strong argument that they should do just that if they want to help bring about significant change. By doing so they will have opportunities to influence corporate policies and practices for the better while earning a reasonable living, indeed fitting with the notion of doing good and doing well at the same time. The numerous business schools offering courses in sustainable development and social entrepreneurship mentioned in Part III have begun intensive programs for a new generation of employees. They are preparing such individuals with the knowledge and determination to bring about fundamental changes in corporate behavior.

The jury is still out as to whether corporations will indeed become major players in finding solutions to the issues raised in this book. The extent to which they do will depend in part on the pressures they face from the media, consumers, investors, employees, governments and multilateral agencies.

Philanthropreneurs—
Using Their Wealth to Bring About Systemic Change

Philanthropreneurs, on the other hand, are individuals with considerable wealth who seek to use their resources in highly entrepreneurial ways. Jeff Skoll, the former president of eBay, is an excellent example. He left the presidency of eBay in 1998 at the age of thirty-three with an immense fortune and ever since has committed himself to addressing social challenges both with his money and with very entrepreneurial ideas. He established the Skoll Foundation, the largest foundation for social entrepreneurship in the world, and the Skoll Centre for Social Entrepreneurship at the Oxford University Business School. He established Participant Productions, which funds feature films and documentaries that promote social values while still being commercially viable. The films he has funded include *An Inconvenient Truth* about global warming, featuring Nobel Peace Prize Laureate Al Gore; *Syriana* about petroleum politics; *The Kite Runner* about life in war-torn Afghanistan; *Angels in the Dust,* a hopeful film about an AIDS orphanage in South Africa; and *Jimmy Carter Man From Plains.* Each film is tied to a social action campaign that helps turn the awareness generated by the films into concrete actions by individuals to address the issues.

Pierre Omidyar, the founder and chairman of eBay, is also a philanthropreneur. His Omidyar Network seeks to "enable individual self-empowerment on a global scale" and to employ "business as a tool for social good." Other philanthropreneurs include Bill Gates and his wife Melinda, who are using their fortune to address health and educational concerns; Richard Branson, founder of the Virgin group of companies, who is funding the Elders, a group working to solve difficult global conflicts; Ted Turner, whose fortune came from CNN, who gave $1 billion to the United Nations; George Soros, who created the Open Society Institute and Soros Foundation Network that supports the development of civil societies around the world; and Steve Case, the founder of AOL, who invests in innovative solutions to social issues such as PlayPumps (profiled in Chapter 3). With the massive amounts of wealth being accumulated by successful entrepreneurs, it is likely that many more such individuals will choose to become philanthropreneurs over the next few years.

Former U.S. President Jimmy Carter does not use his money, but rather his visibility, credibility and tireless energy to champion causes he feels strongly about, such as the promotion of fair elections, values, and his effort to help build low-cost housing through Habitat for Humanity. Former U.S. President Bill Clinton started the Clinton Global Initiative (CGI) to match philanthropreneurs with people and organizations who have demonstrated successful models and high-impact results around the world in education, energy, climate change, global health, and poverty alleviation. Over the past two years, nearly 600 commitments have been made by CGI members, totaling nearly $10 billion and benefiting the work of more than 1,000 organizations. Larry Brilliant leads the philanthropic arm of Google Inc., which was set up as a for-profit entity to fight poverty, disease and global warming. He has a $1 billion endowment to draw upon to invest in initiatives that can bring about systemic changes in these areas.

Celebrities—*Using Fame to Raise Global Awareness*

A number of celebrities are also getting involved. They are increasingly interested in having their name associated with social and environmental challenges of concern to them. That is a change for some. Two decades ago, Bono was quoted as saying, "How can you be a spokesman for a generation if you've got nothing to say other than 'Help!'" Now Bono is known around the world for his commitment to dealing with poverty, AIDS and debt relief in Africa. Angelina Jolie has also demonstrated a serious commitment to poverty elimination in Africa, while Leonardo DiCaprio is a major spokesman around the issue of global warming. George Clooney starred in the film *Syriana,* which Jeff Skoll funded, to shine a light on the dark side of big oil. Andre Agassi has created a school system for at-risk children in southern Nevada. Robert Redford, a social entrepreneur notable for starting the Sundance Institute to give greater opportunities to under-represented independent filmmakers, has more recently focused on the preservation of the natural world and traditional cultures. Oprah Winfrey has given enormous sums to charitable causes, including the construction of a girls' school in Africa. She always promotes the notion of people taking responsibility for their own lives while celebrating many guests who are dedicated to improving the lives of others. Quincy Jones is very active in helping underprivileged children in the United States and South Africa connect with technology, education, culture, and music. Celebrities are yet another example of individuals using their particular skills to address various social challenges of concern to them.

PART III

RESOURCES

Champions and Funders

Behind any great social movement there are those individuals and organizations that champion and help fund the effort. Champions publicly support and fight for a cause; funders provide financial backing that supports those who have the vision and commitment to make things happen. Martin Luther King Jr. was a champion of the civil rights movement. Susan B. Anthony was a champion of the abolitionist movement. Many of the social entrepreneurs you have read about are indeed champions for their specific cause, whether girls' education in Africa, preserving the Amazonian rainforests in South America, or removing land mines from killing fields in Asia.

This section moves beyond the suggestions mentioned in Chapter 1, which were about how to discover your passion and take first steps, to such questions as how to fund and collaborate with others to develop your initiative. The section is designed to help steer those interested in the field of social entrepreneurship to organizations that can help them better understand the needs to be addressed, fund their initiative, and identify other initiatives and possible partners in their area of interest. The section also notes some of the leading graduate schools on the topic, magazines, and other books pertinent to the topic. Much of the material below comes directly from the websites of the organizations mentioned. This is not an exhaustive listing of resources but will provide a good basis for further research. You can take a closer look at these organizations by going to their websites and to www.TacticsofHope.org.

Grants, Support, Fellowships and Awards

- **Ashoka**, founded in 1980 by Bill Drayton, is continuously building an infrastructure that supports the growth and expansion of the field of social entrepreneurship, including seed financing and capital, bridges to the business and academic sectors, and strategic partnerships that deliver social and financial value. Ashoka Fellows receive a living stipend for an average of three years, allowing them to focus full-time on building their institutions and spreading their ideas. Ashoka has long recognized the importance of collaboration with other sectors, particularly business, whose models of competition and innovation provide critical lessons for citizen organizations. Work in this area is focused specifically on closing the historical gap between the business sector and civil society, creating important avenues for integration and synergy between both communities. In order to succeed and become sustainable, social entrepreneurs—much like business entrepreneurs—require support structures tailored to their needs.

- **The Skoll Foundation**, founded in 1999, celebrates, connects, funds and gives visibility to select social entrepreneurs. The Skoll Foundation invests in social entrepreneurs through its flagship award program, the Skoll Awards for Social Entrepreneurship. These three-year awards support the continuation, replication or extension of programs that have proved successful in addressing a broad array of critical social issues: tolerance and human rights, health, environmental sustainability, economic and social equity, institutional responsibility, and peace and security. The Skoll Awards are generally structured as a $1 million award paid out over three years, and in most cases the grant is provided to help organizations expand their programs and capacity to deliver long-term, sustainable equilibrium change. The Skoll Awards are formally presented each Spring at the Skoll World Forum, a major gathering of social entrepreneurs and others in the field that takes place at Oxford University's Saïd Business School in England. A number of the social entrepreneurs featured in this book have received a Skoll Award.

- **Echoing Green** was founded in 1987 by the senior leadership of General Atlantic LLC and the Atlantic Philanthropies, a leading global private equity firm. Its mission is "to spark social change by identifying, investing, and supporting the world's most exceptional emerging leaders and the organizations they launch." Through its two-year fellowship program, Echoing Green helps its network of 450 entrepreneurs with technical assistance, consulting, and growth management. Echoing Green invests mostly in younger social entrepreneurs who have a promising vision.

- **The Schwab Foundation for Social Entrepreneurship** was cofounded in 1998 by Klaus Schwab, the president and founder of the World Economic Forum, and his wife Hilde. The Schwab Foundation does not give grants or invest financially in the organizations of its selected social entrepreneurs; rather, it uses its resources to create lateral partnership, internship and fellowship opportunities for its chosen social entrepreneurs who have successfully implemented and scaled their transformational idea. The foundation thus seeks to further the legitimacy of social entrepreneurs' work, giving them access to high-level networks and contacts in finance, business, academia and policy-making, and enabling them to strengthen and expand their core strategy and mission.

- **The Acumen Fund**, founded by Jacqueline Novogratz in 2001, seeks to prove, in its own words, that "small amounts of philanthropic capital, combined with large doses of business acumen, can build thriving enterprises that serve vast numbers of the poor." The fund provides extraordinary young professionals with fellowship opportunities to use their skills to effect real social change through the organization's market-based approaches in Kenya, Tanzania, South Africa, India and Pakistan, encouraging collaboration with local entrepreneurs on price performance, logistics, distribution systems, scaling and technology.

- **The Draper Richards Foundation for Social Entrepreneurship**, founded by Bill Draper and Robin Richards Donahoe in 2001, provides funding and business mentoring to social entrepreneurs who are just getting started. As the offshoot of its venture capital partner firm, Draper Richards LP, the foundation brings its financial success to a nonprofit portfolio, demonstrating the new kind of hybrid model for venture philanthropy adopted by many philanthropreneurs mentioned in Chapter 10. The organization awards six new grants a year, each for a three-year period.

- **Civic Ventures**, founded by Marc Freedman and John Gardner in the late 1990s, celebrates and funds individuals over sixty who have taken on an "encore career" using their professional career skills to be of service to the community in innovative ways. As noted in Chapter 2, a pilot initiative of Civic Ventures, the Purpose Prize, is one of several programs designed to reframe the debate as to what "retirees" may accomplish in the second half of their lives.

- **Students for the Advancement of Global Entrepreneurship** (SAGE), founded by accounting professor Curt DeBurg, helps high schoolage youth form the belief that it is possible for them to make the world a better place, not only for themselves but for their fellow peers and familial communities. SAGE has created both local and global competitions for high school teams from all over the world to create and present their business and social enterprises. While identifying high school communities to invest in, SAGE believes that education curricula in the twenty-first century should work with students to form ethical understandings of self-reliance, creative business and global citizenship.

- **The Manhattan Institute**, founded in 1978, sponsors the Award for Social Entrepreneurship to honor "non-profit leaders who have found innovative, private solutions for America's most pressing social problems," and those organizations whose guiding purpose and function stem from private individuals doing public good.

- **The National Center for Social Entrepreneurs** is a nonprofit consulting company founded in 1985. Its mission is to increase the effectiveness and financial self-sufficiency of the nonprofit sector by helping individual nonprofits act in a more businesslike and entrepreneurial manner. The National Center offers seminars, consulting, and business services to social entrepreneurs, and offers an extensive collection of resources and learning materials on their website.

- **The Institute for Social Entrepreneurs** provides education and training for social entrepreneurs in the United States and abroad, drawing upon a virtual community of social entrepreneurs and others to collaborate on specific projects.

- **Social Enterprise Alliance**, a membership organization devoted to building nonprofits through earned income strategies, is the product of two organizations merging, the National Gathering for Social Entrepreneurs and SeaChange.

Schools, Books, Magazines and Networks

Graduate Programs Teaching Social Entrepreneurship

Social entrepreneurship has grown rapidly as a field of study at many institutions of higher education. According to a research survey of business schools conducted by Beyond Grey Pinstripes, which spotlights MBA programs leading the way in the integration of social and environmental issues into the curriculum, the percentage of schools that "require students to take a course dedicated to business and society" has increased dramatically, from 34% in 2001 to 63% in 2007. The report continues on to cite, however, that "the proportion of schools requiring content in core courses on how mainstream business can address social or environmental issues remains low."

In many respects, academic institutions are taking the lead to provide a more systemic understanding of social entrepreneurship and its technical terminology. Greg Dees of Duke University, David Bornstein at New York University, Alex Nicholls at Oxford University and Pamela Hartigan who has taught at the University of Geneva and is now helping to lead the Schwab Foundation mentioned above, have all been particularly instrumental in this process. As these individuals have brought about groundbreaking programs at their respective academic institutions, many more are increasingly forward thinking in their desire to integrate new curricula to do the same. Internationally, it is growing to be widely recognized that students are no longer content simply to study international challenges; they want to help discover solutions.

Among the leading educational institutions in social entrepreneurship are the following:

- Stanford University's Social Innovation and Entrepreneurship (SIE) Program
- The Haas School of Business at the University of California at Berkeley
- Columbia University's Research Initiative on Social Entrepreneurship (RISE)
- Duke University's Center for the Advancement of Social Entrepreneurship (CASE)
- Bainbridge Graduate Institute in Sustainable Business
- New York University's Catherine B. Reynolds Program for Social Entrepreneurship
- The University of North Carolina at Chapel Hill – Center for Sustainable Enterprise
- Oxford University's Skoll Centre for Social Entrepreneurship
- The University of Geneva's Entrepreneurial Solutions for Social Challenges Program
- Presidio Business School in Sustainable Management
- The University of California, Davis's Graduate School of Business

BOOKS

- *Strategic Tools for Social Entrepreneurs: Enhancing the Performance of Your Enterprising Nonprofit*, by Greg Dees, Jed Emerson and Peter Economy
- *Enterprising Nonprofits: A Toolkit for Social Entrepreneurs*, by Greg Dees, Jed Emerson and Peter Economy
- *Entrepreneurship in the Social Sector*, by Jane Wei-Skillern, James Austin, Herman Leonard and Howard Stevenson
- *How to Change the World: Social Entrepreneurs and the Power of New Ideas*, by David Bornstein
- *Social Entrepreneurship: New Models of Sustainable Social Change*, edited by Alex Nicholls
- *The Power of Unreasonable People: How Social Entrepreneurs Create Markets that Change the World*, by John Elkington and Pamela Hartigan
- *Blessed Unrest*, by Paul Hawken
- *Unbowed*, by Wangari Maathai
- *Creating a World Without Poverty*, by Muhammad Yunus
- *Giving: How Each of Us Can Change the World*, by Bill Clinton

MAGAZINES

Subscription and free online magazines have become significant champions of social entrepreneurship, celebrating the work of social entrepreneurs and finding new ways to present social entrepreneurship to the public internationally. The following magazines are among the leaders contributing to this literature:

- *Alliance*
- *Entrepreneur*
- *Fast Company*
- *Fortune Small Business*
- *Good*
- *Inc.*
- *Stanford Social Innovation Review*

Online Social Entrepreneur Networks

There is an increasing number of online social networks that champion social entrepreneurs and in some cases, provide consulting services. They are all very different in their look and feel, but equally committed to building an infrastructure to help online visitors, and in some cases clients, access useful information. Some of the most notable social networks include the following:

- **WiserEarth.org**: "A collaborative tool and a comprehensive directory to link and empower the largest and fastest growing movement in the world."

- **SocialEdge.org**: "By Social Entrepreneurs, For Social Entrepreneurs."

- **TakingITGlobal.org**: "The world's most popular online community for young people interested in making a difference . . . a platform for expression, connection to opportunities and support for action."

- **NetImpact.org**: "A global network of 7,000 emerging leaders changing the world through business."

- **Omidyar.net**: "Committed to unleashing human potential."

- **UniversityNetwork.org**: "A resource hub and an action-oriented discussion forum to expand social entrepreneurship education and participation around the world."

- **YouthVenture.org**: "Building a Global Movement of Young Change-Makers."

- **TacticsofHope.org**: A companion website to this book designed to help all individuals, including emerging entrepreneurs, turn their concerns and passion into concrete actions. It also provides access to additional resources. The graphic below is a key feature of the website, enabling visitors to take action to turn their concerns into their own Tactics of Hope.

Online Resources

A

ACCION .... www.accion.org
AccountAbility www.accountability21.net
Acumen Fund.. www.acumenfund.org
Afghan Institute of Learning .... www.globalgoodspartners.org/producers_ail
Afghan Red Crescent Society (ARCS) .... www.arcs.org.af/en
Agassi, Andre .... www.agassiprep.org
Aid to Artisans .... www.aidtoartisans.org
Alliance magazine .... www.alliancemagazine.org
American Apparel .... http://americanapparel.net
An Inconvenient Truth .... www.climatecrisis.net
Angels in the Dust .... www.dolfilms.org/angels
Architecture for Humanity .... www.architectureforhumanity.org
ASEAN (Association of Southeast Asian Nations)............ www.aseansec.org
Ashoka .... www.ashoka.org
Aveda .... www.aveda.com
Aventis Foundation............................... www.aventis-foundation.org
Avina Foundation.. www.avina.net
Awakening the Dreamer,
   Changing the Dream Symposia .... www.awakeningthedreamer.org

B

Bainbridge Graduate Institute in Sustainable Business.......... www.bgieu.edu
Bali Institute for Global Renewal .... www.baliinstitute.org
BeadforLife .... www.beadforlife.org
Ben & Jerry's.. www.benjerry.com
Benetech .... www.benetech.org
Beyond Grey Pinstripes .... www.beyondgreypinstripes.org
Bill & Melinda Gates Foundation...................... www.gatesfoundation.org
The Black Sash.. www.blacksash.org.za
Blecher, Taddy .... www.cida.co.za
Blessed Unrest .... www.blessedunrest.com
The Body Shop .... www.bodyshop.com
Bonnie Clac... www.bonnieclac.org
Born into Brothels.................................... www.kids-with-cameras.org
BRAC (Bangladesh Rural Advancement Committee)............. www.brac.net
Bright Kid Foundation...................................... www.brightkid.co.za
Brighter Planet Visa.. www.brighterplanet.com
Bring Me A Book .... www.bringmeabook.org

How do I begin?

Create your profile at www.TacticsofHope.org

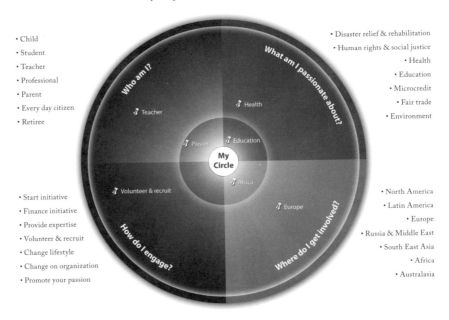

- Child
- Student
- Teacher
- Professional
- Parent
- Every day citizen
- Retiree

- Disaster relief & rehabilitation
- Human rights & social justice
- Health
- Education
- Microcredit
- Fair trade
- Environment

- Start initiative
- Finance initiative
- Provide expertise
- Volunteer & recruit
- Change lifestyle
- Change on organization
- Promote your passion

- North America
- Latin America
- Europe
- Russia & Middle East
- South East Asia
- Africa
- Australasia

C

M

Maathai, Waangari .... www.thegreenbeltmovement.org
Mackey, John .... www.wholefoodsmarket.com
Magic Yeti Children's Library .... www.alexlowe.org
Mandela, Nelson .... www.nelsonmandela.org
The Manhattan Institute for
    Social Entrepreneurship .... www.manhattan-institute.org
Mapendo International .... www.mapendo.org
Marks, John .... www.sfcg.org
Marks, Susan Collin .... www.sfcg.org
McKibben, Bill .... www.billmckibben.com
Médecins Sans Frontières (Doctors without Borders) .... www.msf.org
Mercy Corps .... www.mercycorps.org
MicroCredit Enterprises .... www.mcenterprises.org
Middlebury College .... www.middlebury.edu
Middle East Consortium on Infectious
    Disease Surveillance .... www.ghsi.org/projects/mecids.html
Millennium Development Goals (Millennium Goals) .... www.undp.org/mdg
Mitchell, Edgar www.edmitchellapollo14.com
The Monitor Institute .... www.monitorinstitute.com

N

The National Center for
    Social Entrepreneurs .... www.missionmoneymatters.org
National Outdoor Leadership School .... www.nols.edu
*Native*Energy .... www.nativeenergy.com
Net Impact .... www.netimpact.org
New Profit Inc. .... www.newprofit.com
Newman's Own .... www.newmansown.com
The New York Times .... www.nytimes.com
Next Level Foundation .... www.nextlevelfoundation.com
Nobel Prize .... www.nobelprize.org
Novagratz, Jacqueline .... www.acumenfund.org

O

Omidyar, Pierre .... www.omidyar.net
One Laptop Per Child .... www.laptop.org
OneWorld Health .... www.oneworldhealth.org
Open Society Institute/Soros Foundation Network .... www.soros.org
Osberg, Sally .... www.skollfoundation.org
Osh Kosh .... www.oshkoshbgosh.com
Oxfam .... www.oxfam.org
Oxford University Business School .... www.sbs.ox.ac.uk

U

V

W

INDEX

C

About the Author and Contributing Editor

Wilford Welch, Author

Wilford has a BA from Yale, a PMD from the Harvard Business School and a law degree from the University of California at Berkeley. His professional career has been devoted to understanding and taking actions to address global challenges—as a U.S. diplomat in Asia, as a professor of international business and as the publisher of *The WorldPaper*, a world affairs publication that was carried in twenty-seven countries in six language editions. For many years he was also an international business consultant at Arthur D. Little, Inc., working for multinational corporations on their international business strategies, and governments on their industrial development planning. In 2004 he co-founded the Quest for Global Healing initiative that brings thousands of people together from around the world every other year to help transform their concerns about environmental and social challenges into concrete initiatives.

For the past six years he has served on the board of Columbia University's School of International and Public Affairs (SIPA), and currently serves on the boards of the World Affairs Council of Northern California, the Yosemite National Institutes and the Headlands Institute.

In addition to his lifelong engagement in world affairs, Wilford has a deep commitment to the environment. He was chairman of the National Outdoor Leadership School (NOLS), and a member of the 1994 Sagamartha Environmental Expedition that removed 5,000 pounds of trash from the high camps on Mount Everest. He and the leader of that expedition currently give presentations to corporate audiences that share insights from high altitude mountaineering pertinent to business strategy development and execution and the restoration of a sustainable planet (see www.EverestandEnterprise.com).

In 1988, Wilford took the photo of Mount Everest from the Tibetan side that became the cover photo of the National Geographic Society's climbing map of Mount Everest. He is a member of the Explorers Club.

Wilford and his wife Carole live in Sausalito, California.

David Hopkins, Contributing Editor

David Hopkins is the former director at Middlebury College of the International Affairs Center of the Roosevelt Institution, the nation's first intercollegiate think tank devoted to progressive policy reform. He initiated a new student-led degree in social entrepreneurship at Middlebury College, and graduated with a BA degree cum laude in International Studies, Politics and Economics. He is the first recipient of the Balfour Fellowship for his work on this book and its website. Hopkins has worked and lived with families in several foreign countries, including France, Tanzania and Greece. He has assisted and collaborated with Wilford Welch on projects since 2004. He lives in San Francisco, California.

Photo Credits

p. xiv	© Carole Angermeir-Welch 2008
p. xvi	© Mark Read, CAMFED International 2008
p. xvii	Courtesy of Iqbal Quadir
p. xix	Courtesy of Ashoka
p. 1	© Romano 2008
p. 11	Courtesy of NASA
p. 15	Courtesy of Mark Hanis
p. 18	Courtesy of Phoebe Coburn
p. 31	Christophe Calais, courtesy of Mapendo
p. 35	Courtesy of Saúde Criança Renascer
p. 39	Christopher Pillitz and Fundación AVINA
p. 42	Mark Rosenberg, © Partners in Health. 2001. All rights reserved.
pp. 46–47	© PlayPumps International and Kristina Gubic 2008
p. 49	Diagrams courtesy of PlayPumps International
p. 50	Courtesy of Skoll Foundation
p. 53	© Riders for Health 2008
p. 58	Courtesy of CFWshops Kenya
p. 64	© Room to Read 2008
p. 67	© Room to Read 2008
p. 70	© Mark Read, CAMFED International 2008
p. 72	Courtesy of *The Financial Times*, © Mark Read/CAMFED 2006
p. 76	Courtesy of CIDA
p. 81	Courtesy of CDI
pp. 89–90	Daniel Lemin, © Kiva 2008
p. 93	Dalia Palchik, © Kiva 2008
p. 95	© David Hopkins 2008
p. 97	Courtesy of Fundación San Miguel Arcangel
p. 99	Courtesy of Audrey Codera
p. 100	Courtesy of Audrey Codera, PYEN 2006
p. 107	Courtesy of World of Good
p. 109	© Audrey Seagraves, World of Good: Development Organization, 2006
p. 111	© Sam Kittner 2008
p. 112	© David L. Parker 2008
p. 113	© Romano 2008
p. 115	© Trade plus Aid 2008
p. 117	Courtesy of Trade plus Aid
p. 120	© Wilford Welch 2008
p. 123	© Turquoise Mountain Foundation 2008
p. 128	Christopher Calais, courtesy of Mapendo
p. 133	Courtesy of IBJ
p. 135	Courtesy of IBJ, China
p. 139	Courtesy of SFCG
p. 140	Courtesy of Search for Common Ground
p. 145	Courtesy of Roots of Peace
p. 148	Courtesy of Roots of Peace
p. 154	© Wilford Welch 2008
p. 156	Courtesy of The Idea Village
p. 159	Courtesy of The Idea Village
p. 162	© David Hopkins 2008
p. 165	© David Hopkins 2008
p. 170	Courtesy of the Pachamama Alliance
p. 173	Courtesy of the Pachamama Alliance
p. 175	Courtesy of the Ella Baker Center
p. 177	Courtesy of the Ella Baker Center
p. 183	© Wilford Welch 2008
pp. 184–185	Courtesy of Brighter Planet
p. 199	Courtesy of Audrey Codera and PYEN